DEADFALL

GENERATIONS OF LOGGING IN THE PACIFIC NORTHWEST

James LeMonds

Mountain Press Publishing Company
Missoula, Montana
2001

Third Printing, June 2010

COVER PHOTO

Bill LeMonds (left) and Louie Fanony in the blast zone north of Mount St. Helens, 1981 —AP/Wide World Photos

All photographs from the author's collection unless otherwise credited.

Library of Congress Cataloging-in-Publication Data

LeMonds, James, 1950–
    Deadfall : generations of logging in the Pacific Northwest / James LeMonds.
        p. cm.
    Includes index.
    ISBN 978-0-87842-421-4 (alk. paper)
    1. Logging—Washington (State)—Castle Rock Region.
2. Logging—Northwest, Pacific. 3. Loggers—Washington
(State)—Castle Rock Region. 4. Loggers—Northwest, Pacific.
5. LeMonds, James. 1950–   I. Title.
SD538.2.W2 L46 2000
634.9'8'09795—dc21

                                                        00-051114

PRINTED IN THE UNITED STATES OF AMERICA

MP Mountain Press
PUBLISHING COMPANY
P.O. Box 2399 • Missoula, MT 59806 • 406-728-1900
800-234-5308 • info@mtnpress.com
www.mountain-press.com

For Dad, who has been my encyclopedia and inspiration during this project. And for Bob and the others who didn't come back.

PRAISE FOR

DEADFALL

GENERATIONS OF LOGGING IN THE PACIFIC NORTHWEST

by James LeMonds

"Loggers have been both glorified and villainized in Pacific Northwest literature and neither extreme rings true. Jim LeMonds's Deadfall, in contrast, is a clear-eyed classic: an objective book that captures the true pride and pain of working in the woods and the mixed emotions loggers have about the recent eclipse of their dangerous industry. No matter what view readers have about the spotted owl and Big Timber, they'll find Deadfall to be first-rate reporting by a skilled writer who tells it like it is."

—William Dietrich, Pulitzer Prize-winning
former correspondent for the Seattle Times
and author of The Final Forest: The Battle for
the Last Great Trees of the Pacific Northwest

"In a voice as clear as a tree-topper's cry, Jim LeMonds has given us an honest, insightful, steely-eyed vision of Pacific Northwest logging, and loggers, past to present. And, ultimately, he has shown us what we have become."

—Spike Walker, author of Working on the Edge

"Deadfall doesn't offer easy answers, but Jim LeMonds's sensitive yet unsentimental account of logging in the Pacific Northwest through the experiences of three generations of his family should be required reading for everyone who wants to know just how complicated are the public policy questions, together with the damage to the environment and the human costs after a hundred years of wrangling and litigation."

—Mary Clearman Blew, author of Sister Coyote

"Honest, erudite, passionate, poignant, meticulous, and written with enormous grace and love for a dying craft and way of life, Deadfall is a fine writer's personal elegy for the timber life that once characterized the Pacific Northwest. Jim LeMonds's book takes its place alongside Stewart Holbrook, James Stevens, and Robert Heilman on the shelf of necessary texts for readers who wish to understand and savor the logger—a brave man in the most dangerous job in American history."

—Brian Doyle, editor of *Portland Magazine*

"No one who reads Deadfall *will ever again romanticize the logger as some superhuman mythmaker, or condemn him as a heartless woods-wrecker. In clear, plain, and precise prose, this talented writer portrays the everyday humanity of men who work in the woods and of their families—their courage, tedium, fears, and cold, wet, painful exhaustion—the price they pay to be out among the evergreens instead of behind a desk. I highly recommend* Deadfall *to anyone who would rather have the real thing than the tall tale."*

—Robert Michael Pyle, author of *Wintergreen*

Contents

Acknowledgments *xii*

Introduction *xiii*

Welcome to Timber Country *1*

Old Values in the New World *7*

Farm Boys in the Green Timber *25*

No Looking Back *41*

Aiming for Sixty-Five *59*

Trying to Keep a Little Cushion *75*

The Heart of a Champion *89*

Profile of an American Worker *103*

More Than the Money *117*

Even the Best Expect the Worst *133*

The Best We Had to Give *151*

Will the Last One Out Please Turn Off the Lights? *165*

Eyes Forward *179*

Glossary *183*

Selected References *191*

Index *195*

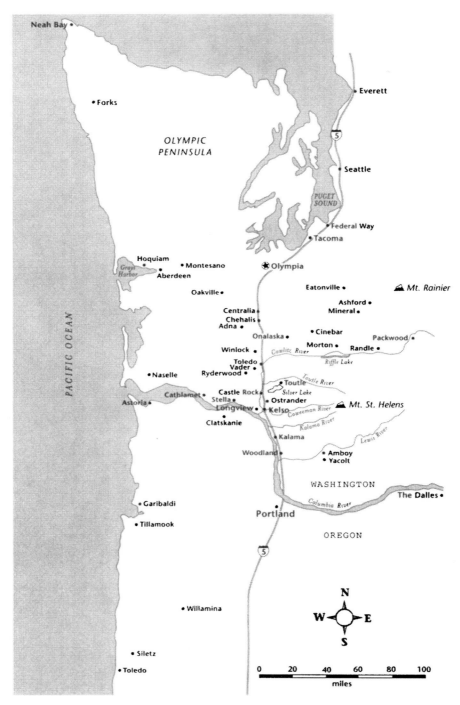

The timber country of western Washington and northwestern Oregon

Logging towns and camps of southwestern Washington

THE BERNDTS

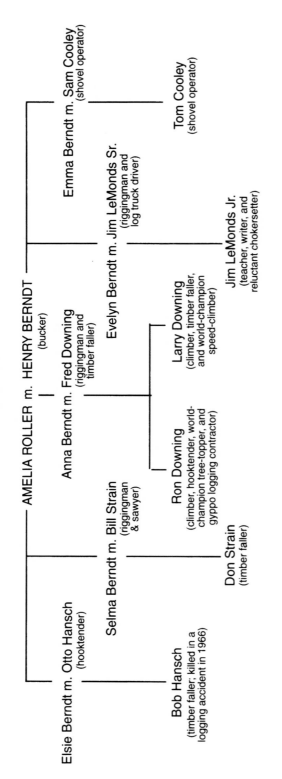

AMELIA ROLLER m. HENRY BERNDT
(bucker)

Elsie Berndt m. Otto Hansch
(hooktender)

Anna Berndt m. Fred Downing
(riggingman and timber faller)

Emma Berndt m. Sam Cooley
(shovel operator)

Evelyn Berndt m. Jim LeMonds Sr.
(riggingman and log truck driver)

Selma Berndt m. Bill Strain
(riggingman & sawyer)

Bob Hansch
(timber faller; killed in a logging accident in 1966)

Ron Downing
(climber, hooktender, world-champion tree-topper, and gyppo logging contractor)

Don Strain
(timber faller)

Larry Downing
(climber, timber faller, and world-champion speed-climber)

Jim LeMonds Jr.
(teacher, writer, and reluctant chokersetter)

Tom Cooley
(shovel operator)

THE ROLLERS

Bill Roller
(roadbuilder; brother of Amelia Berndt)

Ernie Roller
(gyppo logging contractor)

Ed Roller
(gyppo logging contractor)

THE JANISCHES

Bertha Berndt m. Frank Janisch
(sister of Henry Berndt)   (bucker)

Henry Janisch
(timber faller)

Alvin Janisch Sr.
(gyppo logging contractor)

Alvin Janisch Jr.
(shovel operator)

THE LeMONDSES

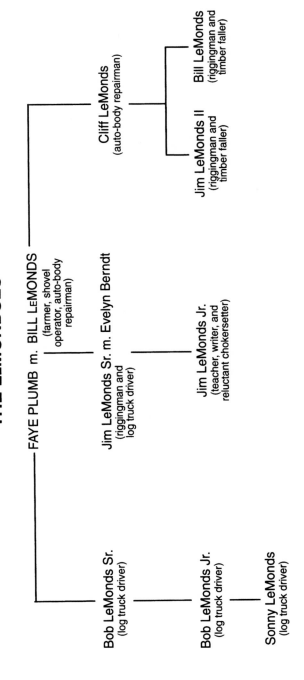

FAYE PLUMB m. BILL LeMONDS
(farmer, shovel operator, auto-body repairman)

Jim LeMonds Sr. m. Evelyn Berndt
(riggingman and log truck driver)

Jim LeMonds Jr.
(teacher, writer, and reluctant chokersetter)

Cliff LeMonds
(auto-body repairman)

Jim LeMonds II
(riggingman and timber faller)

Bill LeMonds
(riggingman and timber faller)

Bob LeMonds Sr.
(log truck driver)

Bob LeMonds Jr.
(log truck driver)

Sonny LeMonds
(log truck driver)

Acknowledgments

Thanks to the following for providing information or assisting with research:

Scott Bailey, Cheryl Borgaard, Tom Bredfield, Jim Carter, Tim Crouse, Fred Dorn, Anna Downing, Fred Downing, Tom Ford, Roger Gallow, Garry Gardner, Ross Gilchrist, Kevin Godbout, Allen Gould Jr., Richard Grabianowski, Elsie Hansch, Ann Johnson, John Keatley, Cliff LeMonds, Dave LeMonds, Sonny LeMonds, W. R. LeMonds, Grace Mack, Don Maddux, Bud May, Margery McKay, Walt Mezger, Betty Phillips, Tim Quinn, Greg Richards, Terry Ruff, Dick Sadler, Margie Wells, Del Whinery, and Donna Yardley.

Thanks to Mom, Kim, Kami, and Sherry, the best women a man could hope to have in his life.

Special thanks to David Freece and the Cowlitz Historical Society for their support of the project during its earliest stages.

And, most of all, thanks to the following men for sharing the stories of their lives: Tom Cooley, Larry Downing, Ron Downing, Bill LeMonds, Bob LeMonds, Jim LeMonds II, and Don Strain.

Introduction

I was three when I took my first ride in my father's log truck. That year, he was driving a 1952 International with a big Cummins diesel engine. We picked up a load at a landing outside Mossyrock, Washington—thirty miles northwest of Mount St. Helens—and hauled it south past our home in Castle Rock to the Exeter dump in Longview. As we came into town, we crossed the Pioneer Bridge, a rickety, high-arching, two-lane structure that spanned the Cowlitz River. The truck barely fit in our lane, and when I stood on the seat to improve my view, my side of the cab seemed to hang in space above the water. Overcome by vertigo, I clung to the back of the seat.

Despite my aversion to narrow bridges and high places, each summer when school was out I rode with my father at least once, hoping to glimpse something of the mysterious working life that kept him away from home during the daylight hours. I loved cruising in that vibrating cab high above the traffic, the engine roar and highway noise providing conversation. Passenger cars below seemed puny and irrelevant by comparison. They lacked the ruggedness and power that extended from the truck's muscular engine to Dad and me. I was young and the equation was simple: we were hauling logs; we were real men, doing real work.

By early afternoon, I was usually worn out, so if a trip took us near Castle Rock, Dad would drop me at our house just off U.S. 99 on his way to or from Longview. Though I rarely made it through an entire day, there were two things I never tired of: watching Dad use both hands simultaneously to throw multiple shifts, manipulating the three levers between us on the floorboard as we geared down to climb the steepest hills; and seeing him signal other truckers when their rigs passed ours, his fingers flashing messages that the scales were open, that the weigh-up cops were lying in ambush just down the road, or that everything was clear for flat-out flying.

Other visuals are hazy, but the olfactory memories of those trips have never left me. It's as though I breathed so deeply of air saturated with diesel and dampness, with the scent of fresh-cut cedar, hemlock, and fir at the landings and log dumps, that the smells never left me when I exhaled. I suppose every child whose father worked in the woods retains a set of images that define logging: scraped knuckles and squashed fingernails; dented hard hats; long underwear; hickory shirts and stagged-off pants stiff with dirt and dried sweat; the smells of chain oil, calk leather, and tobacco; and the lunch bucket that might, at the end of the day, hold a candy bar or cookie Dad had saved as a special treat.

We can't often pinpoint the experiences or scraps of conversation that influenced a decision or set a course. But the events that routed me away from a job in the timber industry are clear in my mind. It began in March 1970 when, as a short-sighted nineteen-year-old, I ran my mouth at the wrong time. I was a sophomore at Western Washington University in Bellingham and had come home to Castle Rock for spring break. The previous summer, I had worked as a shoe salesman at Gallenkamp's in Longview. That week, I stopped by the store to say hello. Jim Tolle, the manager, asked if I wanted to work again in June. He said the position was mine if I wanted it; he also mentioned that the company was looking for trainees for its management program, and he wondered if I might be interested. I told Jim I'd think about his offer.

When my brother Dave and I were growing up, Mom and Dad made it clear that we would finish college. This was not just a hope; considerable family sacrifice had, for years, accompanied this focus, and Dave and I understood what our parents expected of us. But that spring I wasn't in the mood for reason. I had taken a credit overload winter quarter and had just finished a rough set of final exams. I was discouraged that I still had nearly two and a half years of school ahead of me. The evening after I spoke with Jim Tolle, I commented off-handedly at the dinner table that I might return to Gallenkamp's as a salesman during the summer, then give their training program a whirl in the fall. I was only venting, exerting my independence, eliciting a reaction, contemplating, supposing. Surely they knew me well enough to realize I wasn't serious about quitting school. At the time, they merely raised their eyebrows in silence.

Two months later, I learned the details of their deferred response and began to suffer the repercussions. In May, my father phoned me at college and jauntily announced that he had secured me a job: I would be setting chokers for a local independent contractor or gyppo named George Ells. I'd never worked in the woods, but I knew enough to understand that I was in for a great deal of pain. Before I could protest, Dad explained that this was a sensible course of action. The year had been a slow one for him and, as usual, the family savings account was running on empty. I'd make more money working on the rigging than selling shoes at Gallenkamp's. In fact, if I was careful, I could save enough to pay for tuition and books my junior year. My father said nothing about wake-up calls or valuable lessons, but I began to understand how much trouble my brassy talk about a career in the shoe business had gotten me into.

My first day as a chokerman was a Monday in mid-June. Skip Mezger, a neighbor with whom I'd graduated high school, was home from Washington State University for the summer and had hired on as a chaser with the Ells outfit. We rode together to the high-lead tower the crew had set up west of Winlock. When we got to the job site, George Ells introduced us to the hooktender, a grizzled man named Larry, whose name everyone pronounced "Laurie." Larry was in the middle of what Skip and I would learn was his morning ritual: drinking coffee from a badly dented stainless-steel thermos and devouring a package of Hostess Sno-Balls. Pink coconut frosting smeared his face like boldly colored shaving cream. Skip and I decided Larry had spent his life isolated in some hill country "holler." When he later informed us that the hooktender was the brains of any outfit worth its salt, we were extremely skeptical.

Fortunately, after George handed us over to Larry, Larry put me in the care of a soft-spoken riggingman in his forties named Bob. Bob led me to the edge of the landing and pointed out a spot nearly a thousand feet away at the bottom of the deep canyon. That was where we would be working. I immediately envied Skip, whose duties as chaser would keep him on level ground at the top of the hill. Bob and I plunged down the ridge, our spike-soled calk boots digging in as we walked across limbs and debris and followed skid roads cut by turns of logs that had been yarded to the landing the previous day.

Things went reasonably well that morning. Bob was a veteran riggingman and patiently set about teaching me the basics of the chokersetting trade: how to hook the knob of the choker into the bell; how to "bonus" several logs in a single choker; how to link two or three chokers to "tag out" for logs well off the skid road. More importantly, Bob made sure I was always out of the bight and in the clear when the rigging began to move. After lunch, we were working our way through a stack of logs that had rolled into a thin creek at the base of the canyon. I noticed an uprooted old-growth stump forty yards above us, impossibly balanced in a clump of vine maples. Our road was running right past that stump, and each time a turn went up the hill and brushed the vine maple clump, I could feel my muscles tighten right down to my toes.

For the next hour, I had trouble doing my job because I didn't want to take my eyes off that stump. I soon learned I had good reason to be afraid. Bob and I were bending over setting chokers on a turn when I glanced up and saw the stump break free. By the time I had stood and pivoted in his direction, Bob was on his feet staring up the hill. I didn't hesitate or try to sidestep my partner; I ran right over him. I didn't slow down until I was fifty feet up the opposite bank.

When I looked back, I saw that the stump had come to a gentle stop against our cold deck. Meanwhile, my mad rush had sent Bob backwards off the log pile into the shallow creek. I sheepishly made my way over to him, checked to see that he was all right, and apologized for running him down. Rips in his stagged-off pants and hickory shirt marked my calk tracks. Several seeped blood. He shook the water out of his hair, clapped the hard hat back on his head, and smiled. "Jesus, kid!" he said with admiration. "You can really move!"

I lived the rest of the week in fear, constantly on the lookout for maniacal stumps I was certain were lurking just out of sight. To make matters worse, I was so sore from scrambling across the uneven ground that I couldn't keep up with men who were twenty-five years my senior. Larry might have had problems with personal hygiene, but he was at home in this environment. Like Bob, he was rugged and fit and knew his way around. It was a humbling experience for me, and an instructive one. My ideas about the glamour of working in the woods were fading. More lessons awaited me.

One day in July, Larry, Bob, and I were on a sidehill halfway between the landing and the back end of the setting. We'd been sending in nice turns of second-growth firs, many of them forty-eight footers. But the yarder operator was having problems. The landing was so small that he couldn't drag the logs completely onto it. To make matters worse, there was an abrupt rise at the lip of the hill, so the logs tended to tip back off the edge when the operator eased off on the mainline. When the rigging went slack, a log could slide out of its choker and off the landing. Larry had spent a good portion of the day crawling up and down the ridge to remedy these situations, punctuating each trip with colorful language from his expansive hooktender's vocabulary.

Late in the afternoon it happened again, only this time the logs didn't simply tip back off the landing. Two slipped out of the chokers and started down the hill. In an instant, they were coming toward us, end-over-end, like a pair of Mount Rushmore–scale toothpicks. I didn't need to be told what to do; I dove behind a stump and hugged the earth. I could hear those forty-eight footers pounding down the ridge, shaking the ground as they sought us out. I glanced up as one cleared the stump I was huddled behind, flashing a shadow across me like an omen of death as it passed above my head. An instant later, the second crashed into the stump, jolting it so fiercely I thought for a moment it would be ripped from the ground. My knees trembled until the whistle called us out of the brush at the end of the day.

That night at dinner, I told Dad I would finish the job with George Ells, but I made it clear that after that I was done with high-lead logging. The underlying proof of my stupidity shone like a lighthouse beacon when I mentioned in the same breath that setting chokers behind a cat might not be all that bad. When I arrived home from college the next summer, Dad had lined me up with Ted Johnson, a Longview gyppo logging right-of-way near Lake Merwin, southwest of Mount St. Helens. The dangers weren't as dramatic or constant as they had been on the vertical ridges west of Winlock with Larry and Bob, but the bugs and the heat, the chokerjaggers and the never-ending soreness soon wiped away any fantasies that this kind of rigging work might somehow be tolerable. By August, I'd reached two conclusions. First, I would find my own summer job in a different field the next year. Second, I would finish my teaching degree.

I graduated from Western in June 1972. In September, I took a social studies/language arts position at Cascade Junior High in Longview. I have been a teacher for the past twenty-eight years. Those summers in 1970 and 1971 constitute my entire logging experience. Any additional knowledge I have picked up about life in the woods is the result of five decades spent listening to the stories of those who made it their vocation.

Stephen Ambrose, historian and author of *Citizen Soldiers*—a book about the European theatre during World War II—explained his decision to minimize narration and allow the veterans he interviewed to speak for themselves:

> They saw it with their own eyes. They put their lives on the line.
> I didn't. They speak with an authenticity no one else can match.
> Their phrases, their word choices, their slang are unique—
> naturally enough, as their experiences were unique.

In the course of writing this book about logging, I have reread those words many times. They are my personal reminder that this narrative belongs to the timber fallers, truck drivers, riggingmen, and shovel operators who patiently educated me about their working lives. Even though Ambrose's characters were soldiers in a war,

his words fit the loggers I spoke with perfectly. And his counsel—
to let those who have been there supply the story—is incisive and
sound.

Readers expecting a Paul Bunyan treatment of logging have come
to the wrong book. There is a time and place for tall tales and logger lore. This isn't it. I vowed when I started this project that I
would not demean loggers by fabricating or overdramatizing their
experiences. To do so would be a a monumental disservice.

In its summer 1996 issue, *Pacific Northwest Quarterly* published
an insightful essay by Robert E. Wallis titled "Green Commonwealth." Wallis makes the case that in the decade after World War
II, the West Coast Lumbermen's Association, in conjunction with a
number of other Northwest timber companies, spread the Paul
Bunyan legend at every opportunity. They went so far as to hire
James Stevens, author of several collections of Bunyan tales, to
write scripts for extravagant pageants presented at the Shelton Forest Festival in the 1940s and 1950s. Stevens' primary goal was to
generate public support for the industry's nascent tree farm strategy, but he also used the Bunyan character and his mythic feats to
create a trumped-up image of loggers—an image the timber companies propagated shamelessly in what was tantamount to a brain-
washing campaign. According to Wallis, the influence of this American icon was pervasive:

> Bunyan imagery appeared everywhere loggers were: at places they
> visited, in things they read. The workers' hero became a corporate
> contrivance: the industry's quintessential model for labor, a para-
> gon of conformity to an impossible work ethic. Bunyan represents
> the superproductive single male laborer for whom the work and its
> attendant lifestyle are their own reward.

By 1949, the International Woodworkers of America was warning loggers to "forget this proneness to emulate Paul Bunyan and
remember that we are human, our families are human and that
Paul Bunyan and his mighty feats of prowess are just a myth."

But myths die hard. Tell a man often enough that he is too tough
to feel pain, too brave to voice his fears, too stoic to complain about
hazardous conditions, too independent to join a union, too dedi-
cated to his work to do anything other than endure, and he will
begin to believe you. He will accept that "real men" meet this standard and that he is less of a man if he fails to live up to it. Such
thinking is self-defeating, of course. Loggers aren't gods, warriors, or
heroes. They are people, and they are as vulnerable as the rest of us.

I have tried to strip away exaggeration and tell the real story, so
that readers can begin to understand what a logger's life is like and

how economic and political pressures influence that life. There is ample drama in the narratives I have gathered. Some may think I've stretched the truth in places, but that was never my intent. The drama comes from chronicling the history of men who work on the edge—emotionally, financially, or physically—every day.

My family's place in all this is nothing out of the ordinary, but that is precisely why it is worthy of examination. For three generations that spanned nearly the entire twentieth century, my grandfathers, father, uncles, and cousins worked in the timber industry. This is their saga, one in which my role has been to sit quietly and take notes while men I know and love tell a story that stands as a metaphor for loggers everywhere. It is a tale shared by thousands of others who call the Northwest home: a modern-day version of boom-and-bust in a land where timber no longer is king.

Welcome to Timber Country

L IKE THAT OF MOST NORTHWESTERNERS, my history here is a brief
one. Both branches of my family were refugees. My mother's
parents, battered by economic hardship and political repres-
sion, emigrated from the Ukraine to Washington state by way of
Ellis Island and the Great Lakes shortly after the turn of the
century. My father's family came west in the Dust Bowl Depression exodus of the 1930s. Journeys that began more than 5,000
miles apart ended in Castle Rock—a pin-dot timber town in southwest Washington, ten miles north of the confluence of the Cowlitz
and Columbia Rivers. While their cultures, languages, and reli-
gions could not have been more disparate, the Berndt and
LeMonds clans shared an immediate conversion to the timber
lifestyle on their arrival in Cowlitz County. Logging made re-
settlement possible. It paid the bills, bought property, and provided a fragile sense of security, a sense that this time they had
taken hold of something that might last.

Logging was certainly about making a living; it was also about
defining who you were. It was honest work, well suited to people
who didn't mind bending their backs or getting dirt beneath their
fingernails. The ability to stick with it bespoke rough edges, independence, and a tenacity that could garner a person a degree
of respect. My family—both sides of it—bought in from the beginning.

In recent years, rural communities west of the Cascades were
decked out with yard signs that read *This Family Supported By
Timber Dollars.* Had those signs been fashionable during the
1950s and 1960s, you would have seen eighteen in a two-block

1

area of my neighborhood. My father and Les Riffe hauled logs; Howard Stagner, Joe Gunn, Chuck Foster, Jim Slater, Dale Kodad, Al Helenberg, and Orlo Knight worked in the mills; Ivan Golden was a truck boss; George Vernon, Wes Jokela, Max McCoy, Russ McBride, and Chet Hanks cut timber; Sonny Hicks ran loading machine; Frances Piercy was a yarder operator; Walt Mezger was a forester. Eighteen men, eighteen incomes, eighteen households in a neighborhood propped up by logging.

Growing up in a place where logging is woven into the character of the community, you discover that you're part of the culture whether you work in the woods or not. You have uncles, cousins, nephews, in-laws, high school buddies, and friends of friends who are chokermen, truck drivers, and timber fallers. Their work is the topic of conversation at dinner tables and high school sporting events, in restaurants, grocery stores, taverns, and churches. The vocabulary is unique and inescapable, the mythology grounded in tales of human strength and folly played out against a backdrop of harshness, beauty, and grand dimension.

And while logging is less an all-encompassing community force in Castle Rock than it once was, the culture hangs on today with a good measure of resolve. Recently, a friend I teach with bought a pair of *black* Romeo slippers, instead of the traditional brown Romeos—a fashion *faux pas* in these parts on the same level as wearing a bow tie with a hickory shirt. I'm not sure he believed me when I told him there are places in Castle Rock that a man in black Romeos would be wise to avoid. To an outsider, his choice of footwear might seem like a minor transgression, but here, even the clothing is part of the identity, and it is not something that can easily be shrugged off.

Logging has been our way of life for more than a century, but things are different today. Dramatic changes during the last two decades have cut deep. They have shaken our economy, forced us to question the ethics of what we do, and made us pause to wonder where we're headed. During the 1960s, timber-related jobs accounted for nearly 15 percent of Washington's employment. As late as 1979, the industry employed 160,000 people in the Northwest. Ironically, while a bullish foreign market kept harvests relatively stable throughout the 1980s—log exports soared from 210 million board feet a year in 1960 to 4.2 *billion* board feet in 1988—employment dropped almost 20 percent as

2

a result of technological advancements in the industry, and 30,000 people lost their jobs.

Things took an irrevocable downturn in 1990 with the enactment of federal restrictions that set aside habitat for the northern spotted owl. Soon, other species were added to the threatened or endangered list, and the U.S. Forest Service, previously a major supplier of logs for the region's mills, found itself in the impossible position of balancing timber production and species protection. The task of composing separate plans designed to safeguard multiple species in different areas was equally difficult. Endless litigation complicated the issue—environmentalists filed suits to stop logging and timber companies sued for increased access. In an attempt to pacify both sides, the Clinton administration implemented the 1994 Northwest Forest Plan, which removed 88 percent of 24 million acres of federal timberlands from the market. The Forest Service would manage these areas, referred to as "Late Successional Reserves," to provide long-term viability for species dependent on old-growth habitat.

The carrot for timber companies was the implied promise of a steady—albeit sharply reduced—supply of logs from the remaining 12 percent of public forest still available for bid. During the 1980s, timber companies logged 4.5 billion board feet a year on national forestland alone; twenty years later, that number had fallen to 900 million feet. In 1990, the Gifford Pinchot National Forest east of Castle Rock offered 541 million board feet of timber for sale; by 1998, that total was down more than 90 percent to 31 million board feet. The effects of the Northwest Forest Plan were compounded by a 1990 federal mandate that banned the export of logs cut on state land. Thousands of loggers and millworkers lost their jobs in the aftermath of these events.

Millworkers and loggers in Cowlitz County have taken huge hits, with employment falling by half since 1989. And the bad news keeps coming. Changing attitudes about land management and new regulations aimed at protecting watersheds have virtually locked down national forests. Technology continues to minimize the need for hands-on labor. Experts forecast an additional 25 percent reduction in an already decimated work force over the next two decades.

In the meantime, people are looking hard for a way out. My brother-in-law Jim Carter was a logger for twenty-four years. He now attends Lower Columbia College in Longview, where he is studying to become an auto mechanic. When I asked him to name loggers he had worked with who quit or were laid-off, he ticked off nine without hesitating: Ronnie Nolan now works for the county public utilities district; Paul Sebastian controls refrigeration for an orchard in Yakima; Bob Peterson works for Reynolds Metals; Dan Farley, Dick Kleine, and John Stuart work at the Norpac paper mill; Randy Doehne is an electrician; Matt and Mike Meyers do construction work in Portland. "Give me a minute to think about it," Jim said, "and I can come up with a dozen more." Bumped from a job doing maintenance work in the Weyerhaeuser shop in 1999, Jim was given the choice of returning to chokersetting or taking a layoff. He chose the layoff. His hips and knees ache constantly. His doctor has advised him that one shoulder is "worn out" and needs surgery. He can no longer handle the demands of working on the rigging. And with Weyerhaeuser and other timber companies eliminating or contracting out some of the less physical jobs that might have extended his career, he faces starting over. He isn't alone.

The timber industry now employs only 3 percent of the region's workers, though that number is larger in Castle Rock, Morton, Cougar, Onalaska, Randle, Adna, and Shelton—places where enough jobs remain to lure loggers to the notion that they might squeeze out enough years to earn a pension. At times, it feels as though our part of the Northwest is an enclave, separate from the high-tech world inhabited by Boeing, Intel, and Microsoft. Within that isolation we have crossed our fingers and hoped for immunity from change.

At first, loggers and their families refused to admit that things had shifted for good. A handful of diehards continue to deny it, though most of us have finally accepted that the glory days are gone forever. We used up a number of years trying to determine who was to blame: mismanagement or the spotted owl, Earth First or a shrunken export market. It wasn't a particularly productive exercise; it merely diverted our attention from the fact that the present had become a past that would not segue smoothly into the future.

Life goes on in the Northwest, even if what passes for logging bears little resemblance to what we once knew. In towns like Castle Rock, old men retired from the woods still dress in denims and *Loggers World* suspenders when they trek to the post office to pick up their mail, as though in the simple act of selecting their attire they are remembering for all of us, willing us back to those bright days when we knew it was going to last. Clearly, however, we are not exempt. Economic and environmental forces have drawn us into a vortex fraught with frightening possibilities.

It wasn't always this way.

Old Values in the New World

MY MATERNAL GRANDFATHER worked with wood from the time he was a boy. The son of a barrelmaker, Henry Berndt was born in 1887 in Walinigen, a Ukrainian village near the city of Rovno. The Berndt family's roots extended back several generations in Russia—back to the middle of the eighteenth century when Catherine the Great invited German settlers east to farm and settle the rich lands of the Ukraine and Volga. Because their own country was in political and economic disarray, nearly a million Germans immigrated to Russia, enticed by guarantees that they would be excused from military service and allowed to run their schools and churches as they saw fit.

Henry and his father, August, were gyppos in the Old World sense: independent operators producing barrels from start to finish. Because the forest near their Walinigen home belonged to Nicholas II, they could not remove a tree without first securing a government permit. Once they received the permit, they selected a tree—most likely a hardwood such as an oak or ash—felled it, limbed it, and dragged it to the house with a team of horses. The tsar's rules concerning reforestation were stringent: each stump had to be grubbed out and a seedling planted in its place.

At home, Henry and August sawed the log into sections and split it into staves planed narrow-wide-narrow. They soaked and shaped the pieces, then bound them together with strands of split willow. They filled the barrel with water to swell the staves and reduce the potential for leaks. A team and wagon hauled the finished barrels to Rovno, where they were sold to local manufacturers.

By the time he was fifteen, Henry had lost both a mother and stepmother to disease. His remaining family battled poverty and bubonic plague. To make matters worse, a nationalistic movement evolved in Russia that sought to eliminate all traces of "the foreign element." Germans, welcomed to Russia a century before, were now scorned and persecuted. Their exemption from military service was rescinded and government officials monitored their schools, removing teachings about the German culture and language from the curriculum.

Henry's sister Bertha escaped to America in 1906. She lived with an uncle in Racine, Wisconsin, where she met and married Frank Janisch. By 1907, the newlyweds had saved the eighty-four dollars necessary to finance Henry's passage to the United States. He arrived aboard the *New Amsterdam* at Ellis Island in the fall of that year, unable to speak a word of English, and traveled by train to Racine. In 1909, he remet a girl named Amelia Roller, whom he had known in Walinigen, and they married that July.

Amelia had brothers in Castle Rock, Washington, where property was available and affordable. After the Civil War, the U.S. Congress had granted federal land to railroad companies as incentive to extend their lines to undeveloped regions of the Midwest and South. The experiment had worked so well that lawmakers continued the program to encourage building of the transcontinental rail lines. For each completed mile of track, the company received ten sections (6,400 acres) of land. By the early 1900s, the railroad companies were eager to turn their land holdings into cash and to create markets for rail transport. They saturated the eastern seaboard and the Great Lakes region with flyers and newspaper advertisements boasting of cheap land and good jobs out West. The companies' plan was simple: use inexpensive property to entice people to communities along the rail lines; those communities would become customers, reliant on the railroads to bring supplies in and take products out.

Fed up with the oppressive humidity and limited economic opportunities in Racine, the Berndts and Janisches began paying attention to the railroad companies' embellished descriptions of the Pacific Northwest, a land with a moderate climate and lush topography similar to what they had known in the Ukraine. In 1911, they rode the train cross-country to Castle Rock to join Amelia's brothers, who were working in the timber industry.

Northwest logging had gotten its start in 1827, when John McLoughlin of the Hudson's Bay Company established the region's first sawmill at present-day Vancouver, Washington. By 1860, Castle Rock boasted a mill—the second in Cowlitz County— west of town on Arkansas Creek. With so much timber available, every fledgling community west of the Cascades soon had its own logging outfits and accompanying lumber and shingle mills.

During the last quarter of the nineteenth century, San Francisco companies, most notably Pope and Talbot, had dominated the Northwest logging scene, but that was about to change. Once the Northern Pacific and Great Northern railroads reached the West Coast, timber companies could ship lumber to the East without the costly, time-consuming saltwater passage around South America's Cape Horn. This transportation breakthrough, coupled with the depletion of forests in the Great Lakes states, focused investors' attention on the Northwest. Among the speculators was Frederic Weyerhaeuser, who had started in the sawmill business on the Mississippi River during the Civil War.

In January 1900, in one of the largest land transfers in U.S. history, Weyerhaeuser and a group of Midwestern investors bought 900,000 acres of Northwest forest for six dollars an acre. Weyerhaeuser supplied one-third of the capital and brokered the deal with James J. Hill of the cash-poor Northern Pacific Railroad. The total purchase price was $5.5 million. On signing the papers, the Weyerhaeuser Timber Company became the second largest private owner of timberlands in the nation. The company bought 261,000 more acres from Northern Pacific the next year, in addition to acquiring forestland from private sources. By 1903, Weyerhaeuser's holdings in the region totaled 1.3 million acres.

That same year, the company made its initial foray into its Northwest holdings, establishing logging camps south of Mount St. Helens near the town of Yacolt, thirty miles northeast of Vancouver. A huge fire there in 1902 had damaged or destroyed 2 billion board feet of timber on twenty thousand acres that belonged to Weyerhaeuser; logs that could be salvaged were now designated for removal. The company set up fifteen different campsites at Yacolt, operating up to three camps simultaneously with nearly three hundred men on the payroll. Loggers took out an average of 75 million feet of timber annually. The company moved it by rail to the Columbia and sold it to sawmills along the river. The salvage job would eventually wind down, but the company had no intention of stopping there. George Long, head of Weyerhaeuser operations in the Northwest, told anyone who would listen, "Timber is a resource that can be renewed." There was no reason, he said, "why this resource cannot be made perpetual and of sufficient quantity to meet all possible wants." However, several decades passed before Long's ideal made its way into company policy. Weyerhaeuser was preparing to establish a Cowlitz County operation that would rely on logs from an ancient forest stretching between modern-day Interstate 5 and Mount St. Helens. A coordinated effort got underway in the late 1920s involving logging, rail transportation, and milling.

In addition to increasing its burgeoning economic influence, the company began to flex its political muscle. George Long convinced Washington state legislators to establish a state fire warden, county fire wardens, and a system to regulate burning permits. In 1908, the Washington Fire Association was created. Owners of 2.3 million acres of private timberland contributed an annual tax of one-half cent per acre to pay the wages of seventy-five forest patrolmen. Similar legislation passed in Oregon. Forest conservation was now on the front burner in the region's state capitols, and Weyerhaeuser continued lobbying efforts to ensure that it remained there.

Other changes were on the way, as well. In 1905, the Wobblies formed the infamous Industrial Workers of the World, which many government officials and timber company owners would soon view as a seditious organization engaged in criminal activity. Determined to raise wages and remedy the horrendous conditions in logging camps, IWW members were busy sowing the seeds of rebellion among millworkers and loggers throughout the Northwest. Also in 1905, anger resulting from the razing of forests in the Northeast and the Great Lakes region led to the creation of the U.S. Forest Service to manage national forestland. Six years later, when my grandfather arrived in Castle Rock, George Cecil of the Forest Service's Portland office issued this statement about the agency's responsibility:

> Communities will depend upon the national forests for a steady supply of timber and if we cannot meet this demand, we have failed in our mission. . . . [It is] doubly important that we regulate

national forest cuttings with the greatest consideration for the future welfare of the local communities.

The community my grandparents came to in 1911 was hardly a boom town, but Castle Rock's merchants were making a go. H. A. Richards had opened a jewelry store. St. Helens Livery advertised "fine rigs . . . with careful and courteous drivers furnished on request." J. W. Hargrave offered his services as a painter and paper hanger. H. G. Searls was trumpeting the arrival of the new U.S. Cream Separator at his general store. The Castle Rock Lumber Yard, Peabody's Cafe, the Castle Rock Creamery, and half a dozen other businesses were also turning a dollar.

Make no mistake, though; the timber business was the economic, political, and cultural lifeline on which Castle Rock depended. In the years after my grandparents' arrival, the local newspaper, the *Cowlitz County Advocate*, was filled with reports of commercial activity, injuries, and deaths at the Ostrander Railway and Timber Company, the Jensen Mill, the Peabody Shingle Mill, the Silverlake Railway and Lumber Company, the Barnes Mill, and others; the Woodsmen of the World met in Castle Rock on the second and fourth Saturday nights of each month to discuss wages and safety concerns; the Thurston County Sheriff's Department raided three logging camps in the Centralia area, rousting five hundred loggers and arresting six men caught with "Wobbly propaganda" in their possession; and the Secretary of Agriculture informed postal workers that their duties would include keeping an eye out for forest fires along their routes. The scene was essentially the same in hundreds of towns throughout the Pacific Northwest where logging ruled.

Castle Rock was in the very heart of timber country, and that timber was impressive indeed. Only the finest old-growth trees went to the mills; those with even infinitesimal flaws were labeled culls and left to rot. Ground logging—dragging the logs across the ground, as opposed to the later high-lead method that used elevated rigging to lift logs—was the new technology. The steam-powered "donkeys" that Simon Benson and others introduced in southwest Washington to pull timber to cleared landings, had, by 1910, almost completely supplanted the oxen and horses that had previously dragged felled timber from the woods. The first donkeys (also called yarders) were equipped with single-cylinder steam engines. Fueled by a wood fire in a boiler mounted

Single-drum donkeys of the ground-logging era used a "line horse" to return chokers to the rigging crew. —Courtesy Cowlitz History Museum

on the machine, the cylinder turned a winch that wound line around a drum; this mainline pulled the logs to the landing. Initially, a horse dragged the mainline back to the rigging crew. Soon, however, donkeys were upgraded. New models had two cylinders and could generate 200 pounds of steam pressure. These machines also had two drums—one for the mainline, the other for a haulback—eliminating the need for a line horse. A shackle hooked together the mainline and haulback cables, which ran through a pair of blocks called Tommy Moores positioned several hundred feet from the landing. The Tommy Moores, each weighing nearly 500 pounds, were the equivalent of giant pulleys. The crew anchored the blocks to large stumps or trees just beyond the site where the cutters had left the bucked logs. The layout resembled a baseball field, with the donkey at home plate and the blocks positioned at the foul poles. The chokermen secured the logs with cables connected to the butt rigging, which was attached to the mainline; the donkey operator then activated the mainline drum to yard the logs to the landing. Once the chaser had unhooked the logs, the operator reversed the process; using the haulback drum, he returned the rigging to the crew.

Even as early as 1908, new donkeys might cost $5,000, but they were worth the money. They had tremendous power, enabling the operator to yank massive old-growth logs through a landscape strewn with stumps and culls. To withstand the strain, mainline cable measured at least one-and-one-quarter inches in diameter, while haulback and choker cables were often one inch or one-and-one-eighth inches. Because of the tendency of turns—groups of logs lassoed with chokers—to get hung up, rigging crews included a sniper who used an axe to bevel the ends of logs headed for the landing, allowing them to slide over obstacles more easily. The donkey sat on log skids so that the operator could move the machine—even across inconceivably rough terrain—by anchoring the mainline to a distant tree or stump then winding the donkey toward it. The ends of the donkey skids

Two-drum yarders eliminated the need for a line horse.
—Courtesy Cowlitz History Museum

were also beveled as much as forty-five degrees, enabling the machine to ride over logs and stumps like the prow of a ship rides over swells and waves.

Moving the logs to the sawmill created many challenges. In the latter half of the nineteenth century, when Northwest logging began in earnest, sawmills were built on rivers to make the transportation of product easy and inexpensive. While a few outfits experimented with flumes that moved logs several miles from woods to sawmill, most limited their cutting to timber close to the mill site. By the early part of the twentieth century, marketable trees near rivers and existing communities had been cut, and the remaining timber was increasingly difficult to reach. Forced to push back into the surrounding hills, companies laid down rails, built trestles, and eventually created technology that efficiently yarded the logs, revamping the industry's style and strategy in the process.

In 1902, the Silverlake Railway and Lumber Company laid more than five miles of track from a dump on the Cowlitz River south of Castle Rock to its logging sites east of town. It was the first local effort to reach beyond the city limits to gather timber for the mills; it would not be the last. One resulting complication was that transporting men from town to increasingly distant workplaces and back daily was prohibitively time-consuming. Operators began building logging camps on-site, so that their employees would literally wake up on the job each morning. A number of such camps sprang up around Castle Rock in the days after the First World War, including the Stillwater Camp, the Studebaker Camp, and the Silverlake Camp east of Castle Rock where Henry Berndt stayed during the early 1920s.

In 1908, the Whitney Camp on the Columbia River near Astoria, Oregon, boasted hot showers, a library, electric lights, refrigeration, a barbershop, and beds with springs and mattresses. But conditions in most camps were less than comfortable. A few companies housed their men on trains equipped with dining and sleeping cars. Most, however, opted to build bunkhouses on skids, so that the entire operation could be loaded onto rail cars and shipped to new work sites once workers logged out an area. Bunkhouses, typically ten by twenty-four feet, housed as many as sixteen men in two-tiered, wooden bunks that lined the outer walls. Loggers had to supply their own bedrolls.

Because of the close quarters, stories about snorers took on mythic proportions; the sound and volume of one "ground-shaker" were likened to "a one-man dogfight." Rough boards sided the bunkhouses, allowing wind to whistle in through the cracks. One timber faller said it was like "bunkin' inside a picket fence." Kerosene lamps furnished bunkhouses with a dim light that barely reached the corners. In the middle of the room sat a pot-bellied, cast-iron stove around which the loggers hung their socks, underwear, and shirts to dry. In the corners of the bunkhouse, the paraffin-coated wool trousers known as tin pants—rigid with dried mud—stood like half-suits of armor. Because the stove's heat could stiffen leather, calk shoes were kept away from the fire; most loggers preferred that their boots remain damp and flexible.

Boot grease, kerosene, perspiration, pipe smoke, and musty clothing combined to produce a sharp, oppressive aroma. On Sundays, those unable to handle their own accumulated grime and odor heated water on the stove in discarded kerosene cans and gave themselves and their clothes a quick washing. The rest lived with the stench.

Weyerhaeuser's Camp One, northeast of Longview, Washington —Courtesy Elsie Hansch

In addition to the overpowering stink, sanitation was a constant concern. Sometimes the men had to boil their long underwear to kill lice, and infestations of bedbugs made sleeping nearly impossible. At one camp on Grays Harbor, bugs were so thick in the bunkhouse that the crew opted to sleep outside. The loggers used a variety of techniques to deal with the problem, including fogging bunkhouses with steam and sprinkling clothes with kerosene. A riggingman named Pete employed the most inventive measure. He reasoned that because dynamite was so powerful, its ingredients would surely put the kibosh on even the toughest bedbug. After lining his bunk with sticks of TNT, Pete woke the next morning so sick from exposure to sulfur that he couldn't work. By all accounts, the bedbugs suffered no ill effects. Pete, on the other hand, had to spend several days in the sack with the vermin before he was well enough to handle a shift on the rigging. From that day forward, he was known around camp as Dynamite Pete.

Daylight permitting, the workday lasted ten or eleven hours, Monday through Saturday. The men cherished the little time that remained for recreation. Playing cards was a favorite evening pastime; typically, the men played cribbage during the week and serious draw poker on Saturday nights. If you were fortunate, someone in your bunkhouse might provide passable harmonica or violin music. Talk in camp limited itself primarily to logging and romance, the latter receiving increasing emphasis as the weekend approached. The men spent Saturday nights and holidays on booze, women, and blown paychecks, provided they could get to a place large enough to boast a bar. Because forays into the civilized world demanded a certain level of propriety, many loggers owned a suit of clothes for trips to town. Tailors often visited camps to display cloth and take measurements, bringing fifths of whiskey with them as a courtesy to their customers. Missionaries also dropped by on occasion to try and save some souls, but they didn't find many takers.

Practical jokes were rampant. They included short-sheeting beds, filling calk boots with raw eggs, and sprinkling pepper on bunkhouse stoves to set off sneezing fits. Men hoisted bunks off the floor and bound them to the ceiling with heavy wire. They sabotaged bedrolls with crawdads, thistles, and even bear traps. One group of imaginative fellows attached a six-inch fuse to a stick of locomotive grease; its cardboard cover made it look like dynamite. They lit the fuse and tossed the stick through an open window just to see how quickly the bunkhouse would empty. Another stunt involved a billy goat shipped by speeder from one camp to another and left during the day to stink up some poor victims' sleeping quarters.

One perk that seems surprising under the circumstances was that, in general, the men ate like kings. It might seem strange that companies that paid men poor wages and made them work in unsanitary, unsafe conditions would feed them so well, but food was fuel; employers knew that without it their workers wouldn't perform effectively. A few camps tried to cut corners by employing cooks who earned bonus pay by minimizing expenditures; the loggers called such cooks gut robbers. For the most part, crews didn't tolerate poor food or limited quantities. An incompetent cook might find hotcakes nailed to his bunkhouse door, a less-than-subtle message that he'd better seek employment elsewhere. In an attempt to keep the men happy, companies recruited good cooks, paid them well, and gave them free reign to produce enormous meals. Commonly regarded as the most important man on the payroll other than the foreman, the cook had total control of his cookhouse and his crew and immeasurable influence in recruiting skilled loggers. Men might quit a job and take a 20 percent pay cut to hire on with a company that had a reputable cook. Simply put, the outfits that served the best food got the best loggers.

Meals in camp were legendary, comparing favorably to those served in the finest hotels. Even the Wobblies had little to say about the grub, ample evidence that there wasn't much to grouse about. Studies of loggers' diets have found that they commonly polished off between seven thousand and nine thousand calories per day, nearly three times the total today's average man consumes. Riggingmen, fallers, and buckers expended between eight and twelve calories per minute, with bone-chilling weather and heavy gear adding to the caloric burn; by comparison, today's truck drivers and machine operators use up only one-and-one-half to two-and-one-half calories per minute. An incredible 1,200 grams of carbohydrates—essential because they provided instant energy as well as a quick hike in body temperature on cold days—comprised half the calorie total. Despite their tremendous caloric intake, loggers had no need of Slimfast or Fen-phen. Obesity was so rare that if a fat man was spotted in the woods, superstitious loggers believed three accidents would occur immediately thereafter.

While weather conditions, season, and access to markets influenced the menu, a survey of Northwest logging camps in the 1930s found the following items frequently listed on the bill of fare: corned beef, ham, bacon, pork, roast beef, chops, steaks, hamburger, chicken, oysters, cold cuts, potatoes, barley, macaroni, boiled oats, sauerkraut, fresh and canned fruits, berries, jellies and jams, pickles, carrots, turnips, biscuits, breads, pies, cakes, doughnuts, puddings, custards, condensed or fresh milk, coffee, and tea. During the 1930s, as many as 1,200 workers lived in Weyerhaeuser's camps in southwest Washington. Each day, they consumed 250 pounds of ham and bacon, 1,100 pounds of beef, 1,500 pounds of vegetables, 500 pounds of fruit, 3,000 eggs, 225 gallons of milk, and 100 pounds of ground coffee. The weekly total weighed in at twenty-five tons. While there were always leftovers, no self-respecting cook would ever serve them to the men. A cook at a camp in Oregon once told a reporter, "Leftovers is a dirty word." She sent hers to the bosses' lunchroom.

Breakfast and dinner were served in the cookhouse. "Flunkies"—usually women—fired the wood stoves, did prep work for the cook, waited tables, and handled the cleanup. The greatest sin a flunky could commit was failing to thoroughly rinse soap from pots, plates, cups, or silverware. Such neglect could set off a bout of diarrhea, inevitably followed by threats of bodily harm directed at the kitchen staff. The men ate their meals in silence; they were there to feed their bodies, not to run their mouths. Because the cook had to supervise cleanup and begin preparing the next meal, he was anxious to send the men on their way. As a result, it wasn't unusual for crew members to wolf down three thousand calories and be out the door in ten to twelve minutes. As the men boarded the train or speeder for work, they picked up lunch buckets the cook had packed. Meat sandwiches, boiled eggs, fresh fruit, and a dessert of pie, cake, or doughnuts comprised the common midday fare. In some camps, food was laid out buffet-style on a table in the cookhouse, and each crew member assembled his own lunch.

Table manners in the camps were not something Emily Post would have approved. If a meal was bad, it might get tossed through a window. If a logger felt his request for a dish at the far end of the table was being ignored, he might stomp down the middle of it to get what he wanted. For a family man like my grandfather, even good food and a regular paycheck couldn't make camp life appealing.

Every job Henry Berndt held during the thirty-five years of his working life in the New World was in some way connected to logging and lumber. He worked at a sawmill owned by Henry Dierks; as a powder monkey, blowing stumps to clear right-of-way for his nephews, Ed and Ernie Roller; as a riggingman for Jeff Cox; and as a roadbuilder, laying planks for Taylor Brothers Logging Company. For a time, Henry and his brother-in-law Frank Janisch hewed bridge timbers for the McCormick Logging Company. Steam-powered trains transported logs to the mills in Longview, so millions of board feet of prime timber went into trestles that spanned the creeks and canyons. One of the men on the McCormick crew who admired their handiwork referred to Frank Janisch and Henry Berndt as "artists with a broad axe."

Trestles built to span creeks and ravines were essential to rail transportation prior to World War II and the advent of a widespread network of roads that provided access for log trucks. —Courtesy Cowlitz History Museum

19

The "High Bridge" near Ryderwood, Washington —Courtesy Bud May

Although he held many different jobs, Henry's primary employment was as a bucker, charged with sawing the trees cut by timber fallers to marketable lengths. Unlike fallers, who typically worked in pairs, buckers worked alone. Because the huge logs were wont to shift while the bucker was in the middle of a cut, pinching the saw so tightly that he could not extricate it, buckers drove steel wedges into their kerfs to prevent them from closing. It was difficult work that required caution, perseverance, and an eye for the mathematics of angle, stress, and torque. Henry bucked for a number of area gyppos, or independent contractors, including Hilde Lilligren, Rodney Settlemier, and the Barley Logging Company. He was short—only five-four or five-five—and stocky, his physique a reflection of the barrels he had constructed as a boy. His diminutive stature forced him to start his saw at a severe angle on firs and cedars, which commonly measured five to eight feet in diameter. Even while he was talking, eating a sandwich, or smoking his pipe, Henry kept the saw moving, lubricating the blade with an occasional spritz from an oil bottle hung by a hook on the bark of the log. My father couldn't believe how fast Henry finished those cuts.

By the time my grandfather retired in 1947, conditions in the woods had improved markedly. Many camps had electric lights and hot showers; bunkhouse occupancy was limited to eight men; the company provided mattresses and bedding; and cleanliness was no longer viewed as a Sunday-only proposition. Wages had risen sharply with the advent of unionization, and the eight-hour workday for which the Wobblies had fought so hard was now commonplace. Working conditions were still far from safe, but companies had agreed to dispense with the full-speed-at-any-cost high-ball pace that had resulted in thousands of injuries and deaths during the 1920s and 1930s.

Henry and Amelia Berndt raised nine children, seven of them girls. Though their sons, Ed and Walter, did not work in the woods, five sons-in-law did. Otto Hansch was a hooktender; Bill Strain, a riggingman and sawyer; my father, Jim LeMonds, a log truck driver; Fred Downing, a horse logger, riggingslinger, and timber

Long-Bell Company bucker Harold Dobbins at work near Ryderwood. At top, wedges driven into the kerf prevent the log from pinching the saw. An oil bottle hangs nearby for lubricating the blade. —Courtesy Bud May

faller; Sam Cooley, a bulldozer and shovel operator. These were the men who provided for Henry Berndt's daughters and his grandchildren. Like their father-in-law, they saw logging and lumber as their links to a thin corner of the American Dream, and during the 1930s and 1940s, in the wake of the Great Depression, a thin corner was far more than most people were laying hold of.

Everywhere Henry looked, logging made things possible, even becoming a property owner. In the cut-and-run days of the first

A bucker uses a handsaw to muscle through an old-growth giant. —Courtesy Longview Public Library

half of the century, timber companies weren't interested in land, only in trees. When they finished logging an area, they often forfeited it by failing to pay property taxes or sold it at a rock-bottom price. In 1919, my grandfather bought a forty-acre stump farm on Tower Road from the McCormick Logging Company. Soon after Henry made his purchase, McCormick decided to extend its rail line across a corner of the Berndt property. The company bought an easement from my grandfather, who used the money to pay off his mortgage. Even the marvel of having a telephone in the front room was the result of logging. When McCormick established Camp Cowlitz, several miles east of the Berndt home, the company ran a phone line from Castle Rock up Tower Road to connect with the camp. Henry arranged for a hook-up, enabling his family to join a handful of others outside the city limits who enjoyed such a luxury.

In the thirty-six years between my grandfather's arrival in America and his retirement in 1947, the timber industry pro-vided him with enough income to purchase a home and keep a wife and nine children fed and clothed. Henry Berndt was proud of the transition he had made and pleased with the things he had accomplished. He liked to tell his children that three meals a day and a roof above your head added up to a pretty good life.

Like the majority of people living in Washington at the time, he was unaware that timber companies were cutting trees on private lands at a rate four times faster than they could regrow. Even if someone had passed the word along to him and his fel-low northwesterners, it would have been impossible for them to comprehend what this depletion would eventually mean. The land was rich, the climate perfectly suited to growing trees. Once you left the city limits of many towns west of the Cascades, forests of old-growth firs, cedars, and hemlocks, their trunks like columns adorning the temple of some great green god, stretched as far as the eye could see. It was easy to believe that this place offered unending prosperity.

Farm Boys in the Green Timber

MY PATERNAL GRANDFATHER, Bill LeMonds, shuffled his family around Iowa and South Dakota during the 1920s and early 1930s, trying his hand at tenant farming in a variety of locales with mixed success. By 1936, farmers in America's heartland met little success, mixed or otherwise. The cumulative effects of dust storms, drought, and pestilence were simply more than they could endure: payments to creditors put off again and again; children resigned to wearing shirts and shoes held together by patches; and, worst of all, the stomach-wrenching sense that the future was unlikely to bring anything better. That spring, Bill and his wife, Faye, decided to make the break and head west. Although apprehensive about the move, they took heart in the likelihood that earning a living in Washington would be no more difficult than surviving in the Badlands. They'd heard jobs were available—that the region had escaped the Depression's most devastating effects. And while they weren't moving to the Northwest to raise corn, a healthy ration of green in the landscape was certain to buoy the heart of a failed farmer.

They sold their farm equipment and livestock, said good-bye to their friends, and loaded clothes, keepsakes, four children, and a neighbor boy, Elmer Haney, into their 1935 Chevy pickup and a 1930 Oldsmobile that belonged to their oldest son, Bob. Their daughter Lorraine was twenty; Elmer was her sweetheart. Bob was eighteen; Jim, my father, was fifteen; and Cliff was eleven. After reaching Vancouver, Washington, they drove north on Highway 99 and pulled in at a roadside travelers' stop called Come-Back Camp a few miles south of Castle Rock.

Long-Bell Company high-lead machine and crew near Ryderwood
—Courtesy Castle Rock Exhibit Hall

When the LeMondses arrived in 1936, southwest Washington was alive with logging activity. Ground logging, prevalent when Henry Berndt came to Castle Rock in 1911, had given way to high-lead. Crews still used steam donkeys, but they now ran the mainline and haulback cables through blocks hung in giant spar trees. Elevating the lines kept the rigging out of the brush and gave the donkey operator upward leverage that added speed and efficiency. Most importantly, the high-lead method eliminated some of the seemingly endless hang-ups that had plagued ground loggers. In his book *From Jamestown to Coffin Rock: A History of Weyerhaeuser Operations in Southwest Washington*, Alden Jones writes that logging outfits west of Castle Rock experimented with high-lead as early as 1918. According to an article in the *Cowlitz Historical Quarterly*, though, Bob Barr of Kelso was primarily responsible for introducing high-lead logging to the area in 1923. Barr brought in mainline two inches in diameter for his logging operation east of Kelso on the Coweeman River, a tributary of the Columbia. The cable was so heavy it took six wagons, each carrying a coil with line stretching between the rigs, to transport it to the woods. Almost immediately, Barr's operation won over the skeptics, and ground logging soon became a thing of the past.

Long-Bell Company, with a base camp in Ryderwood that housed 2,900 loggers, their wives, and children, was cutting magnificent tracts of timber on the northeast edge of the Willapa Hills. Weyerhaeuser had established camps throughout the Toutle, Kalama, and Coweeman river drainages and was working its way east toward Mount St. Helens. And there were gyppos, dozens of them—independent contractors dreaming of a piece of the financial pie. Pope and Talbot had contracted to log Weyerhaeuser timber north of Castle Rock. They subsequently sub-contracted with Michael and Hiles, Ted Welty, McLean and Shaffer, and others. Lowheed and Boke had set up on Green River, northwest of Mount St. Helens; Julian Rudy had built a mill at Twenty-five Mile, east of Toutle; Lindsay and Schaeffer were logging near Whittle Creek, west of Castle Rock; Eastern-Western and a half-dozen others were working the hills west of Longview, where industry legend Simon Benson, who spearheaded the use of everything from steam donkeys to cigar rafts, had initially set up shop. If you wanted work and didn't mind that it was rigorous, you had come to the right place.

My father's family spent a week or two getting settled at Come-Back Camp, then focused on finding employment. A search of the local paper turned up an ad for pulpwood cutters. Louie Schaeffer, the contact man, was selling white fir to the Strawboard Mill in Kelso and looking for hires with strong backs, no experience necessary. My grandfather got in touch with Schaeffer, who agreed to give Bill and his sons a shot.

Bill had become acquainted with a Castle Rock logger named Fred Moore who claimed to know a good deal about cutting timber. When Bill told him of the job offer from Louie Schaeffer, Moore agreed to help get the newcomers started. The sale of the family's farm equipment and livestock had netted $400; Bill spent $150 of it on a gas-powered drag saw, a requisite for cutting pulpwood. After limbing a downed log, the pulpwood cutters had to wrestle the saw—which weighed close to 200 pounds—onto one end of the log and maneuver it into place. They made cuts every twenty-six inches. Bill and Fred Moore ran the drag saw; my father, Elmer Haney, and Bob limbed the logs and peeled, split, and stacked the wood on a sled—similar to a farmer's stone boat—

owned by Jack Gibson. Louie Schaeffer had hired Gibson's son Hoot to skid the wood to a landing with a team of horses. From the landing, trucks hauled it to the Strawboard Mill.

Beforehand, of course, there was the matter of felling the old-growth white fir. Because white fir is soft, it makes poor lumber; it was considered trash wood, good for nothing but pulp. The timber companies, focused only on top-quality Douglas fir and cedar, had left great swaths of white fir standing. The prairie had supported the occasional oak that, like the farmers, struggled to suck enough life out of the earth to endure another year, but it had none of these evergreens, seven feet in diameter, soaring skyward more than 200 feet, lined out like endless masts on a mythic sailing ship. It was a scene that took some getting used to.

A drag saw used for cutting firewood and pulpwood
—Courtesy Cowlitz History Museum

Timber fallers balance atop springboards near Ostrander, Washington.
—Courtesy Cowlitz History Museum

Fred Moore took charge of the falling; Bob assisted him. Using a two-by-six approximately seven feet long for each of them, they fashioned makeshift springboards; these enabled fallers to work on a level plane above the brush that could interfere with their labor. First, Fred and Bob chopped mail-slot-like holes several feet off the ground on opposite sides of a tree. Next, Fred drove sixteen-penny nails halfway into one end of each board; the protruding heads provided bite when the boards were inserted into the slots. Perched on their springboards, Bob and Fred Moore spent the better part of an hour chopping the face and sawing the backcut in the first tree. The others waited, not sure what to expect. When the huge white fir went over with a siren whoosh that culminated in an earth-shaking explosion, the farm boys were awed to silence.

The pulp-cutting job ended in the spring of 1937, just a year after they had left the Midwest, but the LeMondses discovered that employment was always available in the Pacific Northwest, provided you didn't insist on working at the Weyerhaeuser or Long-Bell mills in Longview. Most jobs in the timber industry, like the stint with Louie Schaeffer, were temporary, lasting only weeks or months. But the Weyerhauser and Long-Bell mills offered long-term employment that could last a working lifetime. "You couldn't buy a mill job back then," my father recalls. Landing one required unusual good fortune, a friend or relative with company connections, or a membership in the Mason Lodge. Fred Moore lined up jobs for Bob, Dad, and Elmer Haney on a section crew at the Crown-Willamette logging camp near Cathlamet. Bob and Elmer were over eighteen and of legal age— but my father was only sixteen and lied to the foreman in order to get hired. They worked for Crown for several months before one of the foremen learned the truth and sent Dad down the road. Soon after, Bob, who had quit when his brother was fired, decided to try his hand at truck driving. He traded his car in on a 1936 Chevrolet log truck with a single-axle trailer. Because he could only work in good weather—few routes were rocked, and the graded dirt roads turned to bog once the heavy rains arrived—he found he couldn't make the payments and had to turn the truck back to the dealership.

After leaving Come-Back Camp, the family stayed for several months at a rental home on Headquarters Road east of Castle Rock. In 1937, they moved to a rental in town, a three-bedroom house on the corner of Fifth and D. The children continued to live at home, but Elmer Haney pulled up stakes and headed back to South Dakota. Elmer never adapted to the confining effect of ridges and trees; he wanted open spaces, flat ground, and a view that extended for a day's ride in every direction. He had hoped to marry Lorraine, who was working as a housekeeper in Longview, but she refused to return to the Midwest with him.

My father got a job cutting shingle bolts at George Schultz's mill on Whittle Creek, less than a mile from his current home. When the job with Schultz ended in 1938, he went to work for forty cents an hour running drag saw at George Lindsay's mill north of Castle Rock. There he got acquainted with a young fellow named Don Slaven, who mentioned that his stepfather, Bill Snyder, was setting up a mill to cut railroad ties for the Kinzua

Logging Company east of the Dalles in north central Oregon. Don bragged of steady work and big money, not to mention the opportunity to leave home and the constraints of family. Dad signed on in January. He caught a ride with several of the crew south to Portland, then east through the Columbia River Gorge to the town of Kinzua, which consisted of little more than a post office, a lumber mill, and a general store.

Accommodations in the Snyder camp, fifteen miles outside of Kinzua, were rustic to say the least. Four men shared a tarpaper bunkhouse framed with rough-sawn boards and heated by a woodstove fashioned from a barrel. They carried their water from a nearby spring and enjoyed the serenity of an outdoor privy in temperatures that dropped below zero. Dad and a partner felled fir and tamarack with a handsaw through the cold, snowy winter and early spring. They limbed and bucked the trees, and a bulldozer dragged the logs to the tie mill, where they were cut into slabs seven inches thick, left rough and wide on the sides.

You'd expect the crew to have spent weekends relaxing and recovering from the demands of falling and bucking timber, but when you're eighteen and full of juice, horizons beckon you. Each Saturday, Don Slaven and my father hiked to Kinzua to pick up the mail. The thirty-mile round trip, sometimes made in knee-deep snow, could use up the light of a winter day. They wandered across an uninhabited landscape of rock bluffs, virgin pines, and jagged ridges. Boyhood in the Midwest had acclimatized my father to harsh winters. The cold was merely an inconvenience for a young, well-conditioned man who had a chance to see some country. In his eyes, hiking a place this big and this raw wasn't work—it was recreation.

My father's adventure didn't last long. Anxious to push rail lines deep into its timberlands, the Kinzua Logging Company was buying ties from every small mill in the region. But even a ready market wasn't enough to keep Bill Snyder's operation afloat. His mill was a ramshackle affair powered by a Hudson car motor that constantly required expensive repairs. When the rear end went out in the flatbed truck that transported his ties to Kinzua, Snyder called it quits. The crew broke camp in early May. There were no paychecks and no apologies.

Once he could see past his anger at losing four months' hard-earned wages, my father focused on dealing with the reality that he was broke and on his own with no means of getting home.

Within a day or two, he hooked up with an elderly contractor in the area who, like Bill Snyder, was cutting ties for Kinzua Logging. The old man was running behind schedule and chomping at the bit to wrap up business matters so he could make his yearly pilgrimage to the Dalles, where he spent several weeks each spring frequenting the taverns and brothels. He'd run the ties through his mill, but they were still in twenty-four-, thirty-two-, and forty-eight-foot lengths. They had to be bucked with a handsaw to eight-footers, then rolled onto a pile with a peavey. When the old man offered Dad a penny-a-tie for bucking and stacking, he jumped at the chance. In ten days of daylight-to-dark work, he finished the job—all 5,400 ties.

When my father asked for his money, the old-timer tore a corner off a paper sack and wrote, "This is Jim LeMonds. I owe him $54.00." He told Dad to take the note to the company office in Kinzua where he would be paid. Needless to say, my father was skeptical. Just stiffed out of four months' wages, he couldn't see a note scrawled on a ragged scrap of paper sack as hard currency, but the old man's word turned out to be good. When Dad got his money, he bought a speeder ticket from Kinzua to Condon, a ticket on a three-coach passenger train from Condon

Jim LeMonds Sr. in front of a tie pile near Kinzua, Oregon, in 1938 —Courtesy Jim LeMonds Sr.

to Arlington, and a bus pass for the final leg from Arlington to Castle Rock.

He arrived home in mid-May with enough cash to buy a few shirts, a mattress for his bed (previously furnished only with springs) and a pair of tires for Bob's 1930 Oldsmobile. He went to work as a whistle punk on a high-lead side north of town run by Louie Schaeffer. The wanderlust that gnawed at him in January faded like the remnants of a storm drifting east toward the Cascade foothills.

Louie Schaeffer, the gyppo who had hired the LeMonds crew to cut pulpwood the previous year, lived across the street from my grandparents on Fifth and D in Castle Rock. During the months my father was in Kinzua, Schaeffer had been gearing up for a new venture. In a lot next to his house, he was repairing a shovel, the loading machine used to set logs on trucks or rail cars. He and my grandfather became friends, and, before long, each time Bill dropped by for conversation he found himself helping Louie with the repair work. Louie taught Bill how to run the machine and promised that once he had wrangled a logging contract, Bill would be his operator. In 1938, Schaeffer moved his equipment to a site north of Castle Rock near the Toutle River, where he'd contracted to log a patch of timber for Pope and Talbot. In addition to hiring Bill to load and my father to blow whistle, Louie set Bob up as a driver for one of his trucks.

After Louie Schaeffer's crew had completed the job for Pope and Talbot, Dad worked on the rigging for Mel McLean and Stan Shaffer and later for Rodney Settlemier, jobs that took him through 1940. He and my mother married in November of that year. In 1941, Lloyd Rainboth, the siderod for an outfit run by Ted Welty near Siletz, Oregon, hired my grandfather and his sons. Bill ran the loading machine; my father did the climbing and head-loading; Bob did the chasing and second-loading; younger brother Cliff showed up when school was out in June and blew whistle.

In late July, my father climbed and rigged a 175-foot spar tree to anchor the mainline and haulback for a new setting. The spar my father rigged for Welty was equipped with a squirrel chunk, a log twelve to fifteen feet long and twenty inches in diameter that functioned as a counterweight for the boom on the loading machine. The squirrel chunk hung approximately 120 feet up the spar from a cable that ran between the spar tree and one of the buckle guys. Line from the haulback drum on the loading machine was run through a pulleylike block that hung from the end of the cable and connected to a boom attached to the tree. The loading machine operator controlled the boom, which he used to swing logs onto trucks, by leveraging the haulback against the squirrel chunk. When the haulback pulled the boom to the right, the squirrel chunk picked up the slack as it dropped, some-times to within fifteen feet of the ground. When the boom swung to the left, the squirrel chunk rose. During some downtime ear-lier in the week, Dad and one of the truck drivers—for no rea-son other than to have something to do—tacked a gunny sack to the bottom of the squirrel chunk. On July 30, 1941, that burlap bag saved his life.

Because the loading boom wasn't positioned correctly, sev-eral men were moving the squirrel chunk's guyline to a stump that afforded a better angle. Dad was standing on the landing, drinking coffee and killing time. He knew they were planning to cut the squirrel chunk loose when they swiveled the loading machine and that when they did, someone would give a holler to let him know it was time to get in the clear. But no one said a word. Dad didn't see or hear the chunk coming—he felt it. He wasn't wearing a hard hat—they weren't standard issue in those days—and when the gunny sack tacked to the bottom of the log touched his head, he flung his upper body back out of the way. The squirrel chunk smashed into his upper thigh and drove him to the ground.

The men rushed him to the nearby town of Toledo in Lloyd Rainboth's 1938 Chevy coupe. They had no splint to keep the shattered bone aligned. Riggingman Paul Coburn was supposed to be steadying the leg, but Coburn was so upset by the accident that he spent most of the ride trying to force his jittery fingers to light a cigarette. My father remembers only the excruciating pain as his leg, seemingly disconnected from his body, flopped with the impact of each bump. When they reached the tiny hospital in Toledo, the lone nurse who staffed it phoned the only doctor in the area, who was on call. There were no attendants, so the crew carried Dad in and lifted him onto the table in the X-ray lab. My grandfather suggested that Dad spend the night at the Toledo hospital, then travel to Portland by ambulance the fol-lowing day to have the leg set. But when the local doctor arrived to assess the damage, he told them a move to Portland was unnecessary; setting the leg would be a piece of cake.

The doctor drilled Dad's femur and clamped the bone together with two steel pins, then fitted him with a chest-high cast. Dad remained in the hospital, but within weeks, infection set in, and he came down with a fever that hovered near 104 degrees for two weeks. He believes that only the availability of sulfa—a nausea-provoking, antibacterial drug that had recently been approved for use—kept him alive. He couldn't hold down solid food and was losing weight rapidly, but the doctor never gave him an IV. In eight weeks, he dropped thirty pounds.

Five months later, the doctor removed the cast and discovered that the bone hadn't healed properly. My father was beside himself, convinced that if he stayed at the hospital in Toledo he would die there. He and my mother arranged a transfer to St. Vincent's Hospital in Portland. Doctors there rebroke and reset the leg, using a plate and bolts to hold it together.

All told, it took Dad a year and a half to get back on his feet. The injury earned him 4-F status during World War II; it also meant he couldn't return to the rigging. In December 1942, he began hiring out as a log truck driver for McLean and Shaffer and other gyppos. In 1947, he and Bob formed a partnership, pooling their resources to buy a 1942 G.M.C. truck and trailer from Les Darr for $6,800. Dad drove the Jimmy, which they named Hustlin' Gal, while Bob hauled lumber with one of Darr's highway rigs. In 1949, Beryl Jackson sold them a new International that Bob adopted, and the LeMonds brothers were on their way to making a tenuous living in the trucking business.

Uncle Bob was a gregarious man with a massive chest, shoulders to match, and a neck that an NFL lineman would have envied; the top button on his dress shirts served only as decoration. Bob was also a practiced rounder whose Saturday night escapades at various bars, taverns, and fraternal watering holes put him in contact with a number of gyppo operators for whom he and my father worked.

While the record they built as independent truckers proves their skill, reliability, and reputation, it also reflects the uncertainty that came with the job. From 1947 to 1974, they hauled for nearly thirty gyppos, including one, Tony Fernandez, who later served time in the state penitentiary for timber theft and murder. In many instances, my father and uncle linked up with

Brothers Jim (left) and Bob LeMonds in 1947 with their first truck, Hustlin' Gal
—Courtesy Evelyn LeMonds

the same gyppo operators more than half a dozen times throughout the years. A few jobs ended in less than a week; others—including those with Allen Gould, Mert Caswell, and Olsen Brothers—lasted more than a year. Although they occasionally traveled to distant places such as Springfield, Oregon, and Forks, Washington, on the Olympic Peninsula, they did most of their hauling within a forty-mile radius of Mount St. Helens, in the Kalama, Lewis, and Toutle River drainages, where the trees were immense and the promise of work seemed endless. Dad and Uncle Bob always believed the timber would last; they were less confident about the solvency of the privately owned logging companies they depended on for their living.

My father remembers a dump truck driver named Don DeGalle who hauled locally during the late 1940s. Frustrated by the trials of making ends meet as an independent contractor, DeGalle complained, "We're goin' broke even faster than we ought to." For truckers like my father, DeGalle had perfectly described the fatalistic feeling that they were on a fast track to nowhere. Steady work was tough to find and equipment failure was as common as December rain; but the most irksome thing about the business was the fear that they wouldn't get their check. Most of the gyppo logging operators Dad and Uncle Bob hauled for were good men, reasonable and dependable, but several didn't pay. Pudge Keller filed for bankruptcy before my father or uncle received a dime. Midland Brothers owed Dad $1,200 when they went bust. Dad and Uncle Bob had fuel bills, parts charges, and mortgage payments that demanded attention, and they had no savings accounts to fall back on when tough times arrived. Polite phone calls to delinquent contractors, who were themselves working on a thin margin, had little effect.

The frustration was enough to set a man's blood to boiling, though he couldn't do much about it. However, when Mert Caswell was slow to pay, Uncle Bob decided on an approach that broke new ground. Well-lubed, he showed up at the Longview Country Club one Saturday evening to suggest to Caswell, a member there, that he write checks to the LeMonds brothers for back wages. Bob didn't mind that he didn't belong to the club and hadn't been invited. He was an imposing figure, gentle on most occasions, but not afraid to say in a very loud voice precisely what he thought of you, even as your country-club friends picked at their steak and lobster and pretended they weren't listening. Caswell wrote the checks on the spot. Thereafter, he paid more promptly.

Collecting wages wasn't their only problem. Because they worked for themselves, Bob and Dad had no medical insurance, no pension plan, and no unemployment benefits to smooth the way when they were between jobs or down because of bad weather. Stability arrived in 1974 when they hired on with Weyerhaeuser, first at Camp Kalama, then at the sorting yard in Longview. For men who had worked twelve- to sixteen-hour days for twenty-seven years, it was a job made in heaven: no more winter layoffs, no more promises of pay somewhere down the line. They worked eight-hour days, five days a week, moving sorted loads to the port dock for transport to Japan, hauling cedar to the nearby Columbia River Lumber Company or hemlock to Weyerhaeuser's Green Mountain Mill in Toutle. Because they made short trips and rarely left the pavement, their trucks suffered essentially no wear-and-tear, so maintenance costs and fuel bills plummeted. During the ten years they worked for

Weyerhaeuser, my father and uncle got their first and only taste of security.

Between his arrival in Castle Rock in 1936 and the day in January 1985 when he sold his truck and retired, my father witnessed far-reaching changes in the timber industry. In the years immediately following World War II, the internal combustion engine revolutionized logging. Chain saws replaced hand-driven crosscut saws. Steam no longer powered the donkeys; diesel trucks moved logs from the woods to the mills, ending the dependency on a railroad system that was both slow and expensive. A vast road network that provided trucks and crew buses, called crummies, easy access to the woods rendered logging camps obsolete. Companies no longer had to bear the expense of running the camps, and the men didn't have to be away from home for weeks at a time to keep a job. In southwest Washington, the Weyerhaeuser camps accessed by rail closed in 1953. A few others accessed by road—including Headquarters, Camp Baker, and Camp Coweeman—hung on until the early 1960s; Coweeman was the last to close in 1964.

Loggers continued to work almost exclusively with fine old-growth firs, many of which supplied enough lumber to build a home. However, change was in the wind. Prior to World War II, the Pacific Northwest Regional Planning Committee had predicted that timber availability would nose-dive once the region's low elevation old growth was logged out. In January 1946, Chief U.S. Forester Lyle Watts reported a shocking decline in harvestable timber on America's private lands, especially in the West. He warned that Northwest mills would have enough privately owned timber to operate for only fifteen more years. "Lack of timber will inevitably force the closing of many mills," Watts said.

The one Northwest company that seemed to be listening was Weyerhaeuser. In 1930, company officials agreed to study the feasibility of a sustained-yield forestry program in the Toutle River Valley west of Mount St. Helens. Research continued through 1936, when the study determined that retaining cut-over lands would ultimately generate profit. Weyerhaeuser announced its new philosophy: timber was a crop to be tended, harvested, and regrown. Breaking with the cut-and-run practice of the past, the company elected to keep its logged-off land, pay local property taxes, and replant. A key step in this process took place in 1941 when Weyerhaeuser established the Clemons Tree Farm—the first of its kind—at Montesano in southwest Washington. An experimental venture intended more to satisfy public concerns with cut-and-run logging practices than to produce revolutionary forestry methods, the creation of the Clemons Tree Farm proved to be a visionary move. Resistance to reforestation was strong, even within the company. President Phil Weyerhaeuser used the Montesano experiment to demonstrate to detractors, both inside and outside the organization, what modern forestry could accomplish. The Clemons Farm introduced ground-breaking techniques—including insect and fire control, fertilization, soil scarification, and hand-planting of seedlings—that transformed the entire industry's approach to forest management.

Most public land managers, timber companies, and loggers themselves ignored evidence that the well was running dry. To the north, the Simpson Timber Company cemented a sweetheart deal with the U.S. Forest Service that gave Simpson virtual *carte blanche* to lay waste to the Olympic National Forest. Closer to home, in the valleys between Mount St. Helens and modern-day U.S. 5, Weyerhaeuser held title to one of the finest forests on the planet and was set to bring it down. The export market was about to open wide, and people still believed that the last great boom lay somewhere beyond the horizon. Like Henry Berndt, my father, my uncle, and other Northwest timber workers maintained a narrow focus. They had bills to pay and families to provide for. They knew only that logs were available, and that those logs translated into paychecks.

The next generation of timber workers would face a very different set of problems. A few experts might have had some inkling of the financial and emotional turmoil that loggers and their families would encounter near the end of the twentieth century, but most people connected with the wood products industry had none. Eight of my cousins—Don Strain, Ron and Larry Downing, Bob Hansch, Tom Cooley, Bill, Jim, and Bob LeMonds—would ride the boom until it went bust, earning their livings as fallers, riggingmen, truck drivers, and equipment operators. At the crossroads in history when forests became farms, these men laid down the last of the big trees.

They have felt the lash of cutbacks and buyouts, of debilitating injuries, of foreign recessions, of the decline of union power, of cut-and-run logging, and of the never-ending environmental legislation and litigation that put their jobs in jeopardy. In the last two decades, the ground beneath their feet has shifted, and nothing indicates that it will ever be solid for loggers again.

No Looking Back

R ON DOWNING IS A MEMBER of logging's vanishing elite, one of a handful of men still living who topped and rigged great spars in the days before steel towers made their jobs obsolete. The oldest of my cousins to make a living in the woods, Ron both witnessed and participated in the wave of change that transformed Northwest logging and landscape after the Second World War. From spar trees strung with wrist-thick mainline to guyless towers operating at midnight, from the cable-snapping muscle of Skagit yarders to the technical finesse of Link-Belt processors, he has seen it all. Retired after more than thirty years as a climber, hooktender, world champion tree-topper, and independent logging contractor, Ron refuses to succumb to nostalgia or Paul Bunyan whimsy. He is just happy to be out.

Ron's father, Fred—husband to my mother's sister Anna—was a riggingman and timber faller his entire working life. Summers and falls during the 1950s, Fred and Harold Huntington worked for Allen and Corky Gould, long-time Castle Rock gyppos, but once winter turned the dirt roads to mud and brought the Goulds' operation to a halt, Fred and Harold relied on horse logging to pay the bills. It wasn't lucrative. In fact, they averaged one load a day—if everything went exactly right. "It didn't do much more than put beans on the table," Fred acknowledged, "but at least we were working."

There was no spar and no yarder; Fred skidded the logs to the landing one at a time with a horse named Bud who weighed in at 1,800 pounds. They also had no loading machine. Fred and Harold used peaveys to roll the logs—most of them eight to eighteen feet in length—up an incline onto a single-axle Chevrolet truck. If a log was too heavy for them to manage, they rigged a line to Bud and used his power to hoist it onto the truck. When Huntington hurt his back in 1952, Ron, who was twelve, filled in for a week and got his first taste of logging. Fred took over Huntington's cutting duties, while Ron set chokers and did the skidding. Ron clearly remembers his place in the pecking order. "Bud was a lot smarter than I was," he said. "He knew what to do. I just walked along beside him."

After graduating from high school in 1958, Ron enlisted in the Air Force. He spent most of his tour as a radarman at Burns, Oregon, tracking aircraft during the paranoia of the Cold War. Although he didn't consider military life particularly oppressive, he didn't like it well enough to re-enlist. After three years and nine months of service, he returned to Castle Rock.

Fred Downing had been unmistakably direct in his career advice to Ron and his brother, Larry. "Whatever you do," Fred had told his sons, "*don't* go to work in the woods." Ron admits it was good counsel, but he ignored it. He was a husband and father now; he needed a job, and the logging industry had plenty available. Hurricane Frieda, which hit on Columbus Day in October 1962, had blown down 15 billion board feet of timber, the equivalent of a year's harvest in Washington and Oregon. The effort to extract the blowdown kept every logger west of the Cascades hustling for months.

In January 1963, Ron went to work setting chokers at a wage of $2.50 an hour for Ed and Ernie Roller, local gyppos and first cousins of his mother, Anna. During the 1940s, the Rollers had employed Henry Berndt, Ron's and my maternal grandfather. "When it came to logging knowledge, I was dumber than dirt," Ron said. "I didn't even know how to put the knob of the choker in the bell." After three months learning the basics with the Rollers, he quit and applied at Weyerhaeuser. Supporting a family made it imperative that he have a good benefits package, something that gyppos like the Rollers couldn't provide. Weyerhaeuser loggers belonged to a union, and that meant medical coverage, a pension, paid vacations, and a chance for rapid promotion.

Because the company was expanding its work force to deal with the Columbus Day blowdown, Ron was able to get a job as a chokersetter. He had worked nine months on the rigging when a climbing position opened at Camp Baker, and he rushed to apply. During the summer, he had gone up a spar tree near Twelve-Mile Camp and assisted climber Paul Myers with the rigging process. Ron had also been using spurs and a climbing rope to scale trees at his parents' place on Tower Road. Though short on experience, he did not lack bravado. He used it to convince Dick Fotheringill, camp superintendent at Baker, to give him a shot at the climbing job. Fotheringill consented and Ron skyrocketed from the low end of the logging totem pole to its very pinnacle in a single day.

While the move from chokersetting to climbing resulted in a sizable raise—from $2.31 to $3.51 an hour—it also involved a large increase in tension and fear. Climbing is dangerous and demanding work; its prerequisites are mental acuity, catlike balance and agility, tremendous arm and leg strength, and, of course, no inclination toward acrophobia. "I was green, and the job was scary," Ron recalls, "but I said I'd do it and I wasn't going to tell Dick Fotheringill I'd changed my mind." His stubbornness had less to do with pride than with the 50 percent increase in wages, something a man with a growing family could not easily pass up.

Weyerhaeuser policy required company spars to be at least twenty-four inches in diameter at the top. Ron says so many big, fine trees were available that he never had a problem meeting that standard. The spars averaged 150 feet in height; the largest Ron topped measured 197 feet where he made the cut. At that point, it was thirty-two inches in diameter! The tree was ten and a half feet through at the base, and Ron estimates that its pretopped height exceeded 250 feet.

High-lead logging, which utilized spar trees, hadn't become commonplace until the mid-1920s. Prior to that, however, plenty of people—operators eager to elevate their rigging and climbers willing to take the accompanying risks—had experimented with the innovation. In 1918, on a setting west of Castle Rock, Peter Walt climbed a sixty-foot spar—barely a stub compared to those used later—with the help of two springboards. Standing on one board, he used an axe to chop a new hole several feet above the previous one. Alternating boards in this manner, Walt gained several feet at a time until he could hang the high-lead and haulback blocks at a height where they would be functional. This high-wire act made Walt one of the region's first high-climbers and certainly one of the boldest. According to Edwin Van Syckle, author of *They Tried to Cut It All*, Sylvester Boling used the same method to climb and rig a spar for an outfit on Grays Harbor in 1920. Ultimately, the move to spurs and belts similar to those worn by telephone linemen enabled climbers to ascend 200 feet up a tree and transformed high-lead logging from an ideal to a reality.

Like all climbers of the high-lead era, Ron "walked" up trees, gripping them with spurs attached to his calks, a loop of steel-cored climbing rope encircling the trunk and his waist; the largest trees required thirty-five to forty feet of rope to encompass their base. The climber wore a six- to eight-inch-wide leather belt secured with a front buckle. The rope ran through a series of loops on the belt. One end of the rope had an eye that was larger than the loops so the rope wouldn't pull out. The climber ran the other end around the tree, threaded it through the eye, and tied it off to another loop in the belt using a cat's paw knot. As the climber ascended, he flipped his rope upward, pulled it tight, took several steps to gain back the slack, then repeated the process. With his spurs dug into the trunk, the climber could lean back in his belt, take up the slack in the rope, and give his arms a rest. He also did all his handwork from this position, including limbing, topping, and rigging.

In 1963, even the lightest chain saw was too heavy to lug to the top of a spar. Ron carried a four-foot cross-cut saw and a double-bitted axe that dangled from short ropes attached to loops on his belt. On the way up the tree, the climber chopped off every limb with his axe. When he reached the highest point where the trunk measured twenty-four inches in diameter, usually between 150 and 200 feet up, he topped the spar. Using the same method employed by timber fallers, he first chopped a face in the trunk—a cut the shape of an open mouth. He had to make the face deep and wide so the top would not split. Next, he moved to the back of the tree and sawed through to the face.

After he'd limbed and topped the tree, the climber came all the way down to begin the rig-up phase. He reclimbed the tree carrying one end of a "pass rope," a lightweight rope drawn from a four-hundred-foot coil at the base of the spar. When he reached the top, the climber fed the pass rope across his climbing rope and down to the ground. The rig-up crew attached a strap—a short cable with eyes spliced in both ends—and a pass block

Climber on the way up
—Courtesy Bud May

weighing about ten pounds to the pass rope. By pulling on the other end of the pass rope, the crew raised these to the climber, who used the strap and a fastener called a shackle to hang the pass block. He then ran the pass rope through the block and sent it back down. The ground crew attached the pass rope to the pass line—seven-sixteenths or half-inch cable connected to a drum on the yarder—pulled the pass line through the block, and unhooked the pass rope. From this point forward, the ground crew sent up all equipment the climber needed to rig the tree via the pass line, which was stout enough to handle the load.

Next, the climber moved down the tree until he was ten feet or so below the pass block and knocked off a swath of bark about five feet wide all the way around the trunk with his axe. When this was done, the crew sent up four tree plates on the pass line. Three feet long by six inches wide and one inch thick, with hooks welded to the top and bottom, the iron tree plates weighed fifty pounds apiece. The climber spiked them vertically to the barked part of the tree, equidistant from each other around the trunk.

By now, the rig-up hooktender would have marked out a ring

of evenly spaced stumps—typically six large ones that showed no signs of uprooting—about 300 feet from the spar and had his men notch them for guylines. The crew laid the eye of each guy at the base of the spar and raised it on the pass line to the climber, who laid it over one of the top tree-plate hooks. These top guylines measured one and three-eighths inches in diameter. The ground crew wrapped the bottom ends of them several times around the stumps, pulling each wrap tight with the mainline before spiking it in place. The spar tree would have to withstand severe stress once the yarding began, so the crew often hung another set of stabilizing lines called buckle guys about a third of the way down the tree from the top guys. The buckle guys were one and one-quarter inches in diameter, and they literally prevented the spar from buckling. The threat of collapse was real. In *From Jamestown to Coffin Rock*, Alden Jones notes that Bud Orley, a Weyerhaeuser yarder operator in the days of steam machinery, worked under nine spar trees that broke under the strain. "I was spending so much time under the donkey sled," Orley commented, "I tried to get 'em to put a bed under there for me."

When the ground crew had tightened the guys and secured the spar, they sent up a high-lead strap, usually made of one-and-three-quarter-inch cable; the climber wrapped it around the tree and laid it across the hooks on the lower ends of the tree plates. He pulled the two eyes at the ends of the strap together and secured them with a huge, horseshoe-shaped shackle that had a bolt that fit across the open end. After this, the crew ran the block up on the pass line. Though the high-lead blocks Ron dealt with in the 1960s were only half the size of those common in the steam-logging days before World War II, they could still weigh 800 to 1,000 pounds. Once the yarder operator had raised the block to precisely the right height, the climber shackled it to the tree. Using another strap and shackle, he then hung the haulback block, which weighed 200 to 250 pounds, about two feet below the high-lead block. Using the pass line to raise the cables, the ground crew sent up one-and-three-eighths-inch mainline, which the climber threaded through the high-lead block, and seven-eighths-inch haulback, which he ran through the haulback block. The ground crew then connected the lines to drums on the yarder.

A rig-up crew often spent a full day topping and preparing a standing tree. Crews assigned to areas with widespread blowdown where no spar was readily available might spend as much as a week locating, moving, rigging, and raising a tree that was already on the ground. In the months after the 1962 Columbus Day wind storm, many crews had to raise their own spars because all suitable standing trees had been blown down.

Once they had the spar rigged and ready to go, the crew could begin skidding logs to the landing. Because they could log only a portion of the 360 degrees around the tree with the mainline and haulback blocks in their original positions, they called the climber back, usually twice, before finishing a setting. He would swing the blocks to the other side of the tree, so the crew could eventually skid logs from around the tree's entire perimeter.

After gaining a few months' experience, Ron no longer fretted about working 150 feet off the ground, but plenty of other things set him on edge. Every climber worried that a treetop might snap off prematurely during topping. If the tree began to break before the climber finished sawing the backcut, some of the wood might hold, causing the top to barberchair, or kick back toward him, when it broke and fell. If the top sprang back and hit the climber, the blow could seriously injure him or knock him out of the tree to his death. Ron had one problem with breakage during his career; it happened while he was topping a tree with a heavy lean. He had faced it up under the lean and sawed the sides to remove the sap wood. When he was halfway through the backcut, an inch-wide crack opened on the side of the tree where he was sawing. The top began to tilt away from him, first in slow motion, then more rapidly, until it finally broke and fell. Keep in mind that Ron wasn't sawing the top off a Christmas tree. He was working at a height where the spar was at least twenty-four inches in diameter, larger than the base of the average tree that today's timber fallers cut. By the time the top broke free, its weight had pulled the spar over at a dramatic angle. The spring back to the vertical position—Ron estimates the distance at twenty to thirty feet—nearly flung Ron off the tree and set the spar rocking like an E-ticket attraction at an amusement park. "That," he comments with a smile that says you had to have been there, "was a pretty good ride!"

Limbs posed perhaps the greatest danger to a climber. Occasionally, a limb grew upward, forming half a U from its intersection with the trunk. Loggers called such limbs suckers. On the way up, a climber could not limb a sucker that measured a foot or more in diameter. Sawing or chopping a big limb from below was foolish because, as it gave way, instead of breaking loose cleanly, the sucker might peel down the side of the tree (a poorly cut top could do the same thing). When the peeling wood reached the climber's rope it would suck him against the trunk with crushing force. A number of climbers were killed in this way in the early days of high-lead logging.

The cut-from-above approach, while markedly safer, left the climber with one major dilemma: how to get his rope over a huge sucker that restricted passage. A few climbers used two ropes: when they reached a sucker, they threw the extra rope around the tree above the limb, hooked it to their belt, then detached the original rope before moving on. Like the majority of climbers, Ron did not want to bother with the extra rope. His technique was to get his rope as close as possible to the bottom of the sucker. Next, he reached over the top of the limb, grabbing the rope tightly enough to hold himself in place. Using only his off-hand, he untied the end from his climbing belt, passed the rope over the limb, then retied it to the belt. Once he retied the rope, the climber had to take a quick step back as the slack came tight. No matter how many times Ron executed this maneuver, the sensation that he was falling never went away. "It could put the hair up on the back of your neck," he says.

As a Weyerhaeuser climber, Ron moved from one setting to another, rigging spars and swinging blocks for the Camp Baker crews. He came to appreciate the skill and endurance of the men he encountered. In particular, he admired the hooktenders who headed the rigging crews and dealt with daily problems ranging from haywire equipment to difficult terrain. "Those older guys were tough, seasoned men," Ron says. "It was a pleasure to work with them." He feels especially grateful for the tutelage of experienced hooktenders Stud Curtis and Little Vic Thompson. Curtis, solid and predictable, provided exactly the guidance a rookie climber needed to gain confidence. Thompson, a wizard in the art of raising a spar from the ground when no tree stood on the designated setting, also knew a few things about climbing and was happy to share his knowledge. Both men valued mental power over physical force, and their advice was not lost on Ron. "At first I tried to muscle things," he says, "but it didn't work very well. Once you've been around for a while, you learn the little stuff that makes the job much easier."

By his own admission, Ron is self-reliant, inclined neither to wait for higher-ups to trek to the job site when problems arose nor to listen to their advice once they arrived. "If you talked to the people I worked for, they'd probably say I was independent," he says with a smile, "but I imagine they'd also put a few colorful words in front of *independent*." In 1964, that independence led to a conflict between Ron and a siderod at a setting near Camp Baker. Because the yarder had been positioned at a bad angle, the haulback and mainline were constantly "out of lead," preventing the cables from spooling smoothly onto the drums on the yarder. The siderod refused to acknowledge that the placement of the yarder was causing the problem. He accused Ron of rigging the tree incorrectly. By the time the argument ended, Ron was no longer employed by Weyerhaeuser Company.

Ron went to work for Alvin Janisch, who, like Ed and Ernie Roller, was both a local gyppo and a cousin of Ron's mother. Janisch's was a small operation manned by personable people, and Ron felt at home there. Alvin ran the yarder, his boy Alvin Junior operated the shovel and did the chasing, and Alvin's brother Henry did the cutting. Ron doubled as chokersetter and climber. "That year," he says, "I went from high-climber to jack-of-all trades. I was the whole rigging crew. But that was all right. I was young and I didn't mind."

By 1969, Ron had grown tired of working in the brush by himself and was ready for a change. When Camp Kalama's climber was killed in an accident, Weyerhaeuser rehired Ron to fill the position. By now, his high-climbing was not confined to the workplace. When Ron left the Air Force in 1963, his brother, Larry, was already competing at area logging shows. Before long, he got Ron involved. They tried everything from chokersetting to axe-throwing—Larry even gave log-rolling a whirl—before settling on the climbing events. "You learn where you can make your money," Ron says, and for him that was tree-topping. The event requires climbers to scale a 100-foot pole and, using a four-foot saw, cut off a prenotched top forty inches in circumference. Time stops when the block hits the ground.

In the evenings, Ron and Larry went out north of Castle Rock to Barnes Park, where they'd clandestinely limbed two practice trees. By 1967, Ron was hitting his stride. "To win, you had to train and put your guts on the line," he says. After a grueling day of climbing or working on the rigging, he could barely force himself to complete the practice climbs at Barnes Park. But without that additional training, he wouldn't have had a chance of winning, even though he made his living as a climber. The competition was too stiff.

Southwest Washington has produced dozens of world-class competitors and lays claim to two of the best men ever to participate in logging sports. Toutle's Paul Searles was unbeatable in log bucking events from 1932 until he retired from the sport in 1953. Searles' fame earned him appearances on Art Baker's *You Asked For It* and Groucho Marx's *You Bet Your Life*. His greatest moment came when he met the log-bucking champion of California head-to-head as part of a well-publicized ceremony to open the Golden Gate Bridge on May 28, 1937. Searles whipped his saw through a redwood log thirty-four inches in diameter, soundly trouncing his opponent. Castle Rock's Hap Johnson, sixteen times a world champion, was the biggest name in tree-topping and speed-climbing in the 1950s and early 1960s. Like Searles, he appeared on *You Asked For It;* he also performed on a television show hosted by Arthur Godfrey that was filmed at Shelton, Washington. Johnson was John Wayne's double for the climbing segment of the feature film *North to Alaska*.

Each summer at Albany, Oregon, as many as 20,000 spectators pay to see the best loggers on the planet vie for world titles in events that include bucking, axe-throwing, speed-climbing, and log-rolling. In 1970, Dwight Carpenter's time of eighty-eight seconds should have earned him first place in the tree-topping event, but that year, it was only good enough for fourth place behind Ron, Larry, and Louis Kloewer (all four men were from Castle Rock). Ron's time of eighty-one seconds, his fastest ever, earned him both a world record and a world title. The $400 purse may seem like nothing compared to the pay today's professional athletes garner. But to Ron, who was bringing home thirty-five dollars a day working for Weyerhaeuser, it was big money. He finished his career with twelve world titles as a tree-topper, the first five from 1966 through 1970, then, after a three-year hiatus following a broken leg, seven more from 1974 to 1980.

While many who participated in logging sports have fond memories of their competitive days, Ron isn't among them. "It became a job, a way to make money," he says. "What I mostly remember is that it was a lot of hard, hard work. And to make things worse, I used to get incredibly nervous." His daughter,

*Larry (left) and Ron Downing at a logging show
in Estacada, Oregon* —Courtesy Anna Downing

Laura, recalls the competitions at Albany as carefree vacations
filled with restaurant meals, dips in the motel pool, and the car-
nival atmosphere of the timber show. For Ron, it was much different. "After I quit, it took years before I could even drive past
Albany, Oregon, without getting sick to my stomach."

Ron stopped climbing competitively in 1981 and has few regrets. He nearly threw the dozens of trophies and plaques he
won during his eighteen-year career in the trash, but his parents convinced him to store the hardware in their attic. "I liked
the people and the chance to demonstrate the old-time skills,
but if I had it to do again, I wouldn't have gotten involved in
logging sports." Asked why he hadn't quit earlier, he shrugs.
"That's just me. When I start something, I have to see it through."

By the late 1960s, Weyerhaeuser and other timber companies
had begun to phase out high-climbers as they made the transition to mobile, prerigged steel towers. Ron found himself
climbing part-time and tending hook in the interim. In 1970,

he fractured his leg while working on a grapple yarder. A thirty-six-foot log, sixteen inches in diameter, was jillpoked, one end buried in the ground and the other sticking out at an angle. When the yarder operator hooked onto the log and pulled, the buried end didn't move; instead, the exposed end whipped toward Ron. He got his hands up before it hit him, but the log pushed him down and fell across his legs, breaking his left tibia. He wore a walking cast for a month but went back to work in only eight weeks. By then, steel towers completely supplanted spar trees, so he went to hooking full time.

By 1975 Ron was ready to give timber falling a try. Weyerhaeuser was nearly out of old growth, and the smaller trees seemed less intimidating. "I didn't know anything about cutting timber," he admits. "I figured the only way to learn was to do it." He soon found out how difficult it is. "It's a very physically demanding job," he says, and coming from a man accustomed to the fatigue and pounding endured by riggingmen and high-climbers, the comment is particularly noteworthy. But the hard work pales in comparison to the hazards. "Timber falling is far and away the most dangerous job out there," he says. "So many unforeseen things can happen."

A day in April 1976 supplies a perfect example. Ron's partner had taken a job as a bull-buck, so Ron paired with Lonnie Dailey, an experienced head faller, to cut right-of-way near Camp Baker. Ron's brother, Larry, and Larry's partner, Jack Hurley, were cutting an adjacent strip several hundred yards away. Ron and Lonnie were working on an old-growth fir. When it started to go over, they scrambled to what they believed would be a safe spot behind another tree. Ron can't explain how it happened, but a limb, sixteen feet long and five inches in diameter, broke off the tree they'd cut. It ricocheted off other limbs as it descended and fell behind the tree where they'd taken shelter, striking Lonnie Dailey across the back and shoulders. One moment he and Ron were standing together watching the show; the next, Dailey lay collapsed on the ground, moaning and semiconscious.

Fortunately Larry and Jack Hurley had their saws turned off, so they heard Ron running toward them and hollering. They were on the scene quickly. Dailey was in shock, his chest crushed and both lungs punctured. Ron and Jack Hurley stayed with him and did their best to provide comfort while Larry sprinted half-a-mile over rugged terrain to the crummy. He drove to the

Camp Baker transfer where he used the radio to call for help, then returned to the right-of-way strip with a stretcher. Ron, Jack, and Larry loaded Dailey onto the stretcher and started through the timber. Partway to the crummy, other Weyerhaeuser men met them and helped get Dailey to a clearing. From there, a helicopter transported him to a hospital in Longview. Between the moment Dailey was injured and the moment he arrived at the emergency unit, only one hour and fifty minutes elapsed. Doctors later sent word that the quick action taken by Ron, Larry, Jack Hurley, and the others had saved Lonnie Dailey's life.

When Mount St. Helens erupted in 1980, Ron was cutting timber near Dollar Creek, just south of the mountain. Wanting to put as much distance as possible between himself and the volcano, he bid on a hooktender's job that had opened twenty-five miles southwest at Camp Kalama. His reprieve was short-lived. Like virtually every other Weyerhaeuser side working in the Kalama River drainage, Ron's crew was soon transferred to the St. Helens area to help log salvage in the blast zone. "It was miserable work," he says. "It was gray, it was dismal, and there wasn't any life up there. Everybody was depressed."

Ron continued to tend hook for Weyerhaeuser on both highlead and guyless tower operations until 1986. By this time, the company was downsizing and the work force was disgruntled and constantly in flux. As crews were reduced, the remaining men had to change jobs, bumping workers with less seniority. One day, you might be cutting timber out of Camp Baker; the next, you could be setting chokers at Camp Kalama. Ron had loved the pride and awe of working in the big timber, but those days were gone. The atmosphere had changed. The job had lost its magic. "I started dreading Monday morning as soon as I got off work on Friday night," he says. "I knew I had to get out."

At just that time, Ron's father-in-law, a veteran gyppo, was set to retire and anxious to sell his equipment. Ron didn't hesitate. Because his house was paid for, he was able to borrow the $100,000 he needed to get the operation off the ground. Ron purchased his father-in-law's entire outfit: yarder, loader, skidder, fire truck, parts truck, and tools. He bought a six-man bus, hired a crew, and got a contract logging for International Paper west of I-5 between Ryderwood and Boistfort. He didn't run yarder, but he did nearly everything else at one time or another: chased, cut timber, set chokers, and operated the loading machine.

By the late 1980s, however, I.P. had run out of trees. The company laid off its crews and closed up shop. After I.P. bailed out, Ron logged for ITT-Rayonier, as well as a number of private landowners. Most people believed the rashness and neglect of the cut-and-run era were a thing of the past, but many timber companies—as well as state and federal management agencies—could not resist the lure of a wildly expanding export market during the 1970s and 1980s. They cut what they had as quickly as possible, then appeared stunned when supply could not keep pace with demand. Like many contemporary loggers, Ron condemns companies that were in it only for volume, regardless of the consequences. "They over-cut," he says. "Not just International Paper, but a lot of others, too."

Scott Bailey, regional economist for the Washington Employment Security Department, supports Ron's contention. A number of factors have contributed to reductions in timber employment, Bailey says, but the fall-off is mainly "due to the industry harvesting at unsustainable levels. This was true throughout the Northwest. The industry expected that the harvest on federal lands would increase to cover the decline on private lands, but obviously that didn't happen." Cowlitz County is a prime example. Timber harvests on private land here reached 775 million board feet in 1978 but declined steadily to a low of 273 million board feet in 1997. The fall-off in federal harvests has been even more dramatic.

In 1988, Ron was working near Stella, west of Longview. While walking on the landing, he stepped on one end of a small alder log just as his operator rolled the cat across the other. The log kicked up under Ron's foot, applying enough torque to break his ankle. "It launched me into the air," Ron says of the accident, "and it was very painful." In retrospect he sees the injury as a blessing: it forced him to turn his attention to managing the outfit, which made his entire operation more efficient. Now, as he spent his daylight hours talking to people at businesses in town about jobs and parts and equipment, he got his first inkling that there might be things in life other than logging.

Like many independent contractors, Ron suffered a severe blow in 1990 when the state banned the export of logs cut on state-owned land. That same year, the federal government declared the northern spotted owl an endangered species and set aside state and national forestland as habitat, dramatically reducing timber sales there. This did not pose a monumental problem for Weyerhaeuser because its timber holdings are vast. Most independents, however, possessed no forestland. They had long relied on state and federal sales to provide work, but those doors were rapidly closing. With fewer trees available, every timber sale attracted dozens of contractors, mortgaged to the hilt, who were willing to low-bid a job to keep their equipment running. The Park Equipment Company, ten miles north of Castle Rock on Interstate 5, had enough repossessed steel towers in its auction lot to tell the story of the contractors' fate in a single glance. As other gyppos began to go under, Ron could see the writing on the wall. The only way to survive would be to work harder, be more aggressive, but he was already pushing himself to the limit. "I was putting in twelve hours a day, six or seven days a week," he says. "I could see there was no way I was going to make it."

Ron quit logging in 1992 and enrolled at Lower Columbia College. A federal program for displaced workers paid for his books and tuition. A fifty-three-year-old competing against teenagers, Ron relished the opportunity. "It wasn't so much the technical skills that I picked up," he says, describing his liberal arts education. "You just learn a lot more about the world and about life. I grew up in Castle Rock. It was a narrow little environment. When I went to L.C.C. I enjoyed the chance to learn about other people and other ideas." He took three years to earn his associate's degree. It is an accomplishment of which he is very proud.

Like many of today's loggers, Ron does not fit the popular image of the snoose-chewing, cut-it-all timber beast. "I didn't want to cut the last tree," he says. "I just wanted to log." While he admits that he is "a logger first and an environmentalist second," his views on landscape are both surprising and conflicted. The stunning decline of clean freshwater available for humans and wildlife deeply disturbs him. He approves of regulations that keep equipment out of streams and marshes and advocates thinning instead of clear-cutting timber on steep ground as a way to reduce erosion and significantly improve riparian conditions. Unlike many Northwest timber workers and industry spokesmen, Ron does not believe government land must be logged to sustain production. "We don't need to log one stick out of our national forests," he says, "Not if private lands are managed effectively." After pressing him, though, I can tell he is more comfortable with the idea of lengthening harvest rotations on public lands—from the fifty-year cycle prevalent during his career to upwards of one hundred years—than with leaving the trees alone forever. Embracing a no-cut policy would mean allowing timber in state and federal forests to mature and rot, and he has difficulty accepting what he perceives as waste. Retirement and an evolving environmental consciousness cannot wipe away who he was and is.

Today, Ron is semi-retired and debt-free. By 1993, he had liquidated most of his logging equipment and invested the money. He recently bought a house that he is repairing; he may sell it, buy another, and repeat the process. He also owns an "air business"—fifty machines at area service stations and convenience stores where customers pay twenty-five cents to pump up their tires. He stays busy, though occasionally he feels like he is inventing things to do. The old work ethic is hard to dismiss. "Some days," he says, "I feel like I'm treading water."

The broken leg and ankle healed. Ron points to a hearing loss—the result of not wearing ear protection—as the only long-term damage attributable to his career in the woods. "I was fortunate to get out without any physical defects," he says. "When you first start in the woods, you have to be lucky and you have to be around men who watch out for you. After that, you pick up some skills and it's easier to remain injury-free."

Ron doesn't get hung up on sentimental fabrications about the good old days. He does, however, consider himself blessed to have witnessed so much. "I got in on the tail-end of the old spar trees," he says. "That was really something to see. I miss logging in the big virgin timber too. It was just beautiful out there." He remembers a day when his wife and kids wanted to pack a picnic lunch and spend an afternoon at a nearby park; he had difficulty working up any enthusiasm for it. "I thought to myself, 'I get to see things better than that every day.' I guess we got spoiled by it."

Ron and a friend occasionally get together and swap tales about the old days. "Sometimes," he says, "we'll get twenty loads in a couple hours of telling stories!" Those reminiscences aside, he speaks fondly of only one other aspect of logging: "What made the job tolerable was that there were a lot of good men." He was tempted by a number of offers to get back into the business, but he resisted. "My gut told me to stay out," he says. "Every time I thought seriously about going back, I got sick to my stomach."

When I arrived for one of my visits with Ron, he was working on the roof of his carport. My own fear of heights made me wonder if being up there made him nervous. Then I remembered that this was a man who climbed for a living, who raced up hundred-foot poles after the workday was finished, just to improve his conditioning. I imagined him leaning against his climbing belt at the top of a two-hundred-foot yellow fir and considered the world as he must have seen it: a panorama in green stretching to the horizon at every point of the compass. So much timber. So many settings waiting down the road.

It's a long way from the tops of those spars to the roof of his carport, but Ron Downing is not moved by nostalgia. He has no interest in looking back.

Aiming for Sixty-Five

T HE WORD DOWNSIZING calls up images of IBM, General Motors, or other corporate giants slashing middle-management positions, using new technology to eliminate manufacturing jobs, relocating factories to Mexico or Indonesia to maximize profits. Logging might seem like a more locally rooted business, a mom-and-pop enterprise removed from the dictates of brokers and board rooms. Not so. All the homespun mythology can't change the fact that logging is a business, and the bottom line is turning a dollar. It makes no difference how skilled an employee might be, how many generations of his family have been involved in the industry, or how dependent he is on paychecks that never seem to be large enough. He can still wind up as a pawn in a game of stock options and quarterly earning reports played in a corporate office hundreds of miles away.

My cousin Don Strain was laid off in 1982 after having spent twenty years with Weyerhaeuser as a chaser, bucker, timber faller, and cutting supervisor. He works as a faller for an independent contractor now, but the pay and benefits can't compare to those he earned at Weyco. The company justified his lay-off as part of a necessary restructuring after the end of salvage operations near Mount St. Helens. For Don Strain, it has meant restructuring his life.

Don is fifty-nine and some of the spring has left his legs—he can no longer leap up and grab the basketball rim attached to his garage—but he is still in astounding physical condition, lean and leathery from the daily demands of life as a cutter. When I tell him as much, he laughs it off. "Heck, Melvin Wheeler is

59

three years older than I am, and he's still one of the best timber fallers in the woods today." Like an aging pro athlete trying to hang on for one more season, Don has no choice but to stay fit. Either he wins the battle against age, inflexibility, and weakness, or he loses his livelihood.

Although Don's parents never pushed him toward or away from a career in the woods, Don has no difficulty explaining why he settled on the logging life. "It's simple. I've been in love with the outdoors since I was a kid." During his boyhood, Don hunted, picked cones, and peeled cascara; he sold the cones for seed and the cascara for laxative. At fifteen, he began charting the growth of the trees on his family's three-acre place on Tower Road. Once a year, he measured the diameter of every Douglas fir, cedar, and white fir, maintaining careful records in a pocket-size book. He kept this up for more than a dozen years—not for any pragmatic adult reason, but because he has always been curious about the lives of trees.

In 1959, Don was dating the daughter of Ed Ashe, personnel manager at Longview Fibre. Each summer, Ashe hired a handful of senior boys from Castle Rock to work at the pulp mill, and that year Don made the list. He was employed as a millwright's helper, and he detested the job. It lasted only a summer, but it convinced him of what he had previously only suspected: he would never be satisfied with a job that kept him indoors.

After high school graduation and the stomach-turning summer at the mill, Don attended Lower Columbia College in Longview for two years. He considered pursuing a career in forestry but decided against it. He lacked the money to continue at a four-year school, and he admits that he also lacked the drive to see it through. Or perhaps the seduction of the woods was simply too great.

Bill Strain, Don's father, had spent his entire working life in the timber industry, first as a riggingman and faller, then as a sawyer. Now Don headed down the same road, hiring on with his mother's cousins, Ed and Ernie Roller, in the summer of 1960 (his cousin Ron Downing would do the same three years later). Don set chokers, learned to run cat, and, by 1961, was also falling timber. His first experience cutting timber shook him up a little. The patch of second-growth he and his partner were working in was imposing, and Don received only generic instructions. "It was sort of a trial-and-error procedure," he says. "I was scared to death, but I also discovered there's nothing that can match the adrenaline rush of cutting a tree and watching it go over."

Don enjoyed working for the Rollers, but their forays into the logging world were sporadic. The majority of their contracts involved building roads—work that depended on good weather. "When November came and we got 'mudded out' I could see the handwriting on the wall," Don says. At the end of 1961, he got a job at Weyerhaeuser as a chaser for $2.41 an hour. During the next five years he would also run skidder and cat.

The 1962 Columbus Day Storm scattered trees from hell-to-breakfast in southwest Washington, and the subsequent salvage operation created myriad employment opportunities. Don began cutting timber on Saturdays and Sundays for area gyppos so swamped with contract work that they were running seven days a week. Beginning in 1964, he cut sporadically for Weyerhaeuser as a fill-in. In 1966, Don went on the saw full-time for the company. Those first years were an apprenticeship, watching and working with veterans Don Vernon, Gene Foister, and Russ McBride. Three decades later, Don still considers them the best cutters he's ever been around.

Don's pay at Weyerhaeuser was hourly because of a momentous change in company policy in June 1961, just before he hired on. Beginning in 1919, the company paid its cutters "by the bushel," their wages calculated per thousand board feet cut or bucked. In 1961, fallers earned sixty-seven cents a thousand and buckers seventy-three cents. Because they were working in old-growth timber, partners could often fall and buck 75,000 to 100,000 board feet in a six-hour shift. This translated into a wage of $50 to $70 a day—huge money in 1961. Don Vernon and his partner, Herman Kwandt, once racked up 625,000 board feet in a five-day week.

Weyerhaeuser's decision to put their workers on hourly pay deeply impacted company-employee relations and the timber-falling trade in general. Beliefs vary as to what precipitated the change. The company complained that paying by the thousand board feet was not cost effective. Cutters contended that the white-shirt-and-tie crowd at Weyerhaeuser's Tacoma headquarters resented earning less each year than hundreds of uneducated, backwoods timber fallers working out of places like Castle Rock, Washington. Whatever the reason, the company put an end to busheling and began paying cutters a flat rate of $3.30 an hour, a wage reduction of 50 percent or more for nearly every timber faller in the vicinity.

The physical and emotional fallout was immediate. Men who had been making and spending big money could no longer maintain their lifestyles. Don Vernon's brother, George, was also a timber faller. George and his wife Eileen lived across the street from us in Castle Rock. A few months after Weyerhauser implemented the new pay system, I watched the repo men carry away the Vernons' piano. The policy change generated a tidal wave of bitterness. Weyerhaeuser expected the fallers to produce at the same rate as before the wage cut, breaking their backs for half the money. The men refused. In the end, the fallers won a small victory: as the export market blossomed in the wake of the Columbus Day Storm, the company had to hire more cutters to maintain volume.

Despite their anger over the cut in pay, Don Vernon, George Foister, Russ McBride, and many other seasoned timber fallers refused to do sloppy work. A young cutter learning the ins-and-outs of a craft that required both endurance and intelligence could not have asked for better mentors. "They planned, and they made things work," Don recalls. He was stunned by their ability to fell old-growth trees, typically 180 to 220 feet tall, within a yard or two of where they intended. To minimize breakage, they had to avoid sending their trees over stumps or windfalls. The game was to lay the trees out parallel to one another, like carefully placed sticks in a giant's game. "It was like watching pool players who are always thinking several shots ahead," Don says. To this day, he remains amazed by their artistry and efficiency.

In late 1969, Don paired with Keith Hall. They cut timber together until July 1974. During that five-year span, the company offered three times to move Don to a salaried position. He turned them down twice, but when they asked again in 1974, he was married and had a son, and he decided the time was right for change. He had hoped for something safer and more secure than timber falling, and his new position seemed to be the answer: he was to evaluate the work of the company's cutters, checking to see that they got the maximum value out of every log.

When Don made his move, the company was in transition, too. Walt Mezger, who started with Weyerhaeuser as a forester in the late 1940s and eventually became the woods planning coordinator for the St. Helens Tree Farm, remembers the 1970s as an evolutionary period. "It was an exciting time. The company was trying to finish up the last of the old growth and get geared up to deal efficiently with smaller trees." As the old growth disappeared, Weyerhauser phased out the mammoth yarders and rigging, replacing them with faster, lighter, more mobile machines. And, with the gift of the big timber used up, waste was no longer acceptable; the company emphasized recovering a greater share of each tree. (The new focus paid off. By 1990, Weyerhaeuser was utilizing 98 percent of the wood in each tree, an increase of 33 percent within three decades.)

After six months of monitoring the company's cutters, Don took a position as "contract cutting supervisor." In response to an increased demand for wood products on the international market, Weyerhaeuser had begun supplementing its union crew with a large number of independent fallers. By the late 1970s, gyppos were cutting more than 40 percent of the company's timber. It was Don's responsibility to keep tabs on the work of the independent contractors, making sure they didn't take unnecessary risks or break too much timber. His job site encompassed several hundred square miles in the Kalama, Toutle, and Green River drainages west and north of Mount St. Helens.

The position took some getting used to. Responsible only for himself and his partner six months earlier, Don now supervised the performance of 150 gyppo cutters. He spent his days mediating disputes, relaying orders from management, and evaluating the work of his men. The headaches didn't end when he got home. "I was spending two hours on the phone every night," he says, "laying out jobs and trying to answer questions." The quality of the gyppos' work also plagued him. "Company cutters were starting to tune in to the new emphasis on getting the most out of every log and minimizing damage," Don explains, "but the work of the contract cutters wasn't at the same level. There were some excellent independents, but overall the work of the gyppos wasn't as good as what I was used to seeing from the company men. Those older guys had more experience and were just better at what they did."

Weyerhaeuser aimed its decision to rely on contract fallers not only at increasing volume but also at reducing costs, a movement still in vogue today. Factoring in wages, medical benefits, vacation time, and holidays, Weyerhaeuser currently pays its cutters approximately $40 per hour—nearly $250 in a six-hour day. Gyppo operators don't provide the same level of benefits to their men, so subcontracting can generate enormous savings. During the 1970s, Weyerhaeuser's Camp Baker had more than 100 cutters on the company payroll. With the crews working out of Twelve-Mile and Camp Kalama, the total approached 250. By 1998, Weyerhaeuser had sliced its cutting force to 25 men. Independent operators and newly developed machines—feller-bunchers, roto-saws, and harvesters—that work more quickly, cheaply, and efficiently than a man with a saw took up the slack.

The eruption of Mount St. Helens in 1980 briefly delayed Weyerhaeuser's transition to nonunion contracting. The timber blown down in the blast zone had to be removed quickly before it was lost to decay. Just like after the Columbus Day Storm in 1962, this meant bringing in more cutters, riggingmen, operators, and truck drivers—both union and nonunion. But even before the company finished its salvage extraction at the end of 1982, executives were formulating a plan to downsize Weyerhauser's woods operation: it would be the opening salvo in a labor skirmish that has continued for two decades.

When the cutbacks began, Don was supervising eleven sides. Rumors of reduction-in-force flew, but Don's boss assured him that his job was safe. On April 13, 1982, the company gave Don two options: transfer to Arkansas or go back to cutting. Every year, on the company evaluation, Don answered the question "Would you be willing to relocate?" with a definite "No." A northwesterner his entire life, Don couldn't accept a move to Arkansas. He considered going back on the saw for the company, but returning to his job as a union faller would have meant giving up the vested pension he'd built up in his salaried position. He decided to keep the pension, invest the severance pay, and look for work elsewhere. Don believed he had done a good job for the company and been a loyal employee. He did not forget the company's betrayal overnight.

During the next five years, irony ran deep in Don Strain's life. In May 1982, he went to work for Castle Rock Stihl, a local gyppo firm he had previously hired and supervised. The fact that Stihl was cutting Weyerhaeuser timber contributed an additional dose of dark humor. Stihl put him in charge of a six-man crew, paid him $140 a day—more than he would have earned had he re-

Don Strain, a logger for forty years —Courtesy Kathy Strain

turned to falling for Weyerhauser—and supplied him with one saw annually. Nothing, however, could make up for the loss of six weeks' paid vacation each year or the unpredictability of working for an independent. Don stayed with Stihl until 1986, when a slowdown forced him to take a summer off. Meanwhile, another Castle Rock gyppo called him—Allen "Whoopy" Gould Jr. of Gould-Sunrise. Whoopy needed a cutter and offered Don $21 an hour.

In 1991, after watching Weyerhaeuser save big money by contracting with independents such as his own firm, Whoopy Gould decided to experiment with the same strategy of subcontracting his cutting. He laid off his five-man cutting crew, explaining that the cost of insuring them made it difficult for him to stay in the black. U.S. Department of Agriculture reports verify that a high incidence of death and injury in the timber-falling trade has caused Washington Department of Labor and Industries (L & I) and workers' compensation insurance costs to skyrocket. Costs vary; the amount employers pay is tied to a formula that factors in their previous accident rates and the type of work they do. The average in Washington is $5.50 to $6.00 an hour per employee. In the Pacific Northwest, insurance costs logging companies $90 million in overhead each year. In 1991, Whoopy Gould doubted he could stay in business. Don was disappointed but not bitter. Unlike Weyerhaeuser, Whoopy Gould told his crew straight-up what the situation was.

After the layoff, Don scrambled to fill the financial gap. He bought a 350 John Deere cat and began taking on small contract jobs for private landowners. Timber prices had soared as high as $850 to $1,000 per thousand board feet, more than double the rate in 2000, which fluctuated between $260 and $420 per thousand board feet. As a result, twenty- and forty-acre family holdings suddenly became lucrative and many private landowners were looking to sell their timber. Don functioned as a one-man crew, cutting and bucking the timber, setting chokers, and running the cat. He hired a truck driver with a self-loader to haul the logs. Despite modest success, the lure of independence never snagged Don the way it did Ron Downing and others. He could work steadily during good weather, yarding logs with his John Deere, but he knew a year-round operation of his own would require serious investment in a tower, loading machine, and crew. The risk didn't interest him.

In January 1995, Whoopy Gould called again. His cost-cutting experiment had failed because cutters that subcontractors sent his way performed poorly. Don went back to work for Gould-Sunrise, where he still works today. He enjoys cutting for Whoopy, who treats him fairly, but the work is erratic. Weyerhaeuser has its own timber and a long-term plan for harvesting it. It can keep its union crew working virtually year-round by moving the men to low-elevation settings when snowfall closes operations in the mountains. Things don't run as smoothly for independents. In 1997, for example, bad weather kept Don out of the woods for a week in February, another in March, and another in April, and he had no way to make up the lost wages. In May 1998, the cutters put more timber on the ground than the rigging crew could handle and had to take a four-week layoff. Work was steadier in 1999, but only because private landowners, who knew that forthcoming environmental regulations would further restrict or eliminate logging near streams, were standing in line to have their timber harvested.

Whoopy Gould offers an insurance plan and a week of paid vacation each year, but these are a far cry from the fully paid medical coverage and exceptional vacation and holiday pay Don enjoyed at Weyerhaeuser. And, once inflation is factored in, his hourly wage doesn't come near what he made fifteen years ago. Unfortunately, talking about how things were doesn't change the way they are.

Don Strain still appreciates working outside. He shakes his head in wonder at the beautiful timber and the sublime setting that have blessed his life as a logger. "The real timber is gone," he laments. "There's a twinge of melancholy in knowing that we'll never see anything like it again." A universal irony among loggers is their love and admiration of the landscape they helped destroy. Despite his regrets about the loss of nearly all the region's old-growth forest, Don is a strong proponent of the tree-farm system. He likes what Weyerhaeuser has done and admires its proficiency. Each year, the company logs 2 percent of its timber. In theory, a fifty-year cutting rotation—each site logged once every fifty years—allows for a steady supply of trees.

Rae Johnson, long-time Weyerhaeuser surveyor, commented in Alden Jones's 1974 book *From Jamestown to Coffin Rock* that the biggest revolution in the timber industry during the twentieth century was *not* the change to growing timber as a crop; it was the compression of the harvest rotation schedule. "As late as 1960," Johnson says, "one hundred years was considered a likely rotation for our timber. Then someone suggested sixty years as an attainable rotation. . . . The sixty-year cycle [was] adopted as a management policy for most of the private and public timberland-owning operations. . . . This amazes me every time I think of it."

During the 1960s, company executive and wunderkind Charles Bingham led a campaign to lop ten more years off the cutting cycle and Weyerhaeuser soon eclipsed the sixty-year rotation that had boggled Rae Johnson. At a meeting in Tacoma in October 1966, Bingham convinced the company's board of directors to back a concept that became known as "high-yield forestry." The plan was to compress the life span of Douglas firs from five hundred to fifty years. Weyerhaeuser scientists, who had been conducting research since the company established the Clemons Tree Farm in 1941, could now produce genetically superior trees that were taller and faster growing. These "super trees" would produce nursery stock that would seed every acre of Weyerhaeuser timberland. Previously, pickers had gathered cones and the company had scattered the seed aerially, with little regard for elevation, soil, or terrain. The new method would eliminate the randomness. High-yield forestry meant hands-on management of the most stringent kind. With the help of herbicides, fertilizer, and thinning, the super trees would grow at an unprecedented rate, making Bingham's fifty-year cutting cycle feasible. One scientist at Oregon State University went so far as to predict that the new trees would grow at a rate *twenty-two times faster* than native stock. "Charley Bingham was an extremely bright and personable man," says Weyerhaeuser forester and woods planning coordinator Walt Mezger. "You had to have somebody in the power structure to beat the drum for change, and Charley was the one most capable of doing it."

Before Weyerhauser could implement its high-yield forestry program, the company had to make a detailed inventory of more than two million acres of its Northwest land and timber, including a comprehensive evaluation of forest soils, which were broken into four hundred different types. This information became the basis for decisions involving what to plant and where to plant it. Once the company finished its initial assessment, it began to shape an overall design for harvest and reforestation. Referred to as the Forestry Inventory System, the computerized program continues to play a significant role in the company's forest plans, most notably by determining which seed stock is best suited to a particular area. "It's unbelievably sophisticated," Mezger says. "It can tell you acquisition history, logging history, soil type, plant species, stream temperature, timber size. You name it, it's there. Most importantly, it allows you to make real decisions, not just guesses."

High-yield forestry represented a total commitment to the tree-farm philosophy. "It was a specific program with steps and policies that everyone would adhere to," Mezger says. "That had never been done before." Currently, Weyerhaeuser employs the world's largest private silvicultural and environmental research staff and operates eight nurseries where genetically superior stock is cloned to produce seed. The results have been spectacular. Jerry Gutzwiler, Land and Timber Manager at the Clemons Tree Farm, recently boasted, "Intensive forest management is producing almost twice as much wood per acre on our western Washington lands as could passive forest management."

One prominent critic of the move to a fifty-year cutting cycle is William Dietrich, author of *The Final Forest*. The decision to compress harvest rotation was based on financial rather than biological reasoning, he explains. Studies have shown that Douglas firs grow rapidly for the first seventy-five to one hundred years of their lives, not just the first forty to fifty. But investors don't want to wait an additional twenty-five to fifty years for a return. With the average investment per acre at $300, Weyerhaeuser has emphasized reduced rotations, which means cutting the timber as quickly as possible and returning the profit. If the company's tree-farm laboratories can produce even faster growing trees, Weyerhaeuser may be able to reduce the growth cycle to thirty-five years, translating into a 3 percent annual harvest of company timber that would make stockholders very happy. The trade-off, William Dietrich and other ecologists say, is that forest health and biodiversity will be pushed even farther into the background.

In *Timber Country Revisited*, author Earl Roberge praises Weyerhaeuser's genetically enhanced "super trees." He includes a photo of the stump of one tree that "achieved a diameter of twenty-four inches in twenty-seven years, about half the usual time-span for such growth." Timber companies continue to use cross-breeding and gene-splicing to spur maturity rates and increase both volume and profit. Like Roberge, Don Strain sees this as the wave of the future.

Don acknowledges that past logging practices caused serious environmental problems. He points to roading on steep hillsides as one of the primary transgressions. He also remembers when operators routinely ran logging equipment through creeks filled with salmon returning to spawn, and he is pleased that the Forest Practices Act of 1974 put an end to such abuses. He believes strongly in monitoring stream temperature and ensuring that it is low enough to sustain fish runs. However, to those who suggest thinning—as opposed to clear-cutting—as the way to maintain soil stability, prevent erosion, and minimize stream damage, Don responds that it is not a pragmatic approach. "Thinning older stands of Douglas fir doesn't make sense. What's left will blow down. Also, Douglas fir only thrives in the kind of open area you get when you clear-cut. It doesn't regenerate as an understory tree." He believes just as strongly that some environmental restrictions are absurd. Portions of Washington's 1999 Forest and Fish Agreement require leaving untouched buffer zones adjacent to creeks and rivers. "Why in the name of God's green earth do they make people leave shade trees on the *north* side of a stream running east and west?" he wonders, asserting that this would in no way reduce the amount of sunlight that reaches the water.

Excessive regulations that "take" from private landowners also bother Don. His cousins, the Rollers, own eleven acres of prime timber on their family farm that they can't touch because the federal government has classified it as a roost area for eagles. A friend of his can't remove trees in the vicinity of an eagle's nest on adjacent Weyerhaeuser property, even though the nest has been unoccupied for eight years. In such instances, Don believes the government should compensate property owners who must forfeit the income the trees would have generated.

Don and his wife, Kathy, own a ninety-acre ranch west of Toutle. Sixty acres are in timber. They do some thinning and remove the windfalls, which results in several truckloads of logs that they sell to Weyerhaeuser every year. Currently, they have no plans to harvest the rest. "I don't want to cut it," Don says. "This is our nest egg in case something goes wrong." Layoff and injury are possibilities he can't discount. Keith Hall, Don's former falling partner, was one of the best Don ever worked with. In September 1987, a dead top was hung up in the limbs of several trees near where Hall was working. He knew the top was there, but forgot about it when he went in to make a cut; the top came down and struck him across the back. Keith Hall now walks with a cane.

Amazingly, Don has never suffered a serious injury. He complains of "white finger"—the numbness of the fingertips that afflicts so many fallers after years of gripping the saw—but his greatest regret is not wearing ear protection at an earlier age; he isn't deaf but his hearing is diminished. His back has begun to bother him, but the nine years he spent as a supervisor, removed from the rigors of falling, have likely prolonged his ailment-free career.

The work has always been hard, but Don believes today's smaller timber translates into tougher conditions than ever before. "The saw is always in your hands," he says. "There's never a chance to rest." He also thinks timber falling is more dangerous now than in the past because the men cut so much alder, a tree ignored in the days dominated by old-growth Douglas fir. "Alder is brittle wood. It tends to shatter. You can hardly saw fast enough to keep it from barberchairing. It can definitely get your heart to racing."

Don can name half a dozen men he's worked with or known who were killed falling timber. And he's had his own share of close calls. One came shortly after he and Keith Hall finished falling a strip of trees in the early 1970s. Hall had started bucking while Don was moving their tools. Don heard a cracking sound and glanced up to see a snag, 150 feet tall and 6 feet at the base, crash out of the standing timber on a direct line for their position. It came up forty feet short.

Cutting snags is a faller's nightmare. Early in 1998, while working for Whoopy Gould east of Woodland, Washington, Don cut thousands of snags as part of a job Gould contracted on the northern fringe of the Yacolt Burn. The cutters worked at their regular hourly rate; evidently, no one would concede that cutting snags warrants hazard pay. The snags, some sixty to eighty feet tall and four to six feet in diameter, were left from the massive 1902 fire that jump-started Weyerhaeuser operations in the Northwest. Typically a snag is little more than a wood shell holding in soft, pulpy rot. Once a faller slices through the outer layer, the inside can crumble at any moment, bringing the entire snag down on him. If the wood is solid, a good study of the tree's lean and a deep undercut can minimize the danger, but nothing can make the job completely safe.

Don's closest call came in 1996 when he was cutting fir with an inexperienced partner near Ryderwood. Timber fallers are supposed to stay at least two tree lengths apart. This rule is designed to prevent accidents to fallers when trees unexpectedly go sideways or fall into other trees, creating a domino effect. Unbeknownst to Don, his partner had closed the gap. "He cut the corner out of a 130-footer," Don explains, "and it went sideways on him." Don glanced up just in time to see it coming his way. He managed to duck behind a standing tree an instant before the 130-footer hit it dead center. "You wanna talk about being shook up," he says. "I took the rest of the day off and sat in the pickup. That evening when I got home, I called Whoopy and told him that guy had to go. You've got to have a partner you can count on. If you're watching out for somebody you don't trust, then you aren't paying one-hundred-percent attention, and you start making mistakes of your own."

The most obvious changes Don has witnessed during his career are the decline of timber size and the downsizing of machinery to handle the smaller logs. When he started, a faller and his partner averaged five to eight trees a day; now a single cutter working in alder might put down 200 to 250 trees a day. Don once cut a yellow fir that scaled out at more than 30,000 board feet; today, he'd be lucky to cut half that much during an entire shift.

The need to produce volume makes speed the central focus now. Don agrees that young fallers can do the "hurrying," but too often they are poorly trained, careless, and unconcerned about doing a good job. "They don't make clean undercuts, and that affects where the timber goes and how much damage is done. Backcuts are supposed to be made at least two inches above the undercut, but half the time they're not, and that increases the likelihood the tree will come over backwards." Worst of all, he says, fallers nowadays often ignore the rule that two or more tree lengths must separate men working a strip together. No one enforces the rule either, and unnecessary deaths and injuries result.

Although the Department of Labor and Industries (L & I) monitors the safety practices of timber fallers, fallers have no certification process. They need no permit or license, only a saw and the ancillary equipment. Don acknowledges that L & I is understaffed, but he believes the agency could do a much better job of instructing and supervising cutters and enforcing rules. Don has seen outfits draw fines because a faller has a small hole in his chaps. "Meanwhile, the violations that can kill people are taking place every day, and L & I doesn't get around enough to catch those things."

Tom Ford, logging safety specialist for Washington's Department of Labor and Industries, says the friction between L & I and contract loggers compounds the difficulty of working cooperatively to improve safety. "This state has nine regulatory agencies that govern logging practices." Because contractors are fearful of bureaucratic interference, Ford says, "they tend to do everything possible to avoid contact with us." From Ford's perspective, the answer is not as simple as instructing L & I representatives to be more vigilant. "It's the employers' responsibility to make sure their cutters are properly educated," Ford says. L & I provides training for the employees of contractors interested in making the job safer. Unfortunately, he admitted, not many take advantage of it.

Don says caution and experience are the keys to avoiding injuries. "You don't take chances. You do things the right way. I can't move as fast as I used to, but I know what I'm doing." Don's wife, Kathy, may share his confidence, but the danger is always on her mind. "I say a prayer for him every morning," she says. "I want him to get out as soon as possible." But at fifty-nine, where would he go? Staying in the business will not be easy either. Asked how many cutters he knows who remained healthy enough to stay on the job until sixty-five, Don just smiles and says, "Not many."

In the meantime, Don goes to work each morning for Whoopy Gould. He rides in a king-cab pickup to patches of alder and hemlock that wouldn't have qualified as decent firewood when he started in the woods. He straps on ear protection, chaps, and hard hat. He picks up the Stihl 066 with the thirty-six-inch bar that weighs nearly twenty pounds and grabs the gas and oil cans, wedges, tapes, wrenches, and axe that add another thirty pounds to his load. Then he heads over the hill, trying not to think about the fact that he's been both good and lucky for all these years.

"You get to see a lot of great country," he says. "I won't miss the nasty, windblown days when I retire. But I will miss working outside, the smell of the fresh air. When spring comes, the sun pops out, and the birds start singing." He leaves it at that, as if he knows that words cannot do justice to the image or the emotion.

Don has six years to go. Six years of dealing with arthritis and back pain. Six years of hoping his partners are careful. Like the timber, Don Strain's job is not what it once was, but he's in it for the duration. This is what he knows. This is what he does.

Trying to Keep
a Little Cushion

I SHOULD HAVE KNOWN BETTER than to try to interview my cousin Bob LeMonds during the summer months. As the son of a gyppo truck driver, I know dry weather means long hours and regular employment, early wake-ups and bedtimes before the sun goes down. When I called in June and talked with his wife, Julia, she said Bob was hauling from Castle Rock to Garibaldi on the northern Oregon coast. If things went smoothly, he made two 250-mile trips a day. Breakfast at the LeMonds house was served at three in the morning. Bob and I finally connected one day in early July when the contractor he was working for didn't have enough logs ready to justify calling out his drivers. Even the circumstances of our meeting were a statement about the life Bob has lived.

Bob's father was my dad's brother and trucking partner. Dad and Big Bob started working together just after World War II, and despite some rocky times, they always managed to hustle enough jobs to pay last month's bills. When Bob followed in his father's footsteps, he didn't choose a career as much as surrender to the natural flow of things. "I guess I was born with a steering wheel in my hands," Bob says. The easy flow has become a hard-running current he can't escape. Bob has driven truck for thirty-nine years, racking up more than two million road miles. He's fifty-eight and retirement is nowhere in sight.

As far back as Bob can remember, driving and logging were irrepressible, interconnected pieces of his life. His father apprenticed him, breaking Bob in as a driver, showing him how to maintain a truck, and introducing him to the network of gyppo operators that did the hiring. "I was always around it," Bob says. "I rode with my dad and Uncle Jim whenever I got the chance. By the time I was fourteen I was already helping with greasing and lining brakes." After dumping a load of logs, Big Bob sometimes moved into the passenger seat and let his son drive empty back to the brush. "There wasn't a manual or anything," Bob says. "You just had to do it if you were going to learn. When I rode with Dad and Uncle Jim, I paid attention to what they were doing and tried to pick up as much as I could." He learned how to click smoothly through nonstop gear changes, how to save his brakes on long, steep downhills, how to back a trailer around tight bends on mud-slick landings. By the time he was eighteen, he was no longer a rookie.

In the fall of 1960, after graduating from Toutle Lake High School, he attended Lower Columbia College while keeping a summer job driving dump truck for Crystal Pool Sand & Gravel. He liked the work, but part of him wanted to set a course of his own. When winter came, he decided to focus on his classes, become a diesel mechanic, and make his break from the trucking business.

He didn't get far.

In the fall of 1961, my father was hauling poles for Bob Jackson from Pine Creek, southeast of Mount St. Helens, to the International Paper log dump in Longview. Having lost interest in the diesel mechanic coursework, Bob had dropped his college classes and was riding along as my father's flagman. When Dad caught a bad case of the mumps, he asked Bob to fill in for him. Some of the poles were 130-footers, special orders for a company in need of piling. They were too long to fit on the truck in the regular manner, so Jackson came up with a creative solution: he cut a cradle in a large wood block and fastened it to the rooftop of the cab. On top of nine or ten 85-footers loaded in the conventional fashion, Jackson set on a single 130-footer per load, propping the small end in the cradle atop the cab. While the big log didn't restrict the truck's maneuverability, the driver had to take both the overhang—fifteen feet past the front bumper and more than thirty feet beyond the end of the truck—and the sweep of the poles into account when cornering. Despite the potential for danger, Bob never had a problem, and though it lasted only a week and a half, the pole-hauling job demonstrated that he could handle most situations a driver might encounter.

Not long thereafter, Big Bob's friend Walt Settlemier had surgery and couldn't work for several weeks. Settlemier needed someone to drive his truck, and Big Bob recommended his son. Before long, Bob was working for other gyppos who had their own truck fleets, including Mert Caswell and Salmon Creek Logging. "I'm not sure that some of the owners knew how young I was," Bob says with a smile. Men in their forties and fifties dominate the truck-driving world. You see few twenty-year-olds behind the wheel of a logging truck. Loggers like my father who have been injured or are too old for the more physical rigging work often switch to driving; they occupy the majority of the jobs. Moreover, owners have an aversion to putting kids at the controls of expensive machinery.

"Ivan Golden was the truck boss for Caswell and because he knew my dad, Ivan knew I could drive," Bob says. "After I worked for Caswell, I had a little more experience and nobody gave any thought to how old I was." In early 1963, Big Bob hurt his back and Bob took his place behind the wheel of the family's 1956 Diamond T. There would be no more dreams of returning to school. What had begun as a temporary gig was on its way to being set in stone.

Still, it took a natural disaster to cement Bob's career. On Columbus Day 1962, Hurricane Frieda hammered the Northwest with winds that blew down 4.5 billion board feet of timber in Washington and Oregon. Domestic markets could not accommodate the supply. The timber would have been left to rot if not for a booming housing market in Japan that provided logging companies, the state of Washington, and private landowners with a timely outlet for their product. It also guaranteed employment for a new generation of loggers, including Bob, Don Strain, and Ron and Larry Downing.

"One of the company's concerns at that time," Weyerhaeuser forester Walt Mezger explains, "was that the export market was very demanding when it came to quality. Any sign of insect damage would make a log unacceptable. For that reason, there was a lot of emphasis on getting in there and getting the timber out as quickly as possible." As the Japanese market took off, Weyerhaeuser and the whole timber industry went with it. "Once they got geared up and had all those employees and all those buyers," Mezger says, "the export market was so darn good they had to take advantage of it." The ripe foreign market also led the

U.S. Forest Service to approve overcutting of federal forestland on an annual basis through the mid-1980s. The resulting big harvests meant that logging and mill crews expanded at companies, large and small, throughout the Northwest.

By this time, Big Bob had recovered from his back problem. So much work was available that he doubled his operation: he bought a 1956 Autocar, which he drove, and kept Bob on to drive the Diamond T. In the early 1960s, a truck typically made around $100 a day. The driver took home 25 percent in wages. Bob was young and energetic, happy with both the money and the chance to drive. The work was fairly steady, and he and Julia put together enough for a down payment on a house.

The father-son trucking connection continued from 1963 through 1983 with only a three-year interruption. In 1973 Bob went out on his own for a spell, buying a 1966 Peterbilt from his dad, who had purchased it new. At first, the independence was a good fit. Bob was thirty-one. He had plenty of experience, and he knew how to play the game. By 1976, however, the thrill of working for himself had worn thin. The Pete was having engine trouble, and Bob was having difficulty paying his bills. One night over cocktails at the family's truck shop in Castle Rock, Big Bob expressed interest in buying the Peterbilt. After another drink, the deal was done. The following day Bob was back working for his father. "He knew I was disgusted with the way things had been going," Bob says of his father's offer to take the truck off his hands. In one regard, the move changed very little for Bob: his father replaced the engine in the Pete, so Bob was driving the same truck. On the other hand, the pressure of working for himself was gone. Bob quickly reacclimated to a life without the worries of lining up jobs and paying insurance and maintenance bills. Freedom had its price, one he was happy not to have to pay.

By working with his father, Bob avoided some, but not all, of the headaches that haunt gyppo loggers. In particular, Bob worried about having no pension plan or medical coverage. At first, he and Julia simply told themselves they wouldn't get sick. But by the mid-1970s, they had two children, and the talk of brash youth was a thing of the past. In search of a quick fix, they bought health insurance from a friend who was working for New York Life. When Bob broke his leg and, later, when Julia was hospitalized with a severe fever, they discovered the policy didn't cover much of anything.

"We were fortunate never to have a lot of medical problems for ourselves or the kids," Bob says. Julia adds, "When your insurance doesn't pay, you don't run to the doctor for every little thing." The wives of men who worked for Weyerhaeuser told her, "Just go to the doctor if you have a problem. Your insurance will take care of it." But the plan Weyerhaeuser provided for its workers was far removed from the paltry policy Bob and Julia had bought. When their sons needed tubes in their ears and when their older boy got pneumonia, Bob and Julia had to pay the lion's share. At those times, the bills piled up; sometimes it took months to erase the balance. "You just paid what you had, when you could," Julia says. "There weren't any other options." Finally, in the early 1980s, they switched to an improved plan; they now pay $4,800 a year in premiums. "It's still not the greatest," Bob acknowledges, "but it's better than nothing."

Bob worked for his father until Big Bob retired in 1983. At that time, Bob purchased both the trucks his dad had been running: 1973 and 1978 Macks. Bob's older boy, Sonny, then nineteen, went to work for him, and a new father-son cycle began. Despite the rocky road they'd been down, neither Bob nor Julia had any qualms about Sonny going into the trucking business. Bob even agreed to break him in. "As long as it was something he wanted to do, it was all right with us," Julia says.

Bob's father was a commanding presence, both in physical stature and personality. Calling company truck bosses and gyppo operators to line up jobs was easy for him. Bob is shyer than his father, more self-contained, less comfortable carrying on conversations with people he's not close to. One bonus of having Sonny in the trucking business is that he often pulls in work for his dad. "He's a hustler," Bob says with admiration. "If he's not working, he's on the phone trying to line something up. And if he finds a job, he'll pass the word along to me."

Initially, things went well enough when Bob took over the business. In the mid-1970s, Weyerhaeuser had fired a group of drivers employed by Far West Trucking and replaced them with gyppo truckers, including Bob Sr., Bob Jr., and my father. They worked at Camp Kalama, then in the sorting yard at the port dock in Longview. The export market continued to thrive, and, before long, the cleanup effort that began near Mount St. Helens in 1980 was in full swing. As was the case after the Columbus

Day Storm, area loggers and truckers had all the work they wanted during the two years following the eruption.

Hauling for Weyerhaeuser at the port was a gift: no off-road wear-and-tear on the trucks; no long hauls racking up huge fuel bills; and no worries about whether Monday would bring more work. In the mid-1980s, Weyerhaeuser paid $33 an hour, a fat rate for an independent. Regular paychecks and reduced expenses meant relative prosperity for my father, Bob, and Sonny, who had taken his grandfather's place in 1983.

The job in the Weyerhaeuser log yard provided ample work even after the Mount St. Helens salvage ended in 1982. The apparent stability prompted Bob to take a gamble: when my father retired in January 1985, Bob bought Dad's 1966 Peterbilt and hired a driver for it. Almost immediately, the Weyerhaeuser work came to a dead halt. The company had decided to downsize its entire southwest Washington operation; less logging meant Weyerhaeuser could move many of its own trucks—those that had previously worked in the woods—into the Longview yard. The gyppos were out the door. "By 1986, things had really slowed down," Bob says. "For awhile, we were lucky if we had one truck working."

After the Weyerhaeuser layoff, Bob worked for Bornstedts and other independents, doing his best to make a go of it. "I'd watched the way my dad managed the trucks," Bob says. "He always spread them around with different gyppos. That way, if one truck was down at a particular site, one of the other gyppos we were working for might be able to use it to pick up a load or two." It was a constant struggle to keep the trucks busy no matter how he sliced it. "When we had three trucks it seemed like you could keep two working. When we had two, you could keep one working. There never was enough to keep them all going steady for any length of time." At the end of 1986, he had to lay off the driver he'd hired and sell the 1973 Mack.

In 1987, Sonny made the decision to go out on his own. One of Bob's favorite stories tells the results. Joel Olson, a gyppo from Clatskanie, Oregon, owned a fleet of powerful new trucks loaded with chrome, and Sonny was itching to get behind the wheel of one. He had complained frequently about having to drive the well-worn 1966 Peterbilt; that and the growing pains of working for his father had him hungry for freedom. When Sonny left, Bob sold the old Pete to Castle Rock Stihl. Soon, though, Sonny quit working for Olson, hired on with Stihl, and found himself back in the cab of the tired old Pete.

Bob has had to struggle since 1986, but with only one truck to worry about, he has made ends meet. In 1996, he traded in the '78 Mack and bought a 1991 Kenworth T800 with 500,000 miles on it for $41,000. He looked at several new trucks but the asking price was too steep. A rig right off the lot costs $80,000 to $90,000 for the truck alone. The trailer and bunks can add another $20,000. "I didn't see any way possible that I could afford a new one," he says. "The money I spent for the Kenworth was as deep in debt as I wanted to go."

When Big Bob and my father used to discuss the profitability of their trucking business, they could turn sarcastic in a heartbeat, particularly if work was slow or they hadn't been paid. "You truck drivers," one of them would say to the other. "You guys are making nothing but money." Things haven't changed much for independent truckers. The pay never seems to keep pace with the constant outlay for fees, insurance, fuel, tires, and repairs.

Some of an independent's overhead expenses are predictable; others are not. Each year, Bob and Sonny pay $1,350 for

Sonny (left) and Bob LeMonds, third- and second-generation log truckers

permits, nearly all of it for licensing and tonnage fees. Insurance, which Bob purchases through the Trucking Association because it offers a 10 percent discount, exceeds $3,000 per year. Gas costs much more. Sonny LeMonds estimates that he averages nearly 100,000 miles annually. A log truck gets about five and a half to six miles per gallon of diesel. In 1998, fuel was $1.07 a gallon. By March 2000, the price had skyrocketed to $1.60 a gallon. At that price, his fuel bill exceeds $26,000, an increase of more than $7,000 over what he paid in 1998. Yet no increase in pay has offset the difference.

Owning their own trucks is a heavy burden for independents. Tires cost $300 apiece. While the quality of the road and the number of miles they put in affect the longevity of the tires, Bob and Sonny typically go through a front set every four or five months. "Drivers" on the back of the truck—also known as duals—often last a year; trailer tires can make it through two since they get no wear when the truck runs empty with the trailer loaded on top. Still, the annual bill for tires can easily reach $4,000.

To minimize expenses, Bob functions as his own accountant and his own mechanic. He and Sonny share a truck shop west of Castle Rock. Bob and his younger boy, Bill, put in several hours every weekend on maintenance. Bob relines brakes and replaces clutches, seals, and wheel bearings when necessary; Bill does the oil changes and grease jobs. But when the truck needs major repairs, the cost can be staggering. In 1985, Bob's truck needed an engine rebuild; the bill came to $9,000. In 1998, he had a rear-end and transmission repaired for $1,800 and $2,000 respectively. His current truck has racked up 676,000 miles of wear; he has no way to predict what repair bills lurk in the future. "The costs aren't unexpected," Bob says. "The problem is that you just don't know *when* they'll occur."

Bob and Julia do their best to limit expenditures. They have no pricey hobbies, and they don't take costly vacations. "Thirty years ago, Julia and I got into the habit of saving for winter layoffs," Bob says. "We still try to keep a little cushion to fall back on. You need it for repairs and for the times when you're not working." If schedules don't mesh, Bob can be off for several days between jobs. During rare stretches, the work is nonstop, but more often, a full paycheck is just a dream. Insecurity and intermittent layoffs are part of the game. Both he and Julia seem tuned in to that reality; either they are equipped to deal with the stress or are numb to it by now. "I guess you get used to it," Bob says, "but never completely."

Since the Weyerhaeuser layoff in 1986, Bob has contracted with more than half a dozen independent operators. Through much of 1998, he hauled for Diamond Timber, owned by Castle Rock gyppo Jeff Gould. Recently, he has been working for another Castle Rock contractor, Orval Wirkkala of Liberty Logging. Bob would actually rather do contract work for gyppos than for Weyerhaeuser. "The jobs working for the company aren't nearly as good as they once were," he says. "These days, the rate of pay is about the same no matter who you haul for." A frequent complaint of independents working for Weyerhaeuser is that contractors have to start behind the company trucks each morning; that means they always get a later "out" and fewer loads. "With Orval, I start earlier," Bob says. "Because of that, I have a chance to pick up an extra load now and then, and I get to work a few more hours."

Weyerhaeuser's pay rate for independent truckers is in the neighborhood of $42.50 an hour, but Bob says nobody actually makes that much. That figure merely provides the starting point in a formula impacted by volume hauled—calculated in "cunits," each of which is the equivalent of 100 cubic feet of wood—and hours on the road. "With the formula they have, Weyerhaeuser should be paying a fifty-dollar minimum rate," Bob says. By the time the company finishes tweaking the initial wage, truckers are lucky to end up with thirty-five to forty dollars an hour.

On the other hand, what Bob makes working for Liberty Logging won't move him into Donald Trump's tax bracket. Because Liberty contracts with Hampton Tree Farms, Hampton sets the wage. Hampton pays drivers a flat rate for each ton hauled; truckers call this being "paid by the pound." The company has calculated that their truckers can average fifty dollars an hour. That projection is rarely attained. Currently, Bob and Sonny are hauling from a landing near Vader, Washington, to a mill in Willamina, Oregon. Hampton estimates that a roundtrip should take them approximately seven hours. If they meet that timeline, they can average close to fifty dollars an hour. Invariably, however, traffic congestion, slow-downs at the scales, mechanical problems, and other factors make it nearly impossible to stay on schedule. No matter how much they hustle, truckers seem unable to do more than pay their bills and eke out a living.

A local driver in the business for more than two decades who now contracts with Weyerhaeuser told me, "If you want a picture of our situation, think about this: in 1980, when we were hauling out of the blast zone after St. Helens erupted, we were making forty dollars an hour. Now, twenty years later, we're making $42.50. When you factor in inflation, we're making at least 20 percent less than we were in 1980." The deregulation of the trucking industry and the escalating price of fuel have combined to tighten the noose. In addition, competition for jobs is stiff. Weyerhaeuser is reducing its truck fleet, so drivers who once worked for the company are now applying for employment with area gyppos. And as the number of contracts offered on state and federal land continues to decline, the competition for cutting, yarding, and hauling those logs increases, driving pay rates down. Truckers have to take what is offered if they want to work at all.

Bob has noticed that fewer young guys are breaking into the business today. Operators who own multiple trucks aren't looking for rookies, and with things tighter than ever before, a person in his twenties would be crazy to invest in getting a start as an independent. Recently, Bob has seen trucks from eastern Washington come west of the mountains, desperate for work. The days when truckers mainly hauled close to home are past; racking up 500 to 700 miles in a day is no longer the stuff of legend. D & R Johnson Logging owns a stud mill at Riddle in southern Oregon. In the summer of 1999, the company was cutting state timber near Astoria at the mouth of the Columbia River and hauling the logs to Riddle. The drivers' roundtrip was 560 miles. Some truckers predict that longer hauls, higher fuel prices, and lower pay rates will eventually force them to run with two or more trailers in order to maximize load capacity and remain solvent.

In the fall of 1999, the Department of Transportation threw up another obstacle: they started cracking down on the number of hours log truck drivers spend on the road. "There are different ways of figuring it," Sonny LeMonds says of the workday regulations. "Basically, they try to limit you to 500 miles a day or ten hours of driving time." Sonny is thirty-six and can stay behind the wheel for twelve to fifteen hours a day pretty easily. He estimates that the DOT's stepped-up enforcement costs him $350 a week. "The ten-hour rule really limits your options," Sonny says. Once he's made the seven-hour trip from Vader to Willamina and back, he *could* pick up a second load and drive three more hours; but the ten-hour shift might end with him miles from Castle Rock. In the trucking world, you can't simply "clock out" and drive home when the shift is up; you have to stop driving.

In November 1999, the DOT set up a sting operation in southwest Washington. Agents in unmarked vehicles staked out places where truckers parked their rigs overnight. In the morning, they recorded plate numbers and departure times and forwarded the data to state troopers at scaling stations along Interstate 5. That evening, the troopers compared their information to the logbooks the truckers are required to maintain. Those who were caught falsifying hours and mileage received hefty fines.

While the limitation on driving time makes sense from a safety standpoint, truckers see it as part of a Catch-22. Hauling distances and overhead costs are increasing, pay rates have flatlined, and the workday is limited, but the mortgage statement keeps arriving in the mail each month.

In trucking, as in every aspect of the logging industry, the demand for increased productivity has generated improved technology. Truckers, like loggers, have much more powerful equipment than they did in 1961, when Bob started driving. The 1956 Diamond T he drove in the early 1960s had a 740-cubic-inch Cummins engine that produced 200 horsepower. By comparison, his 1991 Kenworth sports an 855-cubic-inch Cummins that churns out 430 horsepower. Bob's father told the story of a low-geared Chevrolet truck he drove for Louie Schaeffer in 1938 that moved at a snail's pace on steep grades. On a long, mean hill south of Toledo, Washington, he could shift to his lowest gear, pull out the choke, bail out of the cab, jog to the rear of the load, check to see that his warning lights were working, then run back and climb into the cab before the truck had traveled fifty feet! Today's trucks glide up steep inclines and mountain passes like a passenger car. Their tubeless radials can withstand much more heat than the old-style tube tires. In the years after World War II, many trucks ran so hot the manifold glowed cherry red, turning the floorboards into a griddle. Curt Jarrett, a veteran truck driver and a friend of Bob's father, once said the heat from the engine "could melt the grease right off your shoes." The new rigs have superior cooling systems and better insulation between the engine and the cab that prevent temperatures from rising to unbearable levels. Today's drivers are on the road for longer hauls, and comfort is less a luxury than a necessity. "It's nice if you've got cruise control and plenty of power," Sonny LeMonds says, "because you're definitely going to be covering plenty of ground."

Speed and power don't keep a truck out of accidents; in fact, they may amplify a driver's mistakes. And a trucker who owns his own rig wants to avoid fender-bending. Driving in snow and ice is always tricky, but Bob most fears bad weather that comes on unexpectedly. "Late fall and the start of winter—that's when there's a lot of fog, and the ice can surprise you." He's only had one wreck. In 1967, he put the Peterbilt in the ditch on his way to pick up a load east of Toutle. The impact threw him into the steering wheel with such force that the wheel buckled. Bob's upper thighs were severely bruised, and he developed a knot on one leg that he had to have a surgeon remove. Otherwise, his career has been accident-free. While Bob tries to make good time, he doesn't take unnecessary risks. "It seems like the guys who drive for somebody else aren't quite as cautious as the guys who own their own rigs. They pound the truck down the road and figure the company will fix it." He believes that same attitude is responsible for the majority of trucking accidents. "Speed is the main problem. Some guys are careless and just go too fast for the conditions. My insurance bill is already high enough. I try to avoid trouble."

"I don't know that there is a *best* thing about having your own truck and working for yourself," Bob says. "You can write off a personal vehicle as a 'company pickup,' but that's about it. The independence stuff is overrated. Any way you figure it, you're still working for somebody else." He has no problem ticking off the negatives: he lacks steady work, has to foot the bill for health insurance premiums, and has to do his own bookkeeping. Turn back the clock forty years and the grievances my father registered at the dinner table would have been nearly identical.

Since the first twenty years of Bob's truck driving career overlapped the last twenty years of my father's, their histories have much in common. As Bob lists the names of places he's hauled and men he's worked for, my own childhood memories of long days and frequent change come flooding back: Al Kelly near Deep River; Mert Caswell near Pine Creek; Walt Settlemier on the Kalama River Road; Salmon Creek Logging in Spencer Meadows east of Mount St. Helens; Albert Anderson on Lewis River Road; Curt Taft near Montesano, Ostrander, and Toledo; Rosboro Lumber west of Chehalis, in Capital Forest southwest of Olympia, and on Winston Creek near Mount St. Helens; Joe Zumstein near Riffe Lake; Bornstedts out of Mineral, Ashford, and Morton; 7 & 7 near Chehalis; John Germeau at Onalaska, Eatonville, Chehalis, Oakville, and Cinebar; Roy Filla east of Castle Rock; Weyerhaeuser in the Longview yard and nearly every place the company has logged in the Toutle, Kalama, and Lewis River valleys; Diamond Timber at Kalama, Chelatchie Prairie, and Yacolt; Liberty Logging near Germany Creek, west of Longview, and now near Vader.

Bob doesn't see trucking as some romantic calling, destiny, or obligation. "I tried to get out of this a few years ago," he says. "I filled out applications at Pacific Fibre Products and the county, but I never heard anything back." He has considered applying at Weyerhaeuser, but not seriously, since the company is eliminating its truck fleet. Fifty-eight now, he knows it's probably too late in life to make a change. Trucking is so entwined with Bob's family history, and his own career ties so closely to both his father's and his son's, that people around Castle Rock thought he was kidding when he said he was looking for a new line of work. "Even when I was telling people that I wanted out," Bob says, "I don't think anybody took me seriously."

Bob is not sure he'll be able to retire at sixty-five. He contributes to a pension fund, but it doesn't amount to much. He hopes the Kenworth will last until he does retire, but he may eventually have to consider buying another truck. Unlike union truckers, Bob has never known security. His thirty-nine years in the business have schooled him in patience and perseverance and steeled him to unpredictability. Still, his voice betrays his anxiety; he feels he is strapped in for a ride over which he has little control.

Through force of will, other cousins have kept their sons out of logging. But in Bob's family, the chain remains unbroken. Sonny has his own truck and a great knack for finding work; he appears to be in it for the long haul. Bob's younger boy, Bill (W. R.), recently quit his job with the city of Castle Rock and hired on as a driver for Tri-Tex, a local fuel-delivery company. For Bill, it's a halfway step, one that gives him both a measure of security and a chance to drive truck. "It's hard to explain to people why I made the switch, although I suppose you could blame it on genetics," Bill says of his decision to get behind the wheel. "There's just something about being out there, going up and down the road with nobody to bother you. You feel like you're free."

Thirty-nine years ago, his father would have said the same.

The Heart of a Champion

LARRY DOWNING doesn't think of himself as a busted-up logger. At fifty-six, he retains much of the athleticism he possessed as a high school basketball star—one of those quick, fierce types—barrel-chested with calves and thighs like thick pistons. His water skiing days are behind him, but he jet skis, hikes, and hunts with his brother and son in Idaho's rugged Salmon River country, and even climbed Mount St. Helens. But a list of his activities and a dose of his enthusiasm don't tell you the whole story. Larry has had both hips replaced; he has dislocated his right shoulder thirteen times and broken both ankles; he suffers from arthritis for which he will not take pain medication. Yet when he says he would have returned to his job as a timber faller after his second hip surgery if he'd had to, I believe him without hesitation. He retired from logging in 1996 with a permanent disability, but he has no use for sympathy. From world titles at logging competitions to thirty-five years in the woods as a riggingman, climber, and timber faller, he has lived life on his own terms and is satisfied with the results.

Larry always loved the outdoors—not hunting so much as just being outside, picking cones or cascara, hiking, or aimlessly exploring. And Larry didn't restrict his exploring to ground level. When he was fourteen, his parents came home from a trip to town and found him fifty feet up in a second-growth fir near the Downing house. He had an axe with him and was limbing the tree as he descended. His father wasn't particularly upset that Larry was five stories off the ground; what made Fred nervous was that many of the limbs Larry was standing on were rotten.

The next week Fred gave Larry a set of climbing spurs that had belonged to a telephone lineman. Mornings before school during his sophomore year, Larry ran an extension cord from the house to the forest's edge, tuned in to his favorite radio station, and listened to music while he climbed and limbed a tree. For the next fifteen years, his passion for climbing dominated his life.

Larry entered the logging world the summer after his junior year, working as a chokerman for Jim Adams, a small-time gyppo who was logging on Tower Road a few miles from Larry's home. Because he wasn't eighteen, Larry's employment was an off-the-books proposition with no set wage. When Adams got paid, he passed ten or twenty dollars on to Larry.

When he graduated from high school in 1962, Larry briefly considered attending Pacific Lutheran University in Tacoma; he'd received a letter during his senior year asking if he was interested in playing basketball for the Lutes, and that set him to dreaming. After one look at the cost of college tuition, the dream was scuttled. In June, he went back to work for Jim Adams.

When fall arrived, Larry hired on with Ed and Ernie Roller, his mother's cousins who had given Don Strain a start and who would later do the same for Larry's brother, Ron. The Rollers were logging Longview Fibre timber blown down east of Kalama in the Columbus Day Storm. Larry earned $2.50 an hour. Although he primarily set chokers, he got to do some climbing when it came time to rig the spar.

In April 1963, Larry embarked on a journey of discovery, leaving his job and Castle Rock and traveling to Alaska. "People said you could make big money up there," Larry recalls. "To say the least, that was nothing but a rumor." He got work with Ketchikan Pulp at Thorne Bay, one of the last big logging camps in the area. The pay was $3.18 an hour, better than what he'd made with the Rollers but not exactly the "big money" local loggers had touted. The conditions were classic: eight men to a bunkhouse, a pot-bellied stove for heat, flunkies serving the meals. At Thorne Bay, a siren awakened the men each morning at 5:45. Breakfast was served at 6:00: bacon, ham, sausage, scrambled eggs, and pancakes; there were steaks, roasts, and chops for dinner. The loggers assembled their own lunches from a buffet table. The men were logging old-growth spruce, hemlock, and Alaska cedar. The timber was imposing and so was the rigging: the skyline cable measured two inches in diameter. Larry put in six grueling ten-hour days a week; he survived because he was young and tough and fit.

Living and working in a camp full of grizzled loggers had its ups and downs. In his words, Larry was "a homesick, punk-ass kid." He found out there were two kinds of men: those willing to show a new hire how things were done and those more interested in embarrassing a rookie than in helping him. When someone removed an eye from a piece of cable, the big joke was to tell the new guy, "Take this to the eye sack." Then everybody got a laugh out of watching the newcomer search for something that didn't exist. It was also standard procedure to take advantage of new hires by making them work harder than anyone else on the crew when it came time to carry blocks and pull haywire during skid road changes. "I have a strong belief in treating people decently," Larry says. "That's why I never understood why you would humiliate a guy and get him mad at you when it would have been just as easy to teach him how to do things so that he could help you. Fortunately, I was on a good crew. The hooktender was a guy named Fritz Burkhardt. He only had one arm, but you'd have been surprised at how much he could do."

By June, Larry had tired of camp life and wanted to try his luck at the summer logging shows back home. He returned to Castle Rock and worked briefly for the Rollers again before hooking up with Woodland gyppos Wilson & Sutton, who were logging on the South Fork of the Toutle River. In addition to making $2.75 an hour setting chokers, Larry got to go up the spar with veteran climber Stan Lyons and learn a few things about rigging a tree. When December snow shut down Wilson & Sutton's operation, Larry decided to apply at Weyerhaeuser, where his brother, Ron, worked as a climber. Ron took Larry to see Dick Fotheringill, camp push at Baker. Fotheringill wrote Larry a note to give the Weyerhaeuser employment office in Longview; they hired him as a chokerman.

In 1963, starting pay for a Weyerhaeuser chokersetter was $2.41 an hour during a short probationary period; he would get a ten-cent-an-hour increase if he survived that. Larry's first day was on the 2570 Road in Green River country northwest of Mount St. Helens. A foot of snow lay on the ground and the setting's steepness nearly qualified it as a bluff, but Larry had no trouble making the grade. "They liked me," he says. "I had experience and worked hard."

With Weyerhaeuser expanding, new jobs opened weekly. By April 1964, Larry had enough seniority to move from choker-setting to pulling rigging, and his wage went up to $2.83 an hour. His real breakthrough came when Ron quit his climbing job near the end of the year. Larry told Dick Fotheringill he wanted a shot at the vacant position. Though he was only twenty, Larry wasn't just a brash kid with no experience. After his father brought those spurs home in 1958, Larry had made climbing a part of his life. He climbed in several regional logging contests in 1962, won the novice speed-climbing title at the big show at Albany, Oregon, in 1963, and began to establish a reputation as a world-class competitor. He'd gained more climbing know-how working for the Rollers and Wilson & Sutton and had been up several trees with Ron, who gave him valuable tips on how to rig a spar.

Paid $3.64 an hour, the climber earned more than anyone else in camp. Virtually every Weyerhaeuser logger in southwest Washington had more seniority than Larry and could have had first crack at the job. However, his was the only bid.

Climbing isn't for everyone.

Dick Fotheringill assigned Larry to rig spars and swing blocks for the half-dozen sides working out of Camp Baker. He believed he had boarded the gravy train. "I thought, 'This is it,'" he says. "Things can't get any better." He was outside; he was doing what he loved; he was traveling to a new place each week and working with a variety of people. Times were changing, however. The telescoping steel tower found favor at Baker in 1964, and everyone knew spar trees would soon be obsolete. Workers could move towers quickly; they could set one up within a few hours, saving the several days' wages the climber, operator, and ground crew earned rigging a spar.

Larry continued working as a climber through 1968, though he spent more time working on the rigging than climbing as Weyerhauser phased out spar trees. In the meantime, he satisfied his love for climbing by competing in professional logging shows. "I suppose wanting to be macho was part of it," he says of his motivation, "but more than that, I just like to win." For Larry, the prize money was a bonus. His attitude about the weekend circuit that took him to logging towns throughout the Northwest was less businesslike than his older brother's. "It was a hobby," he says, "a fun thing to do during the summertime." Competing as a professional, he won at several small shows. In 1971, he made his first big splash, capturing the world championship in speed climbing at Albany. In previous years, veteran climbers Dwight Carpenter, Mel Harper, and Kelly Stanley had had the edge on Larry; now he was a step faster and at the top of his game. His newfound success didn't come from any changes in technique or equipment. "I just wanted it more and trained harder," he says. He repeated as world speed-climbing champ in 1972, 1973, and 1974 and also won the tree-topping crown during each of those years while Ron was recovering from a broken leg. In 1972, Larry broke the world speed-climbing record at Vancouver, British Columbia, when he went up and down a 100-foot pole in 32.1 seconds.

Larry was always fast up the tree, but he really smoked the competition on the way down. The rules prohibit free-falling more than fifteen feet without touching, and he pushed that to the limit. In fact, he had broken the world record in 1966 but was disqualified for dropping too far between touches. Not everything went smoothly, even for a world champion. During a competition at Hayward, Wisconsin, that *Wide World of Sports* covered, Larry lost his balance and slid seventy feet down the pole, landing on his tailbone and compressing a vertebrae. At a show in Montreal, his rope hung up while he was descending, popping his right shoulder out of its socket. He has dislocated the same shoulder twelve times since then. After each of the first few dislocations, he went to a doctor to have the shoulder put back in under anesthesia. "I got tired of that," he says. "A guy told me you could do it yourself. You just wad your fingers into a fist and jam it into your armpit, then walk into a wall. I wouldn't recommend that you try it at home," he says with a laugh. "I usually ended up vomiting when I did it myself. I have to admit those weren't some of my brighter moments."

Because of his success, Larry got to travel to places a boy from timber country wouldn't have dreamed of going. He climbed at the 1964 World's Fair in New York; the 1967 World's Fair in Montreal, where he spent six months doing exhibitions; a big exposition in Melbourne, Australia; an exhibition in Tokyo; and several nationally televised competitions at Hayward during the 1960s and 1970s. "I got to go to some great places just because I could climb up and down a tree faster than anybody else," he says. His only regret is that he and Ron didn't have more time for sightseeing. "We always had to hurry up and get there, then hurry up and get back because of our jobs."

Larry has both frightening and fond memories of his summers on the climbing circuit. One year at Albany, Oregon, he watched from the ground as Ron inadvertently flipped his climbing rope over the top of a pole during a topping event; only a safety line kept him from plunging 100 feet to the ground. Larry also remembers when he, Ron, and Dwight Carpenter traveled to Sweet Home, Oregon; the community was hosting its first logging show. When they arrived, the trees for the competitions lay on the ground; Ron, Larry, and Dwight spent the morning helping raise and rig them. The organizers were smart enough to wait until the trees were up and ready before they broke the rest of the bad news: funding was in short supply and the purses would be tiny, only $15 for first place, $10 for second, and $5 for third—80 percent less than what shows of comparable size were paying. The three of them made a pact that the winner would buy dinner for the others. Dwight took first place that day; he said later that it was the only time he ever won an event at a logging show and ended up losing money.

After his speed-climbing and tree-topping victories at the 1974 world championships, Larry retired from competition. He was still in his prime, but he wanted to spend more time with his children. The sport has changed a great deal in the years since his departure. Competition gear is no longer the same as loggers once used for climbing spars at work. Today's climbers wear toe spurs designed exclusively for racing. Also, because the timber industry no longer uses climbers in the woods, the days of loggers, schooled on the job, dominating the competitions are over. The current world speed-climbing champion is a sheetrocker by trade. And, in part because of the new gear, times are faster than ever before.

Larry took risks at logging competitions, but he played it safe when climbing at work. "The most dangerous part was topping the tree," he says, "and I made sure I did it right." He always chopped as wide a face as possible to ensure that when the top went over it wouldn't barberchair and come back at him. And before sawing the backcut, he chopped off the sap wood, two to three inches of the tree's outer layer; the tree's strength lay in this wood, so removing it prevented the top from splitting. In five years of climbing for Weyerhaeuser, Larry didn't break a single top.

Typically, it took around four hours to climb, limb, and top a spar. However, Larry remembers a day when he spent from 7:30 AM until 4:15 PM prepping a tree that was a jungle of thick limbs. Where he sawed it off at 127 feet, the top measured forty-two inches in diameter. Once, his climbing rope got caught on the back side of a spar, and he couldn't move up or down. Larry tried everything to shake the rope loose, but it wouldn't budge; a limb had broken off and the rope was wedged between the remaining splinters of the knot. Because the average spar was four to six feet in diameter, he couldn't just reach around the trunk and free the rope. There was only one solution, and a precarious one at that: he unbuckled the climbing belt, then, leaning back against the rope to keep himself from falling, he worked around the tree until he could free the rope from the

The climber has cut the top out of a spar.
—Courtesy Bud May

knot. "I suppose it was probably no more than five minutes," Larry says, "but it seemed like it took forever to get out of that one."

From the close of his climbing career in 1968 through 1975, Larry hooked for Weyerhauser on both G.T. sides and high-lead sides, which now used steel towers instead of spar trees. Then, in 1975, he went on the saw full time. Prior to becoming a timber faller, Larry, like most riggingmen, had resented cutters, who got a thirty-minute coffee break each morning and worked only a six-hour day. "That really pissed a lot of guys off," Larry says. "I felt the same way until I went on the saw. I found out that timber falling is dangerous work, even more dangerous than climbing."

Larry had tasted life as a cutter in 1966, when he partnered with Jake Luster as a fill-in for a few weeks. They were working in a patch of 250-foot yellow firs near Green River. The first day, Jake put down two trees, and it was Larry's job to buck them. "The chain saws we were using were known as 'Handlebar McCulloughs' because of the shape of the grips," Larry recalls. The saw weighed forty pounds and was impossible for a novice to control. "I couldn't even make it through the first cut. I was out of breath and drenched with sweat. Jake had to finish it for me." After that, Jake taught him how to let the saw do the work. "I was very fortunate," Larry says, echoing the sentiments of other timber fallers who broke in with Weyerhaeuser during the 1960s. "At the time I started cutting, there were still a lot of the old bushelers working for the company. Guys like Jake and Swede Norberg were the ones who taught me the best and easiest ways to do things. Nobody gets that kind of training anymore." Swede showed Larry how to determine if he needed to make an undercut and how to read a log so he'd know which side was safest to work from. After Larry gained experience as a bucker, Swede let him try his hand at falling.

When Larry went on the saw permanently in 1975, he teamed first with Jack Hurley, then with Mike Hinkley, and again with Hurley in 1977. He and Hurley stayed together until the era of partners ended in 1979 and cutters were forced to single-jack. Larry discovered early on that being left-handed posed a problem. The bar on every chain saw is offset to the right; for a right-hander, this keeps the bar away from his body. For a left-hander, however, it brings the bar closer. Larry cut his leg seven times as a result, sometimes seriously enough to require stitches.

*Larry Downing
and Mike Hinkley*
—Courtesy Larry
Downing

Like most loggers involved in the Mount St. Helens salvage operation between 1980 and 1982, Larry hated it. Volcanic ash coated the downed trees; the dust and grit choked men and machines. "I worked for two and a half years in the blast zone," he says. "It was terrible. One cut and you were changing chains. I remember some 'spokesman' saying during a television interview that the mountain had done the loggers a favor by laying out the timber. He should have been there. The only thing that kept me going was knowing it wouldn't last forever." His wife, Gail, had an especially hard time dealing with the knowledge that, had the mountain erupted on a weekday instead of a Sunday, every man in her family would have been killed; not only was her husband working near the volcano, but also her father, her brother, and two brothers-in-law. And now they all had to continue working in the vicinity of an active volcano.

"I always considered myself to be mentally tough, and I'm not one to complain," Larry says. "But that was really a depressing time." One of the concessions Weyerhaeuser made to the men logging in the blast zone was that every crew would have its own crummy, and every crummy would be equipped with a radio. This would provide quick communication in case of an emergency, and if one crummy broke down, another would be near enough to pick up the stranded crew. Soon, though, the company began bunching up the crews—they rode together and were dropped off on the way to the last setting. The changes got under people's skin. If another deadly eruption occurred, one bus would have to gather multiple crews, delaying the escape. In addition, if a particular site had no crummy, that crew would also have no radio and no way to receive or send critical communications. And, the men wondered, what would happen if the crummy broke down? One day, Larry confronted the company's bull-buck and asked him why Weyerhaeuser had gone back on its word. "What do you need a crummy for?" the bull-buck asked. "So you can have a place to eat your lunch?"

Larry exploded, and a heated argument ensued. When the camp push arrived on the scene, he was nonchalant. "Looks like we got a problem here," he said.

"Damn right you do," Larry said before launching into an animated explanation of his grievance. Things cooled down after Weyerhaeuser agreed to furnish Larry's crew with a bus, but the callous attitude of the bull-buck and the camp superintendent bothered Larry and other loggers. The supervisors may not have intended to send the message that the safety of the men wasn't important, but that's what came through.

After the salvage operation ended, turmoil and dissatisfaction within the company continued to build, peaking in 1985 and 1986 when Weyerhaeuser cut hundreds of local loggers and millworkers, offered an additional 250 veteran employees a buyout aimed at further trimming its work force, and, shortly thereafter, forced on the union a Competitive Logging Program (C.L.P.) designed to increase productivity. The security of the 1970s was gone, and the men were both frightened of the ramifications and angry at the company for taking them for granted. "We busted our asses to get the salvage out around the mountain," Larry says, "then we had a couple of good years and were told we were going to have to take a big pay cut." The company's 1986 contract mandated that any timber faller who stayed with Weyerhauser had to take a reduction of $3.91 an hour. In a single day, Larry's salary plummeted from $16.41 an hour to $12.50.

Instead of grabbing the modest severance that accompanied the buy-out, Larry swallowed his pride and accepted the reduction. "What kept me going was that retirement wasn't that far away," he says. "Also, as beat up as I was, changing jobs would have been hard. I'd dislocated my shoulder thirteen times, and I didn't think I could pass a physical if I applied for a job with another company. On top of that, I only had a twelfth-grade education. The thought of changing jobs scared me because I was afraid of failure. Cutting timber was one thing I knew how to do."

The company had eliminated busheling in 1961, but Larry viewed the C.L.P., also known as the incentive program, as a different version of the same thing. The crew members received a base hourly wage, and split a pool of bonus money if they finished a job ahead of schedule or produced more profit on a particular setting than company analysts had projected. When Larry retired in 1996, he was making sixteen dollars an hour, only slightly less than he'd earned before the cut in 1985; however, with bonuses factored in, his pay was closer to $22.50. "We made money," he admits, "but we had to work a hell of a lot harder to do it." His bitterness about the coerced acceptance of the C.L.P. can't mask his pride in being a member of one of Weyerhaeuser's best cutting crews between 1985 and 1996. "They called us the A Team. I guess that says it all." George Lender, Gary Hornkohl, Joe Sullivan, Winston Riddle, and Larry were all experienced, hard-working fallers who pulled down substantial bonus checks under the incentive program.

Though Weyerhaeuser officials cite evidence to the contrary, Larry, like most other local loggers, believes the new pay plan has created its share of safety problems. Everyone is in a hurry and under a great deal of pressure to produce. The only way to gain back the money lost in the wage reduction, which initially cost loggers $400 to $500 a month in wages, is to earn bonus checks. The fast pace can result in foolish actions. Near Yacolt, Washington, a young cutter working on a strip adjacent to Larry's faced up a big second-growth, backed it up, then, when it wouldn't fall, left it. The tree was in a clump, its limbs intertwined with those of several other trees. The rookie not only left it teetering—subject to gravity, wind, and fate—he also failed to mention the hazard to other fallers in the area. Afraid to jeopardize his productivity rate, he simply moved on to the next tree. That evening, Larry noticed the standing death trap on his way out. It terrified him to discover he'd been working near that tree all day. He was fortunate there had been no breeze strong enough to send it over.

Larry shakes his head when he thinks about the close calls. "You look back at all those times you were lucky not to get injured or killed," he reflects. "Sometimes you made mistakes, but most often it was just the result of dangerous situations that couldn't be helped." Like Don Strain, Larry gets chills at the mere mention of snags. "I cut some that were nothing but culvert pipes. Those yellow firs could be five or six feet through. You'd saw in about six inches and the snag would sit down on your bar. The inside was so rotten you'd wonder what was holding it up."

Larry managed to escape critical injury, but the cumulative effect of multiple physical problems eventually wore him down. He broke both ankles in separate incidents. In 1986, he was bucking a log on a hillside near Abernathy Creek west of Longview when the log began to slide. Larry jumped and when he landed, his left ankle buckled. He broke the right ankle near Camp Coweeman in 1995. When the ground gave way on a steep trail, he caught his foot in the crotch of three alders and twisted it. He thought the ankle was merely sprained, and kept working, not only through that day but also those that followed. A trip to a doctor in Longview several weeks later failed to reveal a break, but Larry spent nearly a year trying to work through the chronic pain and swelling. It wasn't until he was examined for a hip problem in 1996 that an orthopedic surgeon discovered a hairline fracture in his ankle. Because the break had not been properly diagnosed, Larry had not given it time to heal. The ankle still bothers him today.

He has also had both hips replaced. His doctor told him the condition was congenital, the result of shallow hip joints, but that climbing and working in the woods had aggravated it. He had the right one done in March 1992 and returned to work—against his doctor's instructions—six months later. Soon, the left hip began bothering him. It was stiff and so painful from arthritis that he had to take anti-inflammatories to be able to sleep at night. One afternoon while walking from his car to his front door with a bag of groceries in each arm, he collapsed. The doctor told Larry the blackout was his body's way of dealing with the onset of a horrific burst of pain. That incident made up his mind: he had the left hip replaced in August 1996. The ankle he'd fractured in 1995 had begun to swell badly on a daily basis, and that, along with the arthritis in his shoulders and hips, contributed to his decision to retire. Still, it wasn't as cut-and-dried as it might seem. "If I hadn't gotten my social security disability, I would have gone back," Larry insists. "I had the knowledge and experience to do things safely."

Looking back at his career in the woods, Larry is quick to say he doesn't think he could have worked anywhere else. "I don't like being confined. That's why I liked logging so much." Ask him if he'd like to see his three boys pursue the same career, however, and he will tell you no, emphatically. He took each of them to work with him for a day during their teen years so they could see for themselves how much charm the job holds. He's happy they have chosen other paths. Kevin and Brian are attending college; Paul works for the Department of Wildlife. Gail also brought Larry's daughters, Jana and Carmen, to the woods to see Larry work. Neither of them married a logger.

Despite a few complaints, he's satisfied with how Weyerhaeuser treated him during the thirty-two years he worked for the company. "There were some assholes who took advantage of people, but for the most part they treated you fair." He can't help but wonder, however, what will happen in the years to come. Company officials boast that the incentive program has created a new atmosphere of cooperation, but from Larry's perspective, the Competitive Logging Program—combined with the wage cutback and the downsizing of the 1980s—has demoralized company loggers. Previously, Weyerhaeuser promoted from within and took time to break men in on equipment such as shovels and yarders. "When I started, Weyerhaeuser was a school for the young and a home for the old," Larry says. But cutbacks reduced chances for promotion, and the C.L.P. discourages apprenticeships. "Guys who are on the incentive program don't want some greenhorn learning at their expense," Larry explains. To increase productivity, Weyerhaeuser is hiring veteran shovel and yarder operators away from area gyppos to fill critical positions. As a result, experienced company riggingmen feeling the effects of age and physical wear can no longer move to an operator's position that might extend their careers.

Union power has suffered a sharp decline as Weyerhaeuser hires more and more independent contractors—part of the extensive cost-cutting strategy that began in the 1970s. Today, the company does none of its own road construction. Only twenty-five union cutters work at the St. Helens Tree Farm. Rumor has it that Weyco drivers may be the next to go as the company jettisons its truck fleet and farms out the work to gyppos. When Larry retired in 1996, he had vision, dental, and medical coverage, as well as five weeks' paid vacation; his wage and benefit package totalled nearly $250 per day. For any company—whether it's General Motors or Weyerhaeuser—moving to a nonunion labor force is the quickest way to reduce such expenditures. In its negotiations with its employees, the company increasingly threatens to contract out all its work to quell rumblings of union action. "Take it or leave it seems to be their attitude," Larry says. He predicts that the trend toward hiring gyppos to handle all phases of the operation will continue. Contractors will compete with each other for the work the company offers; that will mean cutting corners on the wages and benefits they pay their men. For Weyerhaeuser, contracting work out to independents provides an additional bonus: even on its own timberlands, the company is no longer solely responsible for addressing safety and environmental issues; contractors now assume at least a portion of those burdens and serve as a buffer for blame.

Larry has been the guest-of-honor at several Northwest logging shows, and he continues to keep in touch with his cutting-crew buddies. He likes to tell stories. For him, those stories are all the past he needs. "It was hard to get away from it at first," he says of his career as a logger, "but if I went back it wouldn't be a week before I'd miss being off."

The accolades he garnered during his climbing career remain important to Larry, but what satisfies him most is the knowledge that his actions met the standard by which a working man is measured: he worked hard each day from start to finish; he did the job safely and efficiently; he treated his coworkers with respect; and he found time for stories, laughter, and reminiscence.

Last year, Fred Downing decided to log several acres of second-growth behind the Downing home. Larry and Ron agreed to lend a hand. They laid down the same trees Larry climbed as a boy decked out in the belt and lineman's spurs his father had brought home. Cutting those trees closed the circle, melding beginning to end in the story of a man who is a living relic. He is among the last of the full-time climbers and local logging champions, their deeds now relegated to photo albums and museum displays.

Profile of an American Worker

M Y COUSIN JIM is a jack-of-all-trades and a master of many of them. And it's a good thing. He is independent, prone to that gone-to-greener-pastures itinerance that characterized Northwest loggers in the early part of the twentieth century. Jim has been around the proverbial block. He has changed jobs more than twenty times, and it's entirely possible that he's not finished roaming—that either opportunity or circumstance or a combination of the two will one day lead him out on his own again.

Logging was a stopover for Jim, not once but four times, in a love-hate career that spanned twenty-one years as a chokersetter, chaser, timber faller, and log truck driver. When he left the woods the last time, in 1992, it was not of his own accord. He still hasn't gotten over the shock of his dismissal. He's fifty-four now and drives delivery truck for a local freight company. He'd hoped by this stage of his life to have something with more security, but in light of what has happened in the past, security is little more than a word on a wish list.

Jim and I share the same name: James Edward LeMonds. He's my uncle Cliff's oldest boy, a 1964 graduate of Castle Rock High School. During the mid-1940s, my folks tried without success to have children, so when Aunt Joyce gave birth to Jim, she and Uncle Cliff named him after my father. Four years later, I was born. In what must have been a post-birth fog, my parents named me after my father as well. Cousin Jim is James Edward LeMonds II; I am James Edward LeMonds Jr.

One difference between Jim and me when we were growing up was that I knew what I wanted to do with my life: attend college and graduate with a teaching degree. Aside from a brief bout of insanity during which I contemplated a career in the shoe business, I remained committed to my goals. Jim never saw himself working in the woods; yet he ended up there, in good part because he had never envisioned other possibilities. "That was my problem," he admits. "I didn't have a clue about what I wanted to do."

Jim did not follow in his father's footsteps. Uncle Cliff spent one summer setting chokers for McLean & Shaffer before enlisting in the Air Force in 1943. When Cliff received his discharge and returned to Castle Rock, Mel McLean asked if he wanted his chokersetting job back. Cliff declined. "I told him I'd decided to save my calk shoes for hunting season," he says. In 1947, he and his father—my grandfather—opened Bill & Cliff's Body and Fender at the corner of Fourth and A Streets in Castle Rock. Cliff took himself out of the woods and into a territory that very few of my family members inhabited: an indoor job that had no connection to logging. His son, however, fell victim to the siren call of the timber industry—the ready work, the opportunity to be outdoors, the chance to earn decent wages after only a few years on the job.

When you are without a plan, boarding the first ship that passes seems wholly logical, and that's exactly what Jim did. The summer after graduation, he went to work as a whistle punk and chokersetter for a gyppo named Curt Taft. A few weeks later, an argument with a cantankerous catskinner ended with Jim quitting. In spite of the way things turned out, he had found the work appealing. "It was outside," he says. "I loved that part of it." Jim was hooked.

He needed work, and Willie Slagle, the father of one of Jim's high school friends and superintendent at Weyerhaeuser's Camp Coweeman, east of Kelso, got Jim a position in the Coweeman shop. Jim worked the evening shift maintaining loading machines. Working at his father's auto-body repair shop and his uncle Bob's adjacent truck shop and an interest in hot rods had supplied Jim with a broad knowledge of machinery. Changing oil and greasing shovels was a piece of cake, though the wage of two dollars an hour was nothing to brag about. Jim also enrolled in welding courses at Lower Columbia College in Longview during the fall of 1964, but he was never a serious student. The combination of getting home from work at 4 A.M. and attempting to maintain an active love life soon ended his college career.

During the next seven years, Jim's gypsy career gained momentum. He managed a service station, worked in the box plant at Longview Fibre, built canopies, worked at the Weyerhaeuser container division in Olympia, then returned to Longview Fibre. By 1972, he was ready to give logging another go. He called family friend Dick Nesbit, who was supervising Weyerhaeuser's Camp Kalama, and Nesbit got Jim a job setting chokers. Jim was happy to be back in the brush. He was making the same wage he'd made at Fibre and had a good insurance plan. He set chokers for three months, then put in a bid on a job as a chaser. When the bid came through, his pay jumped to just over five dollars an hour.

One day, in the middle of a February snowstorm, Jim stood shivering on the landing, waiting for the next turn to arrive, his fingers and toes numb from the cold. He could see the cutters across the canyon climbing into the crew bus for their morning coffee break. Jim decided cutting was the job for him. When he told Nesbit he wanted a shot at it, Dick suggested he bid on a road-grading job instead. Nesbit had been around the woods for many years; he knew the physical price that timber fallers paid. Jim listened politely but ignored the advice. "I wanted to climb the ladder as far and as fast as I could," he says, and falling timber was the quickest route to more money.

In June 1973, Jim's bid came up on a cutting job, with a wage increase of two dollars an hour. Initially, he partnered with veteran Sam Kreitzer, who showed him the basics. But his second partner, fifty-seven-year-old Earl Hare, really put Jim through his apprenticeship. He taught Jim all the tricks, perhaps the most important of which was using a plumb bob to determine the lean of a tree, a technique critical to directing its fall. Earl also showed Jim how to utilize the lean to bring a tree around— to force it to fall a particular direction without using a wedge. He demonstrated how cutting various types of faces could change the direction a tree fell. He explained how to assess whether the distribution of limbs would influence where a tree ended up. According to Jim, stories about timber fallers being able to put trees precisely where they want them are not exaggerated. "If a good cutter is working with a 220-foot tree," Jim says, "he can drive a stake in[to] the ground with the end of it."

Jim and Earl were cutting yellow fir that was six to eight feet in diameter, but Jim never feared the job. "It didn't bother me at all," he says, "because I had a partner who taught me how to be safe." Like Larry Downing, Jim realized after a few days on the job that cutters weren't pampered prima donnas. "I found out right away that the work was really demanding," he says.

Jim and Earl became close friends. They socialized off the job, exchanged dinner invitations, and helped each other with house painting and other projects. It shook Jim to his shoes when Earl confided that he had terminal prostate cancer. Despite his deteriorating health, Earl refused to miss work. Because he didn't have much of a savings account, he was determined to pay off his debts and leave his wife on sound financial footing when he died. Finally, the rigors of timber falling and Earl's weakened condition combined to nearly incapacitate him. "The last day I

Jim LeMonds II finishes the backcut on a giant fir. —Courtesy Jim LeMonds II

worked with Earl," Jim says, "we were falling snags and he was hurting. The only pain medication he was taking was Copenhagen. He sat down on a stump and told me, 'That's it. I can't do it anymore.' Earl was one tough son of a bitch, and I knew that when he said it was over, it really was." Earl Hare died three months later.

Shortly after Earl's death, Jim was promoted from second cutter to head faller. He was making nearly sixteen dollars an hour, but when a job opened in the saw shop at Camp Kalama, he took it. The work was safe and not physically demanding, and it gave him a chance to do the kind of mechanical work he enjoyed. Falling timber wasn't the same without Earl, and Jim was getting bad feelings about where things were headed. "I could see we were going to cut out the old growth before too long," he says. "That meant smaller trees and harder work." He took a cut in pay when he made the switch, but the overtime that accompanied the nine-and-a-half-hour days in the saw shop made up the difference. Jim's wife, Susan, welcomed the change. "I liked it a lot better," she says. "I finally didn't have to worry about him getting hurt."

When Mount St. Helens erupted in 1980, Jim's first thought was, "There goes my job." Much of Weyerhaeuser's timberland was in the Toutle River valley, directly in the path of the northerly blast and subsequent mudflow. Equipment was ruined, timber was blown down and badly damaged, and the volcano threatened additional eruptions. Rumors flew that the company would shut down its operation in southwest Washington for months, maybe even years. Jack Cody, camp push at Kalama, called company headquarters in Federal Way and told them there was no reason the Kalama sides couldn't go back to work immediately. They were on the southwest side of the mountain, well away from the blast zone. As a result of Cody's efforts, the Kalama crews were up and running after only two days off.

The euphoria was short-lived. While the company waited anxiously for state officials to approve a salvage operation in the blast zone, every Weyerhaeuser logger who had been working out of Camp Baker on the northwest side of St. Helens was temporarily laid off. A chain reaction began, as the loggers used their seniority to bump other Weyerhaeuser men working at Kalama and Coweeman. In an attempt to avoid laying more people off, Weyerhaeuser moved a number of towers from the

Toutle River valley to Camp Kalama. "We started cutting the shit out of the entire Kalama River drainage," Jim says.

Once the company got the go-ahead from emergency officials, in the summer of 1980, it sent virtually every tower, truck, and crew it had into the St. Helens area. The goal was to log the blowdown as rapidly as possible before insects and weather made the wood unfit for market. Suddenly Camp Kalama was nearly deserted. A mudflow triggered by the eruption had wiped out the Baker shop, so the company decided to shift the Kalama shop to Castle Rock, twenty miles closer by road to the operation near the mountain. Castle Rock Stihl rented Weyerhaeuser a room in the back of its building on South Kirby, and the saw shop crew moved in with its grinders and tools.

Jim still had his job, but it was a more difficult one. The ash that blanketed logs and everything else in the blast zone created unique problems, clogging filters and dulling chain teeth far more rapidly than normal. Jim went from sharpening 25 to 30 saws a day before the eruption to rehabilitating 150 to 200 a day after it. The fallers tried using carbide chains with marginal success, and finally settled on round-tooth chains, which lasted longer than the traditional chisel-bits and were easier to sharpen.

In early 1983, after the loggers completed the Herculean salvage effort, the saw shop moved back to Kalama. Things should have returned to normal for Jim, but they didn't. During the Reagan presidency, a new policy forced many people on medical retirement to return to work. A former Weyerhaeuser employee who had previously received a disability for a severe inner ear problem bumped Jim out of the saw shop. Jim has yet to forgive the Republicans.

He went back to falling timber, though a number of things had changed. Now when cutters talked about their "partners," they meant other men on their cutting crew; the single-jack era had begun. Negotiated by the union, the companies, and the state, the new policy gave timber fallers an extra fifty cents an hour for working by themselves.

"What it added up to," Jim says, "was a good way for guys to get hurt. For one thing, you didn't have that extra pair of eyes watching things for you." Worse than that, since the men worked separately, the experienced cutters could no longer break in the rookies, showing them the ropes and ensuring their safety, as Earl Hare had done for Jim. From the companies' perspective, however, something had to give. As timber size decreased with the eradication of old growth, it wasn't cost-effective for two men to work together on a single tree.

Jim's return to cutting did not go well. Almost immediately, he suffered chronic numbness from his fingers to his shoulders. The National Institute of Occupational Safety and Health estimates that "hand and arm vibration syndrome" afflicts 20 to 50 percent of timber fallers and buckers. Each morning, Jim had a little more trouble getting out of bed, until one day he needed help from Susan. "I'd been losing strength in my arms slowly enough that I didn't realize it at first," he says, "but that day when I got to work I couldn't even pick up the saw." He had carpal tunnel surgery and was off work for four months. When he went back, Weyerhaeuser bumped him from cutting to chasing, and his wages fell by nearly two dollars an hour. And that wasn't the end of it. Company downsizing after the blast-zone timber was logged resulted in a chain reaction much larger than the one at Kalama in 1980. As the company eliminated jobs, men with the most years of service bumped down. In 1985, a man with more seniority took Jim's chasing job. Thirteen years after signing on with Weyerhaeuser, he had come full circle: he was now back to setting chokers, the bottom rung on the logging ladder. And once more, his pay took a hit. Like Ron and Larry Downing, Jim believes the downsizing drastically changed the workplace atmosphere. "Everyone resented being bumped," he says, "but we also understood that the guy who bumped us really had no choice."

The 1993 book *The Best Companies to Work for in America* recognized Weyerhaeuser for its outstanding pay and benefits, as well as for the pride its employees took in their work and their company. In a document listing the company's core values, the fifth read:

> Our success depends upon high-performing people working together in a safe and healthy workplace where diversity, development and teamwork are valued and recognized.

If Weyerhaeuser loggers in southwest Washington during the mid-1980s had heard that statement, they would have responded with ridicule and creative profanity. The company's nonstop downsizing and apparent lack of concern for the welfare of its employees turned "core value number five" into a cruel charade.

The incentive program phased in between 1984 and 1986 agitated people nearly as much as the layoffs that began in 1983. Cries of favoritism arose when particular crews were continually assigned the most profitable stands of timber on the easiest ground. "I could see both sides of it," Jim says. "The company wanted their top producers to get the good stuff, and I understand that." But he also saw the gross inequity in the Competitive Logging Program. Crews with the best shows consistently exceeded their production quotas and picked up hefty bonus checks that could total several thousand dollars a year. Others were relegated to impossible terrain or to stands of low-market alder, maple, and hemlock, with no hope of earning the extra pay they desperately needed to offset the 1986 wage rollback. "Some guys made a hell of a lot of money," Jim says, "but some didn't make anything because they were always stuck with the shit."

The eruption of Mount St. Helens was not the sole circumstance that prompted Weyerhaeuser to downsize and impose the incentive pay schedule, but it certainly provided impetus. In 1980, most of the company's remaining old growth was north and west of the volcano; the blast wiped it out. Instead of logging that timber at a moderate rate, the explosion forced the company to step up production and remove the entire chunk at one time; thus, by 1983, Weyerhaeuser had used up harvests it could otherwise have saved for several years down the road. And, because the company had to hire extra help to log the salvage, the workforce was vastly inflated. Timber workers had expected cuts once the St. Helens clean-up was finished, but the extent of those cuts—nearly 1,100 area loggers and millworkers—shocked everyone.

Three additional factors spurred Weyerhaeuser to dramatically reduce its Northwest labor force. The first was the continued transition to lighter, faster equipment to handle the smaller second growth. The speed and efficiency of every machine, from loaders to log trucks, had increased at a startling rate. That meant a smaller crew could get the job done, not just at Weyerhaeuser but throughout the entire industry. Second, as union power increased during the 1970s, company expenditures on medical, pension, and vacation benefits skyrocketed. But corporate

America soon found ways to trim those expenses. In southwest Washington Weyerhaeuser laid off union workers and increased its reliance on gyppo contractors. The final straw was the decline in timber values, which dropped 75 percent during the early 1980s, slowing production dramatically. Unlike most other timber operations in the United States, the Longview woods and mill crews had run at full tilt through 1982, but only because of the salvage job near Mount St. Helens. Once that ended, the economy in southwest Washington felt the jolt.

Jim was not an ardent union supporter. He trusted the IWA leadership only slightly more than he trusted Weyerhauser management. That reluctance to exchange independence for a union card was deeply rooted among Northwest loggers, and timber company owners had taken advantage of it.

At the beginning of the twentieth century, every logger was essentially a temporary employee. In most logging camps, firings were frequent and indiscriminate. Many employers saw nothing wrong with fostering an adversarial relationship with their men. They even believed it was good business for workers to change jobs on a regular basis. If they stayed too long with one outfit, they might start talking about problems they wanted the employer to address, a subject that was completely taboo. For the most part, the loggers didn't seem to mind. Impermanence was a badge for men whose hearts conformed to cowboy-style wanderlust. They accepted the mean conditions as a trade-off for a chance to live independently of polite society and its rules, in a place where hard work alone determined worth.

Eventually, however, the long hours, low pay, filthy accommodations, unsafe conditions, and lack of security combined to make loggers a ripe audience for unionization. Formed in 1905, the infamous Industrial Workers of the World moved into the Northwest to organize the woods crews and recruit converts for the class struggle. That the loggers willingly listened to the Wobblies' revolutionary rhetoric shows how unbearable conditions were. In 1914, J. P. Thompson of the IWW described the timber workers' condition, saying, "The logger finds he is nothing but a living machine, not even treated as well as a horse." More than one pundit called the IWW "the union of last resort": it was often the only vehicle for change available to men in conflict with industries unconcerned about their well-being.

In 1917, the Wobblies organized 295 strikes at logging and mill sites in Washington, reducing production to 15 percent of the previous year's total. The federal government sent troops into the Grays Harbor area to "prevent trouble." Despite the organized move to blunt the influence of the 1917 strike, wages doubled within five years, reaching $3.20 to $4.25 per day, and loggers soon averaged nearly $100 a month.

When the United States entered World War I in 1917, unions took a direct hit. Because the military needed spruce for airplanes and lumber for housing, the federal government enacted a plan to keep a lid on labor's discontent: it actively sought nonstrike pledges from workers as a statement of their patriotism, and most of the men agreed to sign. To insure steady production, the military assigned 25,000 troops to work the Northwest's camps and mills, providing both security and a supplementary labor force.

After the war, labor troubles returned. As the IWW gained a following, constant unrest and occasional violence wracked the Puget Sound and Grays Harbor areas. In 1919, members of the American Legion broke from an Armistice Day parade in Centralia and stormed the IWW headquarters. Four Legionnaires were killed, and vigilantes later took Wobbly Wesley Everest—who had fired several of the shots—from the city jail and lynched him.

The Wobblies did their best to keep pressure on the owners, but when a 1923 strike produced almost no results, they began to lose their influence. The Depression further stunted the emerging power of organized labor; people desperate for work were willing to abide low pay and harsh conditions. The logging companies responded to threats of unionization by portraying the Wobblies as "communists" and "traitors." They offered their own ineffectual union, the Loyal Legion of Loggers and Lumbermen, or 4-L, as an alternative to the IWW. The creation of the 4-L satisfied timber workers for a time, but they soon recognized the organization as little more than a tool of the owners. Things reached a head in 1935, when a big strike crippled the timber industry and rebuilt the power of the unions. Once the International Woodworkers of America organized in 1937, conditions and wages improved markedly. Unionism in all phases of American industry continued to gain power after World War II. Wages were up; medical coverage, pension plans, and vacation pay were now a fixture. And loggers believed the increases would just keep coming. During the 1980s, Jim and his coworkers would learn just how naive they had been.

When the IWA struck in 1986 in response to Weyerhaeuser's proposal to reduce wages by 25 percent, Jim contacted Tom Scott, part-owner of Castle Rock Stihl. Stihl's cutting crew was falling old-growth timber on state land near Thirty-Mile Ridge, northwest of Mount St. Helens, and Jim got himself a temporary job with them. Shortly after the strike ended in September, Weyerhaeuser offered its buy-out to 250 loggers in an attempt to further downsize its workforce. "The stuff that had gone on with the company made me ask myself, 'Where's it all going to end?'" Jim says. He and the 249 others decided not to wait for an answer. They accepted the buy-out—the same one Larry Downing had declined. For Jim, it included a $3,000 severance and a pension of $211 a month when he reached sixty-five. Jim went to work full-time for Stihl. He made several dollars more per hour than he'd made at Weyerhauser, but he lost his medical insurance and three weeks' paid vacation each year; he also had to foot the bill for his own equipment, including calks and chain saws. Jim could have bought medical coverage through Stihl for $320 a month, but Susan was able to get family coverage through her job as an educational assistant with the Longview School District.

Stihl's crew was falling nice timber, but the lack of professionalism the contract cutters displayed disturbed Jim. "The men I was cutting with weren't quite as skilled as the old guys like Earl," Jim says, "and that bothered me from a safety standpoint. I'd never been packed out of the brush before and I wasn't going to start then." Once more, he decided it was time for a change. He told Tom Scott he'd like a shot at driving log truck for Stihl, which was running four of its own rigs. Several months later on a Thursday, Scott told Jim, "Be here Monday morning. I've got a truck driving job for you."

There was more to it than simply showing up, however. Jim had no experience; he didn't even have the combination license required to get behind the wheel. After scaring up a copy of the state's test-preparation booklet, he read it Thursday night, re-read it Friday morning, passed the test that afternoon, and obtained a license. Jim was technically legal, but he knew that passing a written test didn't mean he could drive a truck. He got on the phone to the two men he knew could help: his father-in-law, Russ Case, and my father, his uncle Jim, both of whom were retired and available to lend a hand. Between them, they had more than eighty years of driving experience.

Russ rode with Jim on Monday and Tuesday, and Dad rode with him Wednesday, Thursday, and Friday. His education was quick and intense. "My head hurt after that week," Jim remembers. Each day, he made a single trip from Randle, Washington, to Forest Grove, Oregon, as well as one shorter run. He drove fourteen hours a day for $120. Despite the long hours, he was happy with the job for three years. "In 1989, they told me I had to work Saturdays, after promising me I wouldn't have to."

Jim's younger brother, Bill, who had also taken the Weyerhaeuser buy-out, was falling timber for Castle Rock gyppo Greg Horsley at the time. Horsley had contracted with ITT-Rayonier to cut a unit of old growth, and he was looking for fallers who had worked with big timber. Jim hired on at twenty-two dollars an hour. The first few weeks were physically painful as he made the transition from truck driver back to timber cutter, but it felt good to be on the saw again. His hand and arm strength had returned after the carpal tunnel operation, and he felt optimistic about the new job. Horsley told Jim he was setting up profit-sharing and retirement plans for his employees; he was investing the money in mutual funds. But Jim wasn't around long enough to reap the benefits. He was cut loose without explanation in the fall of 1992. Jim believes his age—he was forty-six at the time—had a lot to do with Horsley's decision to go with younger cutters. In terms of seniority, Jim had been the number two man on a six-man crew, yet he was the only one let go. The layoff took him completely by surprise.

Jim drew unemployment during the winter and kept busy painting cars. Over the years, he had racked up valuable experience working part-time at his dad's auto-body business in Castle Rock. He knew how to take the ripple out of a side panel, how to fill dents with lead, and how to lay on a blemish-free coat of paint with a high-pressure sprayer. He had refurbished his own 1950 Chevrolet, and when he and Susan took it to car shows, people often asked who had painted it. Once people knew what he was capable of, Jim had a line of customers waiting to pay top dollar for a show-quality paint job.

But the resiliency that had kept Jim afloat through previous job changes and uncertainty had waned. He found it difficult to rebound this time. He won't say that he suffered from depression, but he acknowledges that he had the symptoms. "As far as the money goes, I was doing all right," he says. "I could collect my unemployment and do side jobs in my shop." But that didn't exorcise the feeling that he was cast adrift, completely directionless. Displaced loggers could access funds for retraining at colleges and vocational schools, but there was no place for men like Jim to get help dealing with the gut-wrenching sense that they weren't making it. "I just kept asking myself, 'Where are you going to go? What are you going to do?'" The days when good jobs grew on trees were gone, and he knew it.

Jim considered returning to driving for Stihl, but he and Susan hated the thought of the long hours and weekend work. In 1992, he decided to apply for driving jobs at local shipping outfits. At Lower Columbia Trucking in Longview, a sign on the door read, "Not accepting applications." He went in anyway, and said he wanted to apply for a driving job. Initially, they offered him four days a week delivering freight. He put in fifty-five hours the first week and worked full-time from then on. But the news wasn't all good. Jim had been pulling down twenty-four dollars an hour cutting for Greg Horsley; now he was making nine dollars an hour. Painting helped make up some of the difference, but the drop in wages was tough to get used to.

Lower Columbia Trucking gave Jim a route along the Oregon Coast and the Long Beach Peninsula, hauling freight classified as L.T.L.—"less than truckload"—in a Ryder-size truck that was easy to maneuver. He kept his route for seven months before applying at Silver Eagle, a freight company that hauled paper rolls to Vancouver, Washington, and fiber stock to Tualatin, Oregon, for Longview Fibre. Silver Eagle paid the same wage as Lower Columbia Trucking, but offered a medical plan as well. In addition, Silver Eagle was a union shop. Jim joined the Teamsters and got a retirement plan and an improved vacation package.

In March 2000, Silver Eagle closed its doors, citing rising fuel and health care costs as contributors to its demise. Jim now drives for Pacific Northwest Motor Freight, which has taken over a portion of the hauling Silver Eagle did for Fibre. Pacific is nonunion, so Jim is no longer a Teamster. He had hoped to put in the twenty years required to earn a Teamster pension, but that dream went out the window. Susan's job with the Longview School District still provides medical insurance, so Jim invests the monthly benefit allocation he receives from Pacific. If the stock market cooperates, he hopes to have accumulated a few retirement dollars by the time he reaches sixty-five.

He likes his driving job, but despite the surgery and the layoffs, he often finds himself wishing he was back in the brush. "I guess what I found out somewhere along the line," he says, "is that logging is something that's in my blood."

Jim still paints cars on the side. Because of his reputation for exactness and quality, he has two years of part-time work lined up. He would love to open his own shop but he isn't prepared to go full-time. "The government's got more rules than the IRS when it comes to painters," he says. Recently, he went online with a website that advertises his newest business venture: straightening and polishing stainless steel trim for antique cars.

Because he has changed jobs so many times and suffered such dramatic wage and benefit cuts, Jim's working life provides an apt profile of today's American blue-collar workers. Silver Eagle, like Weyerhaeuser, assigned Jim an employee number. For him, the practice is more than just a convenient bookkeeping device for the company; it's a blunt metaphor for the way management sees working people. "When it comes right down to it," he says, "that's all employees are—just numbers."

When he was out of work in 1968, Jim left the house one morning after telling Susan, "I'll be back before noon with a good job." He'd never say that now. Not even the highest-placed family friend can open today's doors. "I don't think I'll ever feel completely comfortable with a job again," Jim says. "The days when you could go to work for a company like Weyerhaeuser and retire there are long gone. It makes it hard to feel secure."

One day at a time, he tells me. That's the only way to hold the dogs of doubt at bay. One day at a time.

More Than the Money

B ILL LeMONDS ADMITS it readily: for him, falling timber was a labor of love. He knew the dangers, saw what happened to the men he worked with, understood that he was not immune from injury or long-term debilitation. Yet in spite of the risks, he was hooked so deeply that it took almost getting killed to convince him to get out.

Bill is my father's brother's son, Jim's younger brother. He graduated from high school in 1966, two years after Jim, then spent four years in the Navy trying to determine what he wanted to do for a living. When he left the service in 1970, he still hadn't made up his mind. He came home to Castle Rock and worked at a local gravel company for several months, but when he married Shari Orr in September of that year, he needed to find stable, long-term employment. In October, Bill hired on at Reynolds Metals Company in Longview, where the pay and benefits were good. If things had panned out, he probably would have stayed, but a layoff in January 1971 forced him to find other work. He took a job driving fuel truck for B.L.R.S., a Castle Rock company that delivered diesel to logging outfits throughout southwest Washington. On his route, he often ran into friends from his high school days who were pulling down good money as riggingmen. He started thinking about the disparity between his wage and theirs, and when B.L.R.S. didn't come through with a pay increase after he'd worked there for six months, he decided to make a move. As Jim had done, Bill contacted family friend Dick Nesbit, who was then superintendent at Weyerhaeuser's Camp Kalama. Nesbit wielded considerable influence and quickly got Bill a job setting chokers.

Bill insists he never imagined he'd end up working in the woods. His refrain is familiar: "It was a last resort," he says, "a job I knew would be there if I needed it." It surprises me more than a little to hear him say that. We spent a lot of time together growing up, and his love for the outdoors was impossible to miss. Whether we were hunting for elk west of Mount St. Helens or hiking the woods behind his home on Tower Road in search of railroad trestles left over from the days of steam locomotives, Bill always seemed most at ease when he was close to the land. It made perfect sense to me that he chose to earn his living at a job that gave him the opportunity to be outdoors every day.

Physically, Bill was well-suited to the demands of a career in the woods. He carries two hundred pounds on a five-foot-seven-inch frame. His chest is deep and his legs are thick as alder trunks. My father always teased Bill about struggling over downed logs with those stumpy legs. "Don't you get high-centered?" Dad would say. But in the long run, Bill's compact build served him well. He suffered less stress on his back, less dispersion of his power. He could go hard all day, whether churning up steep hillsides as a chokersetter or lugging fifty pounds of gear through green timber as a cutter.

He set chokers for a year, learning the ins and outs from veteran hooktender Bob Glasgow. Then, in 1972, a job came open for a G.T. hooker on the night shift at Camp Baker and Bill grabbed it. The G.T., or guyless tower, also known as a grapple yarder, was one of Weyerhaeuser's early experiments in the transition to smaller timber and downsized equipment. Lighter and more mobile than traditional steel towers, the G.T. ran grapples on the mainline instead of chokers. Its range was limited to between 600 and 1,000 feet, but two men could run a G.T.: a hooktender to spot the logs and an operator. Bill discovered that on decent ground a skilled operator with sharp depth perception could send a grapple out and pick a log from the brush with essentially no assistance; it made the hooktender's job a walk in the park. On a good shift, they might yard three hundred pieces—not bad considering the company paid out only one-third the wages it would have spent on a typical six-man high-lead crew. While logging at night took some getting used to, light was never a problem—four 1,000-watt bulbs shone from the boom of the G.T. Even 300 yards from the tower, Bill could read a newspaper without squinting.

From 1974 to June 1975, Bill did a brief stint as a high-lead hooktender on the day shift, then his bid came through on a job cutting timber. The move changed everything. As second-faller on the two-man crew, Bill bucked the timber that head cutter Jim Setala put down. Although he didn't use a handsaw as Henry Berndt had in the years prior to World War II, some aspects of the job remained the same. The work was unforgiving. "Make the wrong cut," Bill says, "and it could kill you." On rugged ground, every cut was an adventure, requiring an eye for balance and geometry. Sometimes, on a hillside, a full-length tree would hang up around a stump, its weight evenly distributed, the ends drooping like the tips of a colossal mustache. One cut, judged correctly, could send both pieces safely down the hill; a miscalculation, however, might shift the weight to the far end, swinging the near end of the log up the hill on top of the bucker as he finished the cut. Logs bridged or bowed in the middle were also potentially deadly. The distorted pressure of the bow or bridge could close the kerf, pinching the saw; worse, as the cut deepened and the remaining wood could no longer withstand the strain, the log might snap and break free, plunging down the hill or kicking back toward the bucker.

Despite the danger, the work suited him. He loved the challenge, the independence, and the exacting demands of the craft. In short order, he decided he had found a home. Besides teaching him to buck, Setala schooled Bill in the art of timber falling. "He'd start by explaining the lean and how the wood was going to hold," Bill says, "but when it came to doing the cutting he made sure I got plenty of practice. Jim figured the only way you could learn to cut timber was by doing it."

Bill worked as a second-faller for four years. Then in April 1979, timber companies convinced the union and the state of Washington that the preponderance of smaller trees made a shift from the old faller-bucker system to one known as team cutting practical and reasonable. The job title "bucker" was eliminated. From that point forward, three or more men worked through adjacent strips of timber, each falling and bucking without assistance. According to the new rules, they had to stay within 600 feet of each other and they had to get help from a partner to cut any tree measuring more than thirty-six inches in diameter at chest height. The latter was a concession to those who argued that falling larger trees required two men. Shortly after the transition, the companies discarded this provision, largely because it was irrelevant: by 1979, few trees measuring more than three feet in diameter remained.

Though companies referred to the single-jack strategy as team cutting, it isolated fallers. Bill's brother, Jim, and many other cutters complained about the hazards of the new system. For Bill, it was a good fit. He had always enjoyed tromping the woods alone, and the newfound solitude attracted him. He didn't have to depend on or worry about anyone but himself; it was just him and the timber. He came to love that aspect of cutting even more than the financial security it provided.

Bill's financial situation had begun to blossom. He'd started on the saw at nine dollars an hour in 1975, but the 1970s saw huge gains for loggers and millworkers. After the Columbus Day Storm in 1962, the Japanese market opened up, timber prices soared, and wages went with them. The export market was as lucrative as a gold mine; the companies were making good money and so were the men. Bill and Shari paid off the mortgage on

Bill LeMonds saws the face in an old-growth cedar.

their house in Castle Rock, then used the equity to buy a home west of town on Melton Road, at the east edge of the Willapa Hills.

In May 1980, Bill's crew had just moved to a stand of trees on the west face of Elk Rock, seven miles northwest of Mount St. Helens, when the volcano erupted. Hundreds of small earthquakes and numerous steam and ash eruptions preceded the major explosion, but geologists and company officials had assured the five hundred loggers working in what would later be known as "the blast zone" that they were in no danger. Their lives were spared on May 18 only because the volcano erupted on a Sunday, when nearly everyone was out of the woods.

The eruption dealt Weyerhaeuser a severe financial blow. It obliterated 36,500 acres of timber and destroyed 26,000 acres of young replants. The mudflow and flood that followed the eruption raced down the Toutle River valley, wiping out the company's railroad lines, bridges, logging roads, and millions of dollars' worth of equipment. Several months after the eruption, Weyerhaeuser doubled its work force in the St. Helens area— signing on new hires, pulling in company loggers from Camp Kalama and Camp Coweeman, and contracting with gyppos who rolled in from all parts of western Washington—then rushed the men into the blast zone to log salvage. Many loggers opted to take extended leaves of absence rather than face the desolation, the clouds of dust, and the possibility of another eruption. Others quit Weyerhaeuser and set their sights on jobs in Alaska. Bill, along with nearly one thousand other men, stuck it out, although the daily need to subdue his fear of another eruption raised his blood pressure. He worked in two feet of ash northwest of St. Helens near Green River, the area the blast hit hardest. He wore a mask to keep the ash out of his lungs, a memorable inconvenience, but the real curse for timber fallers was the constant problem with chains. Under normal conditions, a chain lasted an entire day. But the volcanic grit that coated the logs dulled the chains so quickly that fallers went through six to twelve per day, which led to numerous delays and endless frustration.

Each day, truckers hauled six hundred loads of logs from St. Helens to a transfer depot at the Green Mountain Mill near Toutle. By the end of 1982, loggers had removed 850 million board feet of timber and had finished the salvage job. The company immediately declared a major reduction in force; in 1983 and 1984, they sent hundreds of local loggers and millworkers packing. In addition, as the old contract neared expiration in 1985 and negotiations for a new one began, company officials announced that if Weyco was to weather a precipitous drop in timber prices, it would have to reduce wages and benefits by at least 25 percent. President George Weyerhaeuser, speaking at the Columbia Theatre in Longview, told his audience that the company was in dire straits and needed sacrifices from the union in order to stay afloat.

Chuck Wiggins, Weyerhaeuser's regional vice-president, cited figures showing that the southwest Washington operation had lost $4.25 million in 1984. The proposed wage and benefit rollback of more than four dollars per hour was "essential," he said, if the company was to remain competitive. Every timber company on the West Coast echoed Weyerhaeuser's demand for concessions from employees.

On June 16, 1986, negotiations deadlocked and the International Woodworkers of America authorized a strike involving 7,500 loggers and millworkers in Washington and Oregon. Weyerhaeuser responded with a take-no-prisoners approach. Don Rush, vice-president of operations in Washington, said that if the union didn't approve a contract, the company would permanently eliminate the jobs of 3,100 Northwest loggers. As one of only a handful of major timber companies in the United States still employing its own union work force, Weyerhaeuser laid its cards on the table: agree to the reductions or the company will rely on gyppos to do the work.

Union loggers could not fathom a 25 percent pay cut. Their fortunes had been on the rise for two decades, and they were certain the company would cave in. But management held firm in its refusal to compromise. Even though the IWA had rejected the company's contract offer by a four-to-one margin in June, members approved a "new," virtually identical proposal in September in a two-to-one vote. "The union lost its guts," Bill says. "When the company said they'd go all gyppo if we didn't approve the contract, the union should have told them to shove it. Gyppos need people, too. Where were they going to get them if Weyerhauser loggers held out?" The men lost 20 percent of their previous earnings when they accepted Weyerhauser's offer. In an attempt to ease the residual bitterness and take some of the sting out of the wage cuts, the company offered to expand the production-based incentive program it had begun implementing in 1984.

Bill doesn't dispute the company's need to cut employees after the salvage operation, but he wonders why this move had to be accompanied by a huge fall-off in hourly wages. Like many of his peers, he had little faith in the words of George Weyerhaeuser, Chuck Wiggins, Don Rush, and other company spokesmen sent forth to peddle the tale of corporate woe. Like the bushelers who saw their wages slashed in 1961 with the move to hourly pay, the men were resentful and disconcerted. The pay cut stung their pride, and George Weyerhaeuser's predictions of coming uncertainty and turbulence frightened them.

In 1986, in conjunction with the widespread layoffs and wage reductions, Weyerhaeuser offered its early retirement deal to 250 area loggers. Those with the most seniority had first shot at the buy-out packages, which included severance pay and a deferred pension. Betty Phillips, Human Resources Manager at the Longview site, says, "The people who elected to stay with the company [and refuse the buy-out offer] were, in general, the more productive ones." Not a single logger I spoke with agreed.

Before the strike, Bill was making nearly seventeen dollars an hour. After the 1986 contract settlement, Weyerhaeuser offered him the same job at $12.50 an hour, and he opted to take the buy-out. For Bill, the decision hinged on a single factor: "I wasn't gonna do that job for that amount of money." The company paid a severance of slightly less than $300 for each year of service; Bill's total for sixteen years earned him $4,400. He can collect his pension without penalty at age sixty-five. Bill was fortunate to have exited with some compensation. In the final cutbacks, those men who had worked at Weyerhaeuser for less than ten years got nothing but a layoff notice.

Bill and the others who were bought out or laid off told themselves, "We'll just hire on with a gyppo and make comparable wages." But the wave of corporate downsizing would cost them dearly in the long run. Fourteen years later, the buy-out still haunts them. They continue to suffer from the loss of benefits—the paid holidays and vacations, first-rate medical plan, and pension that were part and parcel of a union job—and the unpredictability of working for independent contractors. Perhaps worse was the fact that Weyerhaeuser eventually employed many of those contractors at a cut rate.

While in hindsight, Bill's decision might look like a mistake, at that time, staying with the company seemed as great a risk as going to work for a gyppo. Larry Downing had turned down the buy-out offer with retirement on the horizon, but many younger men saw no future for themselves with the company. Bill was thirty-eight. The old growth was nearly gone, and change was imminent. The lack of big timber and the obvious trend toward downsizing convinced the men that Weyerhaeuser's entire operation in southwest Washington might go under. During contract negotiations, Don Rush had threatened that the company might disband its crews and go completely gyppo. Was this merely a negotiating ploy? What assurance was there that somewhere down the line Weyerhaeuser might not make good on Rush's words? Many felt it would be better to get a start with someone else as soon as possible than stick with Weyerhaeuser only to find themselves out the door a few years down the road.

Bill bounced around during the next year, falling timber for several independents and even trying his hand as a crewman on a tugboat for a four-month stretch. In June 1987, he was hired by Greg Horsley, a gyppo doing contract cutting for Longview Fibre. The work was steady and the pay was good; by 1988, Bill was making twenty-four dollars an hour. For most of his career with Weyerhaeuser, he had worked in marvelous stands of old-growth and second-growth Douglas fir. The same was true of the five years he spent cutting for Horsley. Fibre liked the performance of Horsley's crew, and kept his men working in big, choice timber. When the Fibre work was slow, ITT-Rayonier contracted with Horsley to cut old-growth state timber it had purchased. By now, nearly every other logging outfit in the Northwest was cutting trees of increasingly smaller diameter. While Bill felt the changes to some degree, he remembers falling awesome tracts of old growth several times a year, even as late as 1992.

Work slowed at the end of 1993, and Greg Horsley had to lay off his crew. Horsley learned what Ron Downing had discovered the year before: the recently enacted spotted owl restrictions and the state export ban had severely limited available contracts. For gyppos, work was increasingly erratic. While the entire timber industry has felt the effects of environmental constraints, federal and state bans (passed in 1974 and 1990 respectively) on exporting timber harvested on public land have devastated logging companies that lack their own holdings. Meanwhile, Weyerhaeuser and other industry giants have prospered. Since today's export market is only open to those with access to private timberlands, companies with major land holdings—such as Weyerhaeuser, Hampton, Boise-Cascade, and others—are in the catbird seat, able to ship logs to dozens of countries, most of them on the Pacific Rim. After a severe downturn in the early 1980s, export sales rebounded, peaking in 1988 when the United States shipped more than four billion board feet of timber abroad, primarily to Japan, but also to South Korea, China, and Australia. Oregon and Washington timber companies logged more than three-quarters of the exported timber. In 1996, the United States shipped less than two billion board feet abroad, but the major players in the industry had a stranglehold on those logs. Former Weyerhaeuser forester Walt Mezger says the ban on exporting government-owned timber really boosted company fortunes. "For Weyerhaeuser, it was like having the only tavern in town."

Meanwhile, small sawmill owners and gyppo logging operators like Ron Downing and Greg Horsley were often out of luck and out of work, and so were the men they employed.

After Horsley laid him off, Bill had time to look at his future. For the first time, he seriously questioned whether he would last until retirement. And he wasn't just worried about whether there would be enough timber. He was forty-five, and already his body chronically protested. He'd always known that physical risks and debilitation were part of the job. In 1989, Bill had suffered a broken nose and a concussion when the top came out of a snag he was falling, dropped sixty feet, and struck him on the front of his hard hat. But even that experience hadn't made him fear going back to work. "It just pissed me off because I knew I'd been careless," he says. Now his knees and hips sent out distress signals. Tylenol and DMSO no longer dented the pain, and he asked himself if it was time to move on. He'd expected to feel rested and ready to return to work after some time off. Instead, he felt the opposite: "The longer I was off, the less I wanted to go back."

Bill drew unemployment through 1994, then settled on a radical and improbable course of action: he decided to give the life insurance business a whirl. Bill and Shari trimmed their expenses to the bone and relied on Shari's job at Weyerhaeuser Credit Union in Longview to carry them through while Bill tried to get his feet on the ground. Combined Insurance Company sent him to licensing school in Tigard, Oregon, then for additional training in Phoenix, Arizona. After completing his schooling, Bill returned to southwest Washington and set about making a living, armed with the sincerity and well-practiced gift of gab that had long been his trademarks. Bill enjoyed talking with friends and retirees about their insurance needs—as well as anything else that came up during the course of a conversation—but he soon became disenchanted with the company. A number of his fellow agents seemed far more concerned with making a buck than with protecting the interests of their clients. On top of his frustration with Combined, Bill felt like an alien in the insurance business. Each morning when he saw a man in a dress shirt and necktie in the mirror, he wondered who he was trying to kid.

After four months with Combined, Bill quit and went back to work as a cutter for Bob Harris, who had contracted to thin timber for Weyerhaeuser. Like Don Strain and Bill's brother, Jim, Bill had to swallow some irony. After choosing the buy-out over the pay cut in 1986, Bill was indirectly back with the company—on the company's terms. Weyerhaeuser used many of the same men it had employed before the cutback, and at a substantial savings because the men now worked for contractors who had low-bid the jobs. They paid their own medical and pension costs, and netted considerably less money than they would have if they'd taken the pay cut.

In the spring of 1995, Good Friday coincided with a celebration at Weyerhaeuser Credit Union in Longview. As part of the festivities, Shari had agreed to dress up as the witch from *Snow White and the Seven Dwarfs*. She sprayed her hair until it stood out from her head, applied several layers of make-up to complement the hag's rubber nose she'd rented, and wore a black dress and a classic witch's hat.

Like the wives of so many loggers, Shari lived with the dangers of working in the woods as much as Bill had. "If I thought about it, it drove me crazy," she says. "You always dreaded the possibility of getting that phone call." When the call came on Good Friday in 1995, she ran to her car in the credit union parking lot and sped across town to St. John's Hospital. She laughs when she recalls dashing into the emergency room in her witch's costume, wondering what could have been more out of place in a Catholic hospital on Good Friday.

Bill had suffered a collapsed lung, a broken nose, and a serious concussion. Harris's crew was working near Goble Creek southeast of Kelso. Bill had cut a one-hundred-footer that went partway over before hanging up between two other trees. He knew better than to walk beneath it—a cardinal sin for a faller—but he had spotted a tree just beyond the hang-up that needed cutting and couldn't bring himself to leave it. It would take no more than twenty seconds to go in, put the remaining tree down, and get out. He waited, checked to make sure the leaner was stable, then hurried under it and got to work. He'd made the cut and was ducking back out of harm's way when the leaner came down, catching him on the left shoulder. The portion of the trunk that hit him was only five inches in diameter, but even that was enough to nearly kill him.

The accident ended Bill's career as a full-time logger. He recovered from his injuries fairly rapidly, but a month after the accident he still struggled with what it had done to his mind. He could no longer pretend that death and injury were reserved for others who were careless or unskilled or simply unlucky. He blames no one but himself for what happened; he is quick to say that human error undoubtedly causes most accidents in the woods. "They've tried to make things safer," he says, referring to steps state agencies and logging companies have taken to reduce deaths and injuries, "but so much depends on the individual, on his mistakes and his misjudgments."

In May 1996, after a year off, he took two jobs, one running excavator for Greg Horsley, who had branched out into the construction business, and the other driving dump truck for Jim Heltemes Trucking. He gets no paid vacation, and his wage of thirteen dollars doesn't compare to what he made as a faller, but the time for compromise had come. He does his best to be satisfied with what he has.

When Bill quit cutting timber, his metabolism changed abruptly. As a result, he's had to adjust his diet and keep an eye on his fat intake. Like most former timber fallers, Bill suffers from white finger, a numbness in his fingers and lower arms caused by the vibration of the saws he operated. Seven times, a limb, choker, or chunk rammed the brim of Bill's hard hat down hard enough to break his nose. Bill helped carry out three coworkers killed in logging accidents and saw dozens of others seriously injured. On three consecutive Fridays during his tenure with Weyerhaeuser, a company helicopter flew over his crew's setting on its way to pick up men who had been killed or hurt. He is thankful that he could walk away relatively healthy after nearly twenty-five years in the woods.

Bill doesn't see things getting any easier for timber fallers. As his brother foresaw, smaller trees have made the job even harder. A big old-growth might have taken half an hour for a cutter to work through. The saw was buried in the tree during that time, so most of its weight was off the faller's arms, shoulders, neck, and back. "Now it takes no more than ten seconds to cut a tree," Bill says, "then it's on to the next one." More time supporting the full weight of the saw means more wear and tear on the body. In the new millennium, a faller who stays on the saw through retirement may be as rare as a three-log load.

Bill is anything but a preservationist; he believes that trees are a renewable resource and sees little sense in letting mature timber decay. On the other hand, his proposed strategy for logging responsibly in the future—"Go in, take the big stuff out. Leave the little stuff to prevent erosion"—resembles the view of environmentalists who insist thinning must supplant clear-cutting if we are to achieve ecosystem sustainability.

Talk like that is anathema to timber company officials. Weyerhaeuser's John Keatley says scientific evidence clearly proves that Douglas fir will not grow as a replant in deep-shade areas that have been thinned. "If you can't clear-cut," Keatley adds, "production will go down, costs will increase, and employment will decline." In 1998, timber officials were extremely concerned about Oregon's Measure 64, which would have banned clear-cutting in that state on both public *and* private lands. Weyerhaeuser, along with every other timber company in the Northwest, contributed money and political clout to a campaign that saw the proposal defeated by a four-to-one margin. Some construed the voters' sound rejection of Measure 64 as proof of their overwhelming opposition to stricter regulation of logging practices; however, an *Oregonian* poll revealed that Measure 64 went down because voters viewed it as too extreme, not because they support clear-cutting. In fact, 75 percent of the state's residents want change. Voters are most vehement about growing older forests, protecting streams, guarding against landslides, conserving habitat, and repairing or eliminating existing logging roads. A survey of Washington voters would probably reveal similar sentiments. Timber officials know the current of public opinion runs against them. They rely on television commercials and increased cooperation with government agencies to dispel accusations that they behave irresponsibly.

Bill's primary environmental concern is the health of the region's streams. For this reason, he believes, as many conservationists do, that state and federal agencies should require logging companies to leave a 100- to 200-foot buffer of trees along streams to improve salmon and steelhead habitat. This barrier would block sunlight, keeping water temperatures low enough for fish to survive; it would also provide the woody debris necessary to sustain a healthy aquatic system. Bill will likely get his wish. In 1999, the Washington legislature passed the Forest and Fish Agreement. It establishes three zones adjacent to streams on public and private land. No one may harvest in the core zone, the 50 feet nearest the water on either side. The inner zone, extending an additional 85 to 100 feet beyond the 50-foot barrier, will see very little logging. In the outer zone, which reaches 50 to 65 feet beyond the inner zone, loggers must leave a smattering of trees per acre to soften wind damage in the interior zones. Tim Quinn, biologist for Washington's Department of Fish and Wildlife, explains the agreement: "We're trying to provide mature forest conditions in the core and inner zones. The goal is to make sure that the streams are shaded and that they are supplied with plenty of wood fiber." Quinn concedes that neither he nor anyone else has the answers to the region's salmon crisis, but he adamantly supports immediate action to improve water quality. "Right now, our plan is to go wherever the science takes us. We know there's a lot of uncertainty about what we're doing. That's why we need a strong, well-funded management program to test . . . whether or not the plan we have is working; then we can adjust if it's not. I really believe that the changes we are making will be a huge step in the right direction." The plan will remove a mind-boggling 15 percent of the state's forestland—amounting to two billion dollars in assets—from production once it goes into effect.

Kevin Godbout, Director of Environmental and Regulatory Affairs at Weyerhaeuser's Federal Way office, explains why the company took an active role in negotiating the Forest and Fish Agreement instead of digging in its heels and resisting. "We recognized that there was going to be a series of endangered species listings for salmon in the Northwest and that we were going to be impacted in a major way. It was in the company's best long-term interest to work with people so that we could have an agreement that gave us some stability." Godbout feels good about the final product. "Some parts of the agreement may be a little too stringent," he says, "but at least it's based on science and is protective of the watershed." In return for their cooperation, landowners, both large and small, will receive a 16 percent reduction in the state excise tax on all logs they sell; additionally, the state will compensate small landowners for at least 50 percent of the value of the timber they have to leave standing along streams.

Timber companies shuddered when the federal government invoked the Endangered Species Act to protect spotted owl habitat in 1990. One of their greatest fears was that investors wouldn't fund a venture that might fall victim to more such federal dictates at a later date. Stricter regulations and growing public opposition to clear-cutting have fueled those fears. In a 1999 poll that Evans/McDonough conducted, eight out of ten Washington voters agreed with the statement "protecting our streams, rivers, and lakes . . . should be a high priority." State Senator Karen Frasier, who represents a legislative district near Olympia, says the poll results clearly document strong grassroots support for environmental protection. She also realizes the political realities that accompany this sentiment: "You had better support environmental quality," she says, "or your campaign is in big trouble."

In 1995, major players in the timber industry responded to the receding tide of public support. The American Forest and Paper Association, whose four hundred member companies own 90 percent of the nation's industrial forestland and account for 84 percent of U.S. paper production, drafted the Sustainable Forestry Initiative. Calling the S.F.I. "a bold new commitment to long-term forestry," Association members vowed to support research into sustainable forestry, to minimize the visual impact of logging, and to develop programs to protect habitat for fish and wildlife. "This is about performance," says Laurence

Wiseman, president of the American Forestry Foundation, an affiliate of the AF&PA.

Skeptics eagerly point out that it is also about public relations. They believe the AF&PA's central goal is to deflect public criticism and, thus, head off legislation that could further restrict industry practices and limit profits. Though the measures outlined in the S.F.I. seem promising, some call its wording "fuzzy." For example, although the S.F.I. calls for members to "control clear-cut sizes," it fails to define what is acceptable. And, while independent certification of S.F.I. goals would lend credibility to the association's efforts, the AF&PA has rejected outside evaluation. Melanie Rowland, a professor of conservation biology at the University of Washington, applauds the progress AF&PA members have made in areas such as selective logging and reforestation. However, she worries that the timber companies will not apply the S.F.I. consistently. "The companies vary tremendously in how much of it is lip service and how much of it is real," Rowland says.

Logging companies must follow myriad regulations and overlapping and frequently changing policies that influence such areas as forest chemicals; insect and disease problems; reserve tree selection; road construction; watershed analysis; harvesting practices; stream temperatures; endangered, threatened, and sensitive vascular plants; and spotted owl and marbled murrelet nest sites. "When we plant, we have one set of rules," Weyerhaeuser Human Resources Manager Betty Phillips says, "but by the time we harvest we might be on the fourth or fifth set of regulations. It's very difficult to operate when there is so much instability."

Bill LeMonds would tell you that timber companies like Weyerhaeuser aren't the only ones who have to live with instability. The ability to adapt to a dynamic world is today's most critical survival skill for corporations and individuals alike.

Looking back at his working life, Bill doesn't grouse about missed opportunities in other fields. Instead, he confesses to dreaming the gyppo's dream: in spite of the odds, he would have liked to have run his own logging outfit. "Just a two- or three-man show," he says wistfully. "I think about that sometimes, being on my own and being my own boss. I should have taken the chance and just done it." In the next breath, however, he acknowledges the reality that tempers romantic visions. "Logging is a sucker's game. When you get started you're in your twenties. You're tougher than hell, and the money looks good. What nobody tells you, and you aren't smart enough to figure out for yourself, is that there's a good chance you'll end up a cripple by the time you're fifty."

Bill and Shari have two sons—Jeremy and Glenn—and share the relief that neither of the boys has opted for a career in the woods. Shari is particularly happy that Bill has made the change to running excavator and driving dump truck, and Bill likes the work. Still, he can't completely shake the memories of the way of life that once held him so tightly.

In July 1997, Bill cut timber during a month-long layoff from his truck-driving job. Once incredibly fit from packing a saw and gear over rugged ground each day, now he got so stiff and sore the first two weeks back that he could barely crawl out of bed in the morning. Yet he clearly enjoyed the chance to return to what he loved, if only temporarily.

"In the middle of winter, when the wind is blowing sideways, it's nice being inside the cab of that truck," Bill says. "But when the sun comes out, you find yourself sizing up trees and thinking about which way they would fall. It haunts you because you loved it so damned much."

Even the Best
Expect the Worst

OM COOLEY IS THE YOUNGEST of my cousins who has paid his
mortgage with timber dollars. Logging is the only work
Tom's ever done, but I can't help thinking of Tom as different from the rest. For one thing, he's younger—a 1971 high school
grad—and still in his forties. For another, Tom has always been
more of a technician than a knuckles-skinned man of the brush.
He's a shovel operator. He spends his days in the cab of a hydraulic loading machine—a 4300 Link-Belt that came with a
pricetag of $350,000—setting logs on trucks headed for the port
dock in Longview or one of the area mills. And, according to
nearly every driver who's worked with Tom, he is one of the
best Weyerhaeuser has ever had.

Tom is also an anomaly: after twenty-eight years he is still
with the company. In the past, that kind of tenure wouldn't
have raised an eyebrow, but in the current era of perpetual
downsizing, it's a real accomplishment. My other cousins have
retired or changed careers, or they are close enough to the end
to believe they can hang on in one capacity or another until
social security and pension checks start showing up in the mailbox. Tom has fifteen years to go, and he is more than a little
apprehensive about the changes and hardships those fifteen
years could bring. He's grateful to possess a skill that is still in
demand. If company cutbacks wipe away his union job, he could
almost certainly find work with a contractor. But he knows the
days of the sure thing are over, and that knowledge makes him
a contemporary of every logger working in the Northwest woods
today.

Although Tom never expected to become a logger, he gravitated to the timber industry in much the same manner as my other cousins: it was what remained after a few hastily constructed dreams drifted into the distance. He spent a few quarters at Lower Columbia College and left feeling less sure of himself than when he started. Ironically, for Tom and other loggers of his era, solid, readily available employment proved a detriment of sorts. Through the early 1980s, good work was there for the asking, and that made it easier to shrug off other possibilities. "Getting a job in the woods was no problem in those days," Tom says. "If you knew somebody"—and nearly everybody in southwest Washington did—"bam, you were in the door." Tom's father, Sam, worked for Weyerhaeuser, so when Tom went to the company's employment office in Longview and filled out an application, he was hired without the formality of an interview. In April 1972, he started as a chokerman at $4.50 an hour, working on a high-lead tower out of Camp Kalama under the direction of hooktender Snuffy Caywood. "I remember that we were working in old growth," he says. "There was snow on the ground, and my feet were so cold I couldn't feel them."

After a year of setting chokers, Tom bid on a job as a chaser and found himself working on a side near Wolf Creek where his dad was running shovel. Tom was happy working on the landing. He no longer had to worry about traversing steep terrain, and on days when the precipitation couldn't decide if it would fall as rain, sleet, or snow, a fire always burned close by. In 1973, Weyerhaeuser was logging old growth almost exclusively. Most of it was limb-free for the first one hundred feet or more, so the chaser rarely had to cut limbs the fallers had missed. His job consisted almost entirely of unhooking the chokers when the turns arrived at the landing. As an added bonus, during slack time, Sam schooled Tom in the art of operating a loading machine. Tom caught on quickly and decided he'd found the career he'd been looking for. In 1974, he bid on a shovel operator's position and landed a job working swing shift in the sorting yard at Camp Kalama. Tom worked on the ground for only two years, a scenario that would never play out today.

The Camp Kalama sorting and transfer yard received all the Weyerhaeuser wood from the Kalama River drainage. After unloading the logs, shovel operators sorted them according to grade, dimension, and species, and rebuilt the sorted loads onto bunks.

Stacker operators hoisted the bunks onto trucks headed for the mills in Longview. Tom ran a 98 Link-Belt, a shovel known as a dipper stick that was equipped with pincerlike hydraulic grapples. A single line moved the "stick" and grapples back and forth on the boom; when he had positioned the grapples at the end of the stick over a log, Tom pinched them shut, lifted the log up under the boom of the shovel, and set it on the bunks.

Six months after Tom started at Camp Kalama, Weyerhaeuser decided to cut costs by making shovel operators do the sorting on-site. The company eliminated Tom's position and transferred him to a loading machine in the brush. The adjustment proved painful. Even though the dipper stick at Camp Kalama required the operator to maneuver the stick to position the grapples, the

Tom Cooley,
Weyerhaeuser
shovel operator
since 1974

grapples themselves were hydraulic, and that made the work tolerable. Tom now had to run a 108 Link-Belt, an old-style grapple machine with no hydraulic capability. It was a full-body job, with hands and feet working levers and pedals in a simultaneous, coordinated effort to swing the boom, cast the lines out like a fisherman equipped for Moby Dick, open and close the grapples, and pick up the logs. All this demanded a great deal of skill and experience. Tom had neither. He felt his ineptness crippled the productivity of his entire crew. Weeks of frustration passed, the stress mounted, and Tom told himself he should go back on the rigging. Fortunately, his foreman, Charley Davis, knew that time was the only cure; he convinced Tom to stick with the job. Within a few months, Tom's technique improved, and he was on his way to becoming a skilled operator.

By the late 1970s, the big timber was rapidly disappearing, and the equipment used to log it was becoming obsolete. The only way to maintain production levels with smaller trees was to increase speed. Enter the new technology. In 1978, Weyerhaeuser assigned Tom a 5800 FMC-Link-Belt, the second fully hydraulic shovel in the Kalama area; Tom's father had operated the first. Unlike the dipper stick, this shovel had no cables. It was powered entirely by hydraulics, which meant Tom could accomplish every aspect of the operation more smoothly and more quickly.

Even a top-of-the-line shovel can't eliminate the need for experience and skill, however. And while a novice chokerman has a hooktender to show him the ropes, a shovel operator is essentially on his own. "It was a long time before I really understood how to organize the landing and how to build loads," Tom says. "I'm still learning things." Some people believe he's a natural, a man born with a gift for running shovel. Tom knows better; he insists it took years to develop the skills he has today. A shovel operator, like the driver of a car, can have complete control only when his movements become second nature. "It's all a matter of efficiency," Tom says. "The key is being well-organized and making every move count. You don't want to waste time digging through your piles to find the right log while trucks are waiting to be loaded. If you have your logs sorted properly, you can load the truck quickly out of one pile. I've been moved onto landings where other operators had been working that were such a mess I wondered how anything got done."

Tom Cooley at the controls of a Link-Belt hydraulic shovel —Courtesy Tom Cooley

Keeping things straight can be a complicated matter. After the yarder skids the logs to the landing, the shovel operator must separate each sort, or grade, of wood. A log's sort depends on its species, dimension, and condition. There are three sorts of hemlock, one sort of hardwood saw logs, one sort of hardwood pulp, a cottonwood sort, a cedar sort, a small-diameter fir sort, and an export fir sort. To qualify for export, Douglas fir must have no more than "minimal defect"; it must measure twelve inches in diameter on the small end and at least twenty feet in length. If logs between eight and twelve inches in diameter on the small end are at least thirty-four feet long, they also qualify. The shovel operator has to identify and stack these sorts without climbing out of his machine for a close-up inspection.

Next to maintaining a well-organized landing, building a load is a shovel operator's most important skill. "It's a lot like putting a puzzle together," Tom explains. "I separate the longer logs that will 'bunk' [form the foundation on the truck's bunks] so that when I start loading I can go right to them. Then I use the smaller logs to fill in the middle of the load." Tom takes pride in setting logs on trucks without the slightest damage or disturbance. "You should be able to load a truck so smoothly that if the driver has [left] a cup of coffee on the dash, there won't be a single drop spilled. It just takes time." Tom remains thankful for the patience and confidence of Charley Davis more than two decades ago. "Without time to learn, you can never get the experience you need to really be good."

After Mount St. Helens erupted in 1980, Tom and every other Weyerhaeuser logger in the area moved to the blast zone. Tom worked near Elk Rock where the explosive force of the eruption had knocked down the entire forest. After the cutters had bucked everything near the road, Tom yarded what he could reach with his shovel and loaded the logs onto trucks headed to Green Mountain Mill near Toutle. "There were days that were so dusty you couldn't see the other side of the valley," Tom says. Maintenance crews thoroughly greased every moving part of his machine, but couldn't keep the volcanic grit from working its way in. When they serviced the shovels after several months of operation, they found every pin encased in sand and had to replace every bushing in the booms. Tom gratefully moved back to the green of Camp Kalama when the salvage operation ended.

During the turmoil of 1986—the strike and settlement, the buy-out, downsizing, and paycuts—Tom had just enough seniority to avoid layoff. Unlike Bill and Jim LeMonds, he decided to stay with the company. "The money I would have gotten from the buy-out wouldn't have amounted to much," he says. "On top of that, the word got out that if you took the buy-out, Weyerhaeuser would never hire you back. I thought then, and I still do today, that if you're going to work in the woods, Weyerhaeuser is the best place to be because of the good benefits and because you usually work pretty close to home."

Tom paid a high price for his loyalty. "There was just so much instability," he says. "You could be changing jobs on a weekly basis." As men whose positions were eliminated during the downsizing bumped down, the fall-out became inescapable. In addition to the 20 percent cut in pay that accompanied the new contract, Tom lost several more dollars an hour in wages in 1987 when a man with more seniority took over his shovel job. Tom was forced to return to chasing. Because he and his first wife had divorced, a large portion of Tom's check went to child support. He barely made enough to pay the bills. Besides worrying about his financial obligations, Tom wondered if he had a future as a logger. "I thought a lot about whether I wanted to keep doing this job, or whether I should pursue something else." Since he had worked in the woods his entire adult life, he had no idea what that "something" would be. Eventually, a degree of stability returned, but three years passed before Tom regained his job as a shovel operator. Weyerhaeuser is still downsizing its work force, but so far, Tom has hung on.

During the past decade, Tom's crew has been to every corner of Weyerhaeuser's 420,000-acre St. Helens Tree Farm. In the days of virgin timber, Weyerhauser loggers marched like an army up the Toutle, Coweeman, and Kalama River valleys. When they finished a setting, they simply moved a mile east to the remaining old growth. Now they travel widely to places were the company's second growth has reached harvestable dimension or where hardwoods must be cleared to make way for Douglas fir replants. A crew might spend several weeks at Canyon Creek in the Yacolt Burn, then suddenly move forty miles northwest to Salmon Creek outside of Toledo. The men's sense of camaraderie has diminished, in part because multiple crews no longer board crummies for the trip to and from work. Instead, each crew travels directly to its job site in a seven-person van. The company is trying to group its crews within a few miles of each other, so that one mechanic or foreman can attend to several sides without traveling an hour or more to do so. Tom has noticed that gyppos get the more distant work; Weyerhaeuser keeps its men and equipment, especially company log trucks, as close to Longview as possible in a move to save fuel and travel time.

Like everyone who works in the woods, Tom notes the profound change in the dimension of the trees his crew cuts, yards, and loads. Smaller trees mean less weight, smaller rigging, and different machinery. Modern yarders are far less powerful than those used before 1985. However, because the turns are lighter, the lines run faster, and chokers return to the rigging crew much more rapidly. When Tom broke in, chokers measured an inch and an eighth in diameter; the riggingmen had trouble wrestling them around logs. Today, they are five-eighths of an inch. "I call them shoestrings," he says.

The smaller timber also calls for dramatically different engineering of the loading machine Tom runs. "The shovels now are fast, and they have to be. The first load I loaded this morning was fir fiber, which includes logs that are partially rotten or less than five inches in diameter. That load had at least one hundred logs." When he started in the 1970s, one hundred logs might have totalled twenty to thirty loads. Only the advent of hydraulics makes the work possible and profitable on today's tree plantations. "To load a 100-log load with the old grapple shovel would have taken one to one and a half hours," Tom says, "and you'd have been pulling your hair out the whole time. I finished the load this morning in thirty minutes."

The change in timber dimension has also created new dangers during the yarding process. "Things can happen so quickly nowadays," Tom says. "Small timber is much more dangerous than the old growth because it's so light. Logs can upend, and you never know where they're going to come down." Inside his cab, Tom is safe from many of the hazards cutters and chokermen face. Still, he has had a number of close calls. On a high-lead side, the shovel works right on the landing so that when the yarder pulls logs in, the shovel operator is there to keep the landing area clear and begin sorting and stacking. If a log gets hung up when it's being yarded, it can swing around or upend as it arrives at the landing. If one smashed into the cab of Tom's loading machine, he could be killed or maimed.

In the winter of 1993, Tom saved the company a shovel, but he barely escaped serious injury or death himself. The rigging crews were snowed out that day, but the company brought Tom in to move his shovel down the 124 Road to a lower elevation where he could load it onto a low-boy that would transport it to another location. "The road was so slick you couldn't stand on it," Tom recalls. Very gingerly, he moved the shovel four or five miles; then he reached a point where the road sloped. A pickup was parked in the way, and Tom had to maneuver around it on the lower side. The shovel began to slide, slowly at first, then it broke loose and headed toward the edge of a long drop-off. Tom reacted instantly, swinging the boom of the machine over the edge of the hill and jamming it into the ground. "Fortunately, the heel rack of the boom caught on a big rotten log," stopping the shovel's slide, he says. The shovel was suspended at the lip of the bank, its right side tipped up off the ground. The cab, which sits offset to the left, was on the downhill side. Had the machine traveled another foot or two, it would have rolled over on top of the cab. "I could have easily gotten killed," he says. "I think I used up one of my nine lives that day!"

Like so many others, Tom feels Weyerhaeuser's most disturbing trend today is its increasing reliance on independent contractors. When Camp Baker, Camp Kalama, and Twelve-Mile all operated, the company's truck fleet numbered nearly 150 highway and off-highway rigs; now it has 35. When Weyerhaeuser cuts drivers, it offers them the "opportunity" to return to a job they held previously—most likely setting chokers, since that is where new hires break in. Men in their twenties or thirties might have no problem making the switch, but the company drivers who have survived repeated cutbacks over the past two decades are in their forties and fifties. Many are no longer fit enough to take on a physical job like chasing or chokersetting. Unfortunately, the alternative is to accept a layoff and look for something else.

In the late 1990s, a recession in Asia caused a fall-off in foreign housing starts, and the timber export market took a downturn. As a result, the company is logging less second-growth fir and more alder and hemlock—jobs Tom refers to as "land clearing projects." Smaller trees means fewer loads and less need for trucks. Weyerhaeuser has always assigned some company trucks to gyppo sides logging their timber, but "I talked to the Weyerhaeuser truck foreman one day," Tom says. "He told me they wanted to cut the truck fleet down to a size where they would just cover the company sides." The latest cuts appear to have accomplished that. Now, when busier times create a need for extra trucks, Weyerhaeuser fills in with gyppo rigs. "It doesn't set well with the company drivers," Tom says. "Everybody's got an attitude," agrees Tom Bredfield, the number two Weyerhaeuser driver in terms of seniority. "They feel it's just a matter of time and we'll all be gone. The contract is up this year, and there probably isn't going to be another one [for truckers]." Not only drivers but all Weyerhaeuser loggers wonder if their fears that the era of company logging is over—the same fears that led 250 of their coworkers to take the buy-out and leave the company in 1986—are finally coming true.

Money dictates most Weyerhaeuser decisions, and loggers hear about it more often than they would like. Longtime Weyerhaeuser riggingman Jim Carter says, "The company is always talking about the 'gap' [the difference between the cost of maintaining its own crews and the cost of hiring gyppos]. They're always telling the men, 'You gotta close the gap or company logging is going to fold.'"

Weyerhaeuser research in the early 1980s compared the cost of having its own union crews complete a specified task with the cost of having a contractor complete the same type of job. The disparity was so large that Weyerhaeuser insisted on implementing the Competitive Logging Program as part of the 1986 contract agreement. Under the C.L.P., a price-setter examines the variables that influence the expense of logging a particular setting. This helps determine how much it would cost a reputable contractor to complete the job. Weyerhaeuser evaluates the work of its loggers by comparing expenditures on the job with that figure. "Our crew is charged the expenses the company incurs," Weyerhaeuser Human Resources Manager Betty Phillips explains. Expenses include wages, health benefits, machinery, transportation, repair, and administrative costs. If the Weyerhaeuser crew can do the job for less money than the price-setter forcasted, the company awards them a bonus. "It seems logical," Phillips says. "The crews that are producing the most volume ought to get more money than the crews that are producing less volume." In her view, the program has been an unequivocal success. "Productivity really picked up after we instituted the C.L.P."

Company loggers don't believe that Weyerhaeuser can reasonably expect them to eliminate the gap. Independent contractors don't have to pay for administrative costs, health care benefits, pension plans, and vacation time. With overhead stacked against them, union loggers cannot merely be *equally* productive as independents; they must be significantly *more* productive to earn reasonable pay. "They always tell us we aren't competing with the gyppos," Tom Cooley says, "but because of the benefits, it's almost impossible to compete." Tom, for example, gets five weeks' paid vacation each year, holiday pay, a 401k pension plan, and a solid health insurance package. Gyppo operators aren't obligated to provide any of those perks to their men. Phillips says the bottom line is that Weyerhaeuser expects its employees to outperform contractors. The company insists that is the only way to remain competitive.

Union loggers point to the contract of 1986 as the beginning of the end. "I'm making less money now than I made in 1984," a

Weyerhaeuser riggingman told me. "Anybody who tells you that the bonus money is making up for the wage cuts we took is crazy. At first, the C.L.P. wasn't a bad deal, but it's gotten to the point where the whole thing is ridiculous. As soon as somebody starts making a bonus, the company changes the formula. But what can you do about it? It's their rules, their cards. If you don't want to play, you go home."

John Keatley, Northern Area Team Leader for the St. Helens Tree Farm, says the escalating cost of equipment has made bonus money increasingly difficult to earn. Weyerhaeuser factors a daily fee into the crew's expenses for each machine they use, and the company replaces that machinery at a rapid rate to take advantage of the latest technology on the market, saddling company loggers with phenomenal overhead charges. "Today," Keatley says, "it isn't unusual for a side to have a million dollars in assets sitting on the landing." Despite some kinks in the C.L.P., both Keatley and Phillips believe it has enabled the company to make huge strides. "It's caused a change in the way crews work," Keatley says. "There is more cooperation in order to increase productivity." Tom agrees that the company had to implement the incentive system. "I think it was pretty much essential. I remember taking books to work to read because there was so little production. The company had to do something to stay competitive." Still, he insists that the way the company administers the C.L.P. creates unrealistic expectations.

In 1998, Weyerhaeuser and the union agreed to try a variation on the C.L.P. "It got to the point where the company was making it humanly impossible to make a bonus," Tom says. "That's why guys voted to take a chance with the new system." Betty Phillips agrees. "With the C.L.P., there were situations in which the system wasn't an effective incentive. It was time to try a different approach." The new program lumps all Weyerhaeuser's southwest Washington loggers together. Instead of only some sides making bonus money, the entire work force shares equally. Every three months, the company evaluates how effective union loggers are in narrowing the gap with gyppos. When the gap closes, the men get an "adder" on their paychecks. Thus far, Tom is making slightly more than he made under the C.L.P., but he has no idea how long that will last. "The company does the paperwork," Tom says. "We don't feel like we have a lot of control."

In sharp contrast to the 1970s, the union no longer has much leverage. At contract time, management trots out the usual threat. "We get the word," Tom says. "They tell us that if we don't accept the contract they'll eliminate Weyerhaeuser logging altogether." The frustration is tough to deal with, particularly when the company implies that union loggers lack the heart needed to get the job done. "The guys I work with have plenty of skill and experience, and they work hard," Tom says. "There's a lot of pressure on us these days. More than I can ever remember. When you hear negative stuff all the time, it wears on you, especially when you know they might cut your job at any time."

Contrary to what its fixation on remaining competitive implies, Weyerhaeuser Company is doing well; it is the world's largest producer of softwood lumber and pulp, the world's largest exporter of forest products, and the world's largest private owner of salable softwood timber. During the next decade, as the high-yield forestry plan instituted during the 1960s starts to bear fruit, company executives expect regional harvests to increase. That timber, much of it Douglas fir, will play a significant role in sustaining logging in southwest Washington. Precisely how things will play out for loggers, however, remains to be seen.

"The St. Helens Tree Farm is very solid," John Keatley reports. Because of its low elevation, logging can proceed year-round; good soil makeup ensures a rapid growth rate; and the proximity of mills and river access minimizes transportation costs. Unlike some Weyerhaeuser officials, Keatley sees a need to maintain a company logging crew. "It helps to be flexible, and you need some size in order to do that. For example, if a shovel breaks down on one of our sides, the operator can call in and we can quickly divert the trucks to a different side. Contractors can't do that. It's also convenient to have your own crews to count on when it comes time to plan for the year." Despite his endorsement of company logging in principle, Keatley acknowledges, "This is a very competitive business." His meaning is clear: the industry must focus on profit. Timber companies are not social agencies. Human Resources Manager Betty Phillips feels the expense of maintaining a union work force is burdensome. "Some people would like to see the elimination of company logging," Phillips admits. "Although we've made very good progress in closing the gap, the difference is still significant. Because of that, productivity is an issue that will definitely need to be addressed in the next contract."

In the 1960s and 1970s, Weyerhaeuser hired one hundred loggers and millworkers a year in Cowlitz County. "Now it's competitive just to get a chokersetting job," Tom says. "You have to be interviewed and have experience or they won't even look at you." And shovel operators? "I was fortunate to break in when I did," he says. To the best of his knowledge, nearly ten years have passed since a company logger was able to submit a bid, survive the probationary period, and stick with a shovel operator's position. The company often hires gyppo shovel operators with experience. Independents such as Whoopy Gould of Gould-Sunrise serve as an unwilling farm system for Weyerhaeuser. Gould has hired and trained a number of men who have eventually quit and gone to work for Weyco. The company lets the gyppos provide the training and experience, then selects the best men to fill the few positions that open.

The days Larry Downing remembers, when "Weyerhaeuser was a school for the young and a home for the old," are as much a relic of the past as spar trees and steam machinery. Increasingly, no one is interested in spending the time and money to break in a new man. This impatience extends to Weyerhaeuser loggers. Since the incentive program began, everyone's foremost goal is to keep the wood moving, and rookies only make it more difficult. "To me, the unwillingness to let people try [their hand at machine operation] is sad," Tom says. "I know people who could make it if they were just given the time." But tolerance of the Charley Davis variety no longer exists. "Back when I started you had twenty days to break in," Tom says. "Now there really isn't a true break-in period. A lot of guys don't even bother to bid on shovel jobs because they know there's no chance they're going to be given the time to make it." Tom sees this immobility as one of the most discouraging aspects of logging today. "There's so little chance for promotion," he says. "You're looking at being stuck setting chokers forever."

Tom's crew may envy the fact that he spends his shift protected from the elements in a climate-controlled cab, but they don't resent him for it. The stagnation of wages that began in the 1980s has rendered bonus money a necessity. Everyone depends on the shovel operator to pump loads out with rapid-fire efficiency. The crew might be able to make up for poor performance on the part of a chokersetter, but they can't overcome the liability of an incompetent shovel operator.

In the past two decades, modifications in pay, hiring practices, and union activity pale in comparison to the evolution of the equipment. Twenty years ago, the loading machine, or shovel, was essentially a stationary object on the landing, and the shovel operator had one task: loading the trucks. Technological improvements during the past decade have given birth to shovel logging, in which the operator ventures off the landing to grab logs and skid them to the road. "Today's shovels move through the brush better than a cat," Tom says. "It's amazing where they can go." The undercarriage of the new machines is arched to provide enough ground clearance for passing over stumps. The advent of high-clearance shovels with high-speed hydraulics has almost outmoded logging with cats and rubber-tired skidders. "Because of the small-diameter logs and the extremely brushy conditions, I'll bet a shovel could outlog five or six cats," Tom says. "Plus, when I get the logs to the road with a shovel, I have the capacity to sort and load them."

Tom is surprised that Weyerhaeuser owns no feller-bunchers or roto-saws, which, on flat ground, can cut 250 to 400 trees per hour, eliminating the need for timber fallers. He's seen these machines at work and marvels at the speed with which they cut small timber. The feller-buncher uses scissorlike blades; the roto-saw uses a round sawblade mounted on the front of a machine. For now, Weyco takes a wait-and-see approach; when the terrain and timber call for it, the company prefers to hire contractors who own feller-bunchers and roto-saws, letting the independents bear the overhead associated with purchasing and maintaining the machinery.

For trees no larger than twenty-five to thirty inches at the butt—and few today exceed this dimension—machines called processors streamline the work. Moving on tracks or rubber tires, a processor can pick up full-length trees, limb and buck them to length, sort them, and stack them. Processors can only run on relatively flat sites; they operate in combination with shovels, roto-saws, or feller-bunchers, and are especially effective in limb-plagued stands of hemlock. Sensors on the machine provide the operator with readouts of a log's length and its diameter at various points. Based on this data, the operator decides where to make cuts to get the most scale. He tells the machine to buck the log at a particular point; the operator never has to leave the cab. In the past, loggers cussed snarled chokers or broken mainline; today, they cuss the computer on their processor if it's not reading properly. Where processors can limb and buck the logs, companies use fewer timber fallers. "The new technology is amazing," Tom says. "A man who knows what he's doing can buck 750 to 1,000 logs a day with a processor."

Weyerhaeuser has been looking at ways other than shovel logging to get logs out of the brush. They now use forwarders, usually in conjunction with processors, to minimize yarding costs. Equipped with bunks to hold the logs and self-loading capabilities, a forwarder can transport logs from the brush to the road. This scenario requires no high-lead tower, no buckers, no rigging crew, and none of the expenses that accompany them.

Because forwarders and processors aren't practical on high-lead sides—the landing is simply too small to accommodate them—the chaser on those settings not only unhooks the chokers but also faces an extraordinary amount of limbing. The eradication of the old growth has left a preponderance of limby hardwoods and hemlocks in the woods. "It's so bad in some places," Tom says, "that when you leave a landing the place looks like a giant bird's nest." The excessive demands on the chaser have led to the experimental use of electronic chokers: the yarder operator can press a button in his cab and automatically unhook the chokers at the landing, eliminating that task from the chaser's list.

Another piece of equipment loggers will depend on in the near future, says Mike Crouse, publisher of *Loggers World*, is the Global Positioning System monitor. G.P.S. is a way of precisely determining locations, without the aid of a surveyor. Loggers can use G.P.S. to identify section lines and establish precise layouts for settings. Using G.P.S. could also minimize roadbuilding and help determine how to most effectively log an area, right down to which stumps would make the best tail-holds on high-lead sides. "The bottom line is that G.P.S. can save loggers time and money," Crouse says.

According to Dave and Kirk Conklin, owners of Portland-based Timber Resource Management, the machine of the future is the single-grip harvester. Developed in Finland and Sweden, the harvester combines the capabilities of a roto-saw and processor. Like a roto-saw, the harvester grips trees with a hydraulic arm and cuts them off using an automated saw. The operator, with the aid of three computers, can put down several hundred trees per hour on flat ground. In addition, the harvester strips the limbs and debarks the tree at a rate of sixteen feet per second, then bucks the trunk into lengths. The $450,000 price tag didn't dampen the Conklins' enthusiasm for their machine. Dave says his harvester, working in combination with a forwarder, can produce as much bucked wood as six men with chain saws. The harvester has also allowed the Conklins to extend their work year. Loggers using heavy machinery on tracks must shut down operations when wet weather compounds the soil damage the machine causes. The harvester's fat rubber tires harm the environment far less. Logging practices and conditions have changed: landowners thin their trees more frequently now, removing weaker ones so the healthy ones grow faster, and smaller timber is the norm. The Conklins believe their single-grip harvester addresses today's conditions and was well worth the investment.

Weyerhaeuser's John Keatley says mechanized cutting using roto-saws, feller-bunchers, and harvesters is the wave of the future. "The technology in thinning and clear-cutting is increasing tremendously. Currently, we have a mixture of hand-cutting and mechanized cutting, but productivity, cost, and quality are all positively affected by the move to mechanization. For example, if you have a feller-buncher that can grab the tree, cut it, and lay it down, there will be far less breakage than if you have fallers trying to put trees on the ground without hitting stumps or other logs." Before 1980, cutters had to hand-buck immense old-growth trees into lengths that could be yarded, but processors can buck today's smaller, lighter timber right in the brush. While difficult terrain still necessitates hand-falling, the demand for cutters continues to shrink.

Tom Cooley talks enthusiastically about the new technology, but he sighs when he contemplates his own future. While he hopes to stick it out until he's sixty-two, he knows his job may not last another fifteen years. "Who knows what's going to happen?" he says. "There are so many rumors about the company eliminating its crews and going completely gyppo, I don't feel very secure." Tom's skill and experience make it unlikely he will ever be without full-time employment, but he'd rather not have to work for a nonunion contractor. All the security he's worked so hard to build in the last quarter of a century—the

vacations, the paid holidays, the health benefits, the retirement—
would vanish in an instant.

At forty-seven, Tom is satisfied with his position and his salary. His base wage is sixteen dollars an hour; with incentive bonuses factored in, he averages eighteen to twenty an hour. He's invested too much time and effort in this career to think about jumping to another. He made his decision in 1986 and has little choice but to stick with it. Asked what advice he would give a young man considering a career in the woods, Tom chuckles. "I'd say forget it. I'd tell him to get an education instead. I think there will always be some logging around here, but you can't think of it as a career anymore."

As for himself, he keeps his fingers crossed, hoping Weyerhaeuser will retain some semblance of its union crews and that he will be able to hang on. He is among the last of the local loggers who can harbor such hope.

The Best We Had to Give

I F HICKORY SHIRTS AND CALK BOOTS are the standard apparel for loggers, then scraped shins and bruised thighs are the mean condition. No one gets through enough work in the woods to call it a career without multiple close calls. Narratives of narrow escapes aren't shared with wives and mothers; most often, telling coworkers must suffice. And in that telling, laughter and coarse language typically camouflage the emotion, for any earnest examination of those brushes with death would necessitate a career change the following Monday.

For children growing up during the 1930s in the Long-Bell logging town at Ryderwood, Washington, the greatest childhood fear was that dad might not return from work at the end of the day. Each evening, wives and children listened for the train that brought the men back to town. A long, mournful blast on the train whistle meant someone had just lost a father or a brother. The apprehension was much the same at Shelton, Washington. If there had been an accident, the train from the woods would rumble into town with the whistle tied down and blowing wide open. Wives and sweethearts of loggers would burst into the streets to see whether the train stopped at the funeral home to deposit a body or at the hotel to drop off an injured man.

Safety has improved markedly in the industry, but those who live in logging communities still receive regular news of death and injury. No one is immune. Eventually, everyone loses someone he or she has known, cared for, even loved.

For me, the names come to mind far too easily: Arling Sorenson, father of my college roommate; Owen Woodard, brother of the woman who cuts my hair; Sonny Hicks, father of my best friend from the old Jim Town neighborhood; George Rockett, brother of a kid who graduated from high school with me. And my cousin, Bob Hansch, the son of my mother's sister Elsie and her husband, Otto. Unlike my other cousins who worked in the woods, Bob didn't live long enough to rack up stories of close calls, great deeds, and laughter to fill a memory book. He never had the chance to mow his own lawn, complain about a mortgage payment, celebrate an anniversary, or hold a son or daughter of his own. He was twenty-three years old when he died in a 1966 logging accident near Neah Bay, Washington.

Bob wasn't Wally Cleaver, but we thought of him as the all-American boy. He belonged to the Lettermen's Club and the Science Club, worked on the yearbook staff, played on the base-ball team, and captained the basketball team; his basketball

Rigging crew and climber in the late 1930s. Bob Hansch's father, Otto, stands below the climber.
—Courtesy Elsie Hansch

teammates voted him most inspirational player. When Bob graduated in 1961, he attended college for a year. Then ready work and good pay in the timber industry drew him, like so many others. Bob's father, Otto, himself the victim of a logging accident, tried to discourage him. "Dad did his darndest to talk Bob out of working in the woods," says Bob's sister Grace Mack, "but Bob was a lot like Dad, and he wouldn't listen."

Otto Hansch was a veteran logger, a riggingman trained during the deadly era of high-ball logging, when speed outweighed safety. He lost a leg, and nearly his life, in the early 1950s. Otto was riding a speeder to work at a Weyerhaeuser setting on Devil's Creek, north of Mount St. Helens. A tree several feet in diameter had fallen across the tracks. Otto and another man grabbed a chain saw and went to work on it; saws were so heavy then that two men—one on each end—had to hold them in place. The crew was already late, and Otto and his partner hurried to finish the cut. The tree had fallen into the cutbank where the track was laid and was severely bowed in the middle. Before the men could finish sawing through it, the tree snapped, popped sideways, and rolled onto Otto's lower body as he fell back onto the track. The damage would have been even worse if the rails had not kept the log from flattening him completely. In the hospital, he received incompetent medical care, and gangrene set in. He had to have one leg amputated. Otto spent the rest of his life on permanent disability.

Bob left Lower Columbia College in 1962 and took a job as a riggingman for Wilson & Sutton; then he hired on at Weyerhaeuser. Near the end of the summer of 1966, he got work setting chokers for Gardner Logging, a gyppo outfit operated by locals Art and Rex Gardner. The Gardners had a camp outside Neah Bay on the Olympic Peninsula. They were running five sides, with several dozen men living on-site. Bob knew Rex's son Garry, who was working as a timber faller, and before long Bob had talked the Gardners into giving him a shot at running saw. Because the coastal timber—primarily hemlock and white fir, three to four feet in diameter—was considerably smaller than old growth elsewhere, the cutters were "single-jacking," working on their own instead of with a partner. It was Bob's first job as a faller; he had no experience and no one to break him in.

Bob bunked with Dick Sadler, a fifty-eight-year-old hooktender who had worked with Otto Hansch on a Weyerhaeuser rigging

Bob Hansch (center) with cousins Larry (left) and Ron Downing —Courtesy Elsie Hansch

crew in the days of steam donkeys. Like Bob's father, Dick Sadler did his best to change Bob's mind about working in the woods, specifically about cutting timber. "I tried every way I could to talk him out of it," Sadler says. "I told him he didn't have enough experience. I suggested he go somewhere else where he could get a partner who could teach him what to do. But Bob was ambitious, and he didn't want to hear it."

No one witnessed Bob's death on October 19, 1966. When he didn't come in for lunch that day, Garry Gardner went to check on him. Bob was dead, his tape hooked onto one end of a log and stretched out for a measurement. Apparently, he had cut a tree that inadvertently bumped a snag on its way down. Weakened, the snag fell as Bob started bucking his log. He never knew what hit him.

After Bob's burial at Tower Cemetery, the extended family met at his parents' home. Bob's aunts—my mother and her other sisters—brought fried chicken, sauerkraut, baked beans, potato salad, pies, and cakes. We younger cousins stood on the wide porch out back, shuffling awkwardly, trying to come to grips with the image of Bob, waxen and still, in the casket at the service at St. Paul's Lutheran Church in Castle Rock. We talked about basketball and days we'd spent tunneling through the hay in the Hansch barn with Bob. When Uncle Otto stepped out onto the porch, conversation stopped. Otto was a rugged man, not given to emotion; he trembled with the effort of holding his grief inside. He shook hands with each of us and looked us in the eyes. "Thanks for coming," he said. That moment still haunts me; it defines the tragedy of a loved one lost prematurely.

We experience so much good fortune: accidents averted by inches; medical miracles that extend lives. Every logger I interviewed described numerous near misses. For them, things fell the right way and they were spared. Why not this time? Why not just a close call for Bob? One that would have shaken him up and given him a story to tell? For these questions, we have no satisfactory answers.

The risk of death has always accompanied logging. One study found that from 1870 to 1910, the on-the-job life expectancy of a Northwest logger was seven years. In 1911, the third Pacific Logging Congress met in Vancouver, British Columbia, to address the timber industry's alarming accident rate. Although the conference produced no solutions, it called for documentation to illustrate the severity of the problem. In 1912, the state of Washington began compiling statistics on deaths and injuries. Statisticians charted safety information from forty-two hazardous occupations, including construction and mining. That year, the timber industry accounted for 43 percent of the accidents and 56 percent of the deaths; in Washington alone, 157 men died in logging and sawmill accidents.

A. M. Prouty's book *More Deadly Than War!* contains a 1924 account from a chokerman named Ellery Walter. The young man's story portrays both the callousness and the inconceivable danger associated with high-ball logging, the senseless full-throttle style that prevailed during the early part of the twentieth century. Walter was working at a camp in northern Washington that was averaging dozens of accidents a week when he recorded the following incident:

> One day when our gang was working under the blistering sun, my partner cut across the main cable line to get a drink of water.

> On his way back, he found himself in the path of the returning
> choker blocks. They were coming back at lightning speed, knock-
> ing down small saplings and making the bark fly off stumps. . . .
> The chokersetter ducked, but not quickly enough. The flying
> choker smashed his head. . . .
>
> Instead of calling the ambulance the foreman, or head
> riggingslinger, dragged his body off to one side and threw his coat
> over it. When one of the fellows objected, he said, "The ambu-
> lance won't do the kid any good now. Get back to work."

Schafer Brothers, a major player in the timber business on
the Olympic Peninsula during the 1920s and 1930s, was one of
dozens of companies known for its flippant attitude about the
deaths of its workers. If, after a man was killed, someone had
the audacity to suggest that the body be taken to town, Schafer's
foreman was likely to treat the request with disdain. "Give it a
little longer," he might say. "Maybe we'll have somebody else to
send with him."

In 1920, the Safety Board of Washington State issued a bulle-
tin declaring that logging in the Northwest was "more deadly
than war"—the phrase A. M. Prouty appropriated as the title for
his book. The board based its judgment on statistics covering a
four-month period from May 1 to August 31, 1920. During that
time, timber-related accidents killed 91 men and injured 4,199
more. By contrast, during the six months of the Spanish-Ameri-
can War—from April 21 to October 21, 1898—290 U.S. soldiers
were killed, 2,565 died from disease, and 1,431 were injured.
Casualties per month for logging: 1,072. Casualties per month
for war: 714.

This disgraceful record mirrored conditions throughout the industry. Deaths continued to increase, topping out at 261 in 1923.
In 1925, more than 100 men died in logging accidents in
Washington's Grays Harbor area. Initially, the U.S. Department
of Labor and Industries said the rate of death and injury was
"unavoidable." During the Depression era, L & I changed tactics
and reported that the men were so "distracted" by the possibility
of losing their jobs during hard times that their lack of concen-
tration put them at risk. L & I statistics reveal that from 1912
through 1931, in-state logging accidents claimed 3,512 lives, an
annual average of 175. In 1931, the work-time lost with each
logging accident was six times that of other industries. It wasn't
until 1932 that logging fatalities in Washington dipped below 100
for the first time. After World War II, the state legislature finally

took a more proactive role by allocating money for safety programs. That and demands for improved working conditions made by a conglomeration of increasingly powerful unions that represented loggers and sawmill workers led to a significant drop in deaths and injuries.

In 1902, a millworker sued the Grays Harbor Commercial Company of Cosmopolis for $30,000 over a work-related injury. Noting that the plaintiff had understood the danger when he took the job, the U.S. District Court of Western Washington found the man was entitled to no damages. The ruling set a clear precedent: companies would not be held accountable for negligence when their employees were injured or killed. Taking risks was what loggers and millworkers were paid for; they could either accept the risk or find a new line of work. In 1911, Wisconsin passed a workers' compensation act that required employers to purchase insurance to cover injuries that employees suffered on the job. Today, all fifty states have workers' compensation statutes, but the dangers loggers face remain high.

The U.S. Department of Labor's Occupational Safety and Health Administration (OSHA) reported in 1999 that out of 305,000 firefighters employed in this country, approximately 100 die on the job each year. According to the National Association of Chiefs of Police, 118 out of 700,000 people working as law enforcement officers died while on duty in 1996. During the 1970s, 815 firefighters lost their lives. In those same ten years, 1,143 U.S. police officers were killed. By contrast, in the three Pacific states and British Columbia during that time span, 1,372 loggers died on the job. This figure is especially disturbing because far fewer people work as loggers in the United States than as firefighters or policemen. Yet until improved technology in the 1990s reduced the need for timber fallers and riggingmen, loggers were dying on the job at a rate six times that of firemen and twelve times that of law enforcement officers.

From 1985 through 1989, logging comprised one-tenth of one percent of total employment in the U.S. However, loggers suffered 2 percent of all workplace injuries, a rate twenty times the norm. In 1992, the Census of Fatal Occupations showed that the risk of death for loggers translated into one fatality for every 500 employees. With 158 logging fatalities nationwide in 1992, the risk of death was eight times higher in logging than in mining and fifty-four times higher than in the manufacturing sector.

A 1989 OSHA report revealed that 71 percent of logging deaths occur in the cutting area; 43 percent of those happen when a logger is falling a tree. Forty-two percent of the fatalities noted in the OSHA document resulted from "unsafe work practices, misjudgments, and lack of training or supervision." The report ended with the following statement: "OSHA believes that current logging methods and the inherent dangers posed by work in the woods, such as those caused by inclement weather, uneven terrain, and isolation from health care facilities, present significant hazards to employees engaged in logging operations across the country, regardless of the type of logging being conducted." Hardly a mind-bending conclusion.

OSHA confirmed that loggers have a "substantially higher" risk of injury and death than other workers, including those in "high-hazard industries" such as demolition and explosives making. The *West Virginia Gazette* reported in 1998 that the rate of fatalities in that state is fourteen times higher for loggers than for coal miners. Each year, seven West Virginia loggers of every thousand are killed on the job. In addition, national studies have found that logging injuries are far more serious and result in longer hospital stays and more lost work time than injuries sustained in other occupations. The U.S. Department of Agriculture determined that approximately one in five loggers suffers a "compensable" injury each year. In 1984, a Work Injury Report released by the Bureau of Labor Statistics revealed that 30 percent of injured loggers missed more than ten days of work. The average time lost for a logging injury was twenty-three days.

Technological advances during the past two decades have increased the percentage of loggers whose work involves operating equipment. The risks to operators have decreased enough that insurance companies will cover them at rates comparable to those they extend to warehouse workers. For loggers working on the ground, however, the danger remains extremely high.

So how does a logger make it through the day? How does he deal with the knowledge that despite safety improvements he has a one-in-three chance of being killed or badly injured during his career? Earl Roberge provides an answer in his book, *Timber Country Revisited*.

> A streak of fatalism seems to run throughout the craft. The logger knows he is engaged in a dangerous occupation and that the

chances that he will be killed or seriously injured in his precarious calling are very high. . . . Every logger has seen accidents and is acutely aware that he may be the next victim, but human nature seems to have provided an escape route to what would otherwise be a very depressing situation. Every logger believes that accidents will happen to the other guy, never to himself.

Like a combat soldier in a unit with a high mortality rate, a logger must simply refuse to believe that a bullet has his name on it. Negative thoughts cause hesitation and doubt, a surefire recipe for disaster. I asked a dozen loggers how they handle their awareness of the risks, the statistics that taunt them with crippling probabilities, the fears of their wives and children, the eyewitness accounts of coworkers crushed and mutilated. Their responses echoed one another: *You just don't let yourself think about it.* Everything—including survival—depends on self-confidence and good judgment; you simply can't let paranoia gain a foothold.

At least that's what they tell you. Don't believe it when loggers assure you they are holding the bad thoughts at bay. Press them hard enough and the truth emerges. For loggers, going to work is like playing slots in Las Vegas: the numbers are not in their favor. And beneath the bravado, they know it as well as a favorite story.

You'd think that in a place like Castle Rock, where the means of making a living offered the inhabitants is "more dangerous than war," a list of timber deaths would be published somewhere—that the sacrifices of loggers who put themselves at risk to support their families would be formally recognized. But there is no record that the public can find easily. The Department of Labor and Industries, the union that represents the men, the Department of Health Statistics—all claim to have no complete listing of the dead, no updated files on computer, or no way of releasing the information in light of "privacy concerns." And perhaps a part of us wants to keep it that way. We speak so casually of hospital stays and hearing loss, of broken bones and permanent disability. It is a subject we permit ourselves to talk about, but, as the loggers I interviewed made clear, not to think about deeply.

I extracted the following compilation of logging deaths from newspaper archives and the memories of several local loggers. It takes into account only those fatal accidents that occurred in southwest Washington or involved men from this area. The list is limited to the years after World War II, and it is far from complete. It also neglects to catalog the hundreds of debilitating injuries that range from excruciating arthritis to paralysis. Still, it is the best accounting I have been able to assemble. For now, it must suffice.

These are our dead. This is their memorial.

—**E. E. Moore** of Castle Rock, killed in November 1945 near Toutle when struck by a skyline cable.

—**James McLean** of Kelso, killed in a logging accident near Tillamook, Oregon, in November 1945, his first day on the job.

—**James Allen** of Ryderwood, killed in January 1946 when a log rolled over him.

—**Jacob Sutinen** of Longview, killed in a logging accident near Astoria, Oregon, in April 1946.

—**Gayl Haney** of Castle Rock, killed in January 1950 when a boom on a loading machine broke loose and struck him on the head.

—**Thomas Kelly** of Kalama, killed in December 1950 near the Kalama River when a tree he was falling barberchaired and struck him.

—**Oliver Peabody** of Kelso, killed near Kalama in May 1951 when hit by a tree flung sideways by moving rigging.

—**Earl Edwards** of Kelso, killed near Abernathy Creek in July 1951 when hit by a snag.

—**Hughie Hamilton** of Kalama, killed in October 1953 when a log rolled over him while he was working on the rigging near Kalama.

—**Jim Baker** of Kid Valley, killed near White Creek in June 1955 when a bulldozer he was operating plunged over a cliff.

—**George McClure** of Cathlamet, killed in January 1958 near the Elochoman River when a broken mainline hit him while he was fueling a cat on the landing.

—**Clayton Robinson** of Tenino, killed near Camp Coweeman in April 1959.

—**Fred Warnock** of Toledo, killed east of Camp Coweeman in June 1959 when hit by the counterbalance of a loading machine.

—**John Archer** of Castle Rock, killed near Green River in January 1961 when the top broke out of a tree he was falling and struck him on the head and upper torso.

—**Arling Sorensen** of Woodland, killed near Toledo in March 1961 when a log rolled off his truck and struck him as he was adjusting his binder chains.

—**Oscar Chism** of Castle Rock, killed near Twelve-Mile Camp in August 1963 when a log rolled over him.

—**Wendell Hynning** of Silverlake, killed near Twelve-Mile Camp in September 1964 when a log rolled down a hillside, pinning him against another that he was bucking.

—**Eugene White** of Chehalis, killed near Camp Baker in September 1964 when several logs tumbled down a hillside, crushing him as he was setting a choker.

—**James Whitcraft** of Kalama, killed east of Kalama in November 1964 when a log he was bucking gave way, causing another hung up above it to roll over him.

—**Edward Wickstrom** of Kelso, killed in June 1965 when hit by a falling snag while setting chokers.

—**Robert Chamberlain** of Grays River, killed near Cathlamet in July 1965.

—**Minor Tubbs** of Woodland, killed while blasting stumps on the Lewis River in September 1965.

—**Frank Karnis** of Woodland, killed while blasting stumps on the Lewis River in September 1965.

—**Dean Browning** of Castle Rock, killed in a log truck accident south of Mount St. Helens in September 1965.

—**Dearl Amos** of Longview, killed when crushed by a bulldozer near Kalama in September 1965.

—**Alfred Hiatt** of Longview, killed at the Wasser & Winters log dump in November 1966 when a log rolled off his truck as he was releasing his binder chains.

—**Johnny Parnell** of Castle Rock, killed in February 1967 near Camp Kalama when a log above the one he was bucking on a hillside came loose and crushed him.

—**Sonny Hicks** of Castle Rock, killed near Salmon Creek in March 1967 when a log pulled in by the yarder crashed through the cab of his shovel.

—**James Hubbard** of Portland, killed east of Kalama in June 1967 when a truck he was riding in lost its brakes and overturned.

—**Ray Bohnas** of Longview, killed near Twelve-Mile Camp in September 1967 when the machine he was driving went over a cliff.

—**Harry Iiams** of Montesano, killed at the Gram Lumber log dump in Kalama in April 1969 when logs rolled off his truck and struck him as he was releasing his binder chains.

—**Herschel Bowers** of Winlock, killed near Camp Ten in July 1969 when a limb fell out of a tree he'd cut and pierced his neck.

—**Tom Galt** of Kelso, killed in March 1970 when a crane hit a power line while he was holding a choker connected to the machine.

—**Bob Hicks** of Kelso, killed in July 1974 when a fire truck he was driving overturned near Twelve-Mile Camp.

—**Jim Mason** of Silverlake, killed in January 1975 east of Twelve-Mile Camp when a tree he and his partner were falling came back on him.

—**Richard Caywood** of Toledo, killed near Twelve-Mile Camp in February 1975 when a tree he and his partner had felled toppled down a steep hillside and crushed him.

—**George Rockett** of Castle Rock, killed near Green River in September 1975 when a tree cut by his partner was pulled sideways by the wind and struck him.

—**Ben Snow** of Toledo, killed near Twelve-Mile Camp in June 1976 when a bulldozer backed over him.

—**George Hack** of Winlock, killed near Camp Baker in June 1977 when a rootwad rolled on him as he was bucking a windfall.

—**Don Morse** of Longview, killed near Rose Valley in August 1978 when a top that broke out of a tree he was falling hit him.

—**John Hoepfl** of Longview, killed near Rose Valley in December 1978 when the stump anchoring the haulback uprooted and the falling line hit him.

—**Dee Bond** of Castle Rock, killed while falling timber near Vader in May 1979.

—**Wallace Bowers** of Winlock, killed in the May 1980 eruption of Mount St. Helens while cutting timber near Shultz Creek.

—**Tom Gadwa** of Montesano, killed in the May 1980 eruption of Mount St. Helens while cutting timber near Shultz Creek.

—**Evlanty Sharipoff** of Mount Angel, Oregon, killed in the May 1980 eruption of Mount St. Helens while cutting timber northeast of Camp Baker.

—**Leonard Ledgett** of Kalama, killed in October 1980 when a limb broke out of a tree he was falling and struck him on the head.

—**Ralph Helland** of Vader, killed while setting chokers near Ryderwood in October 1980 when a log being yarded swung sideways and struck him.

—**John Lynch** of Woodland, killed in November 1980 when a yarder he was moving went over an embankment after the road gave way.

—**Dana Keesee** of Woodland, killed in a logging accident in October 1982.

—**Scott Nelson** of Longview, killed near Camp Kalama in September 1983 when a log rolled over him while he was setting chokers.

—**Gary Wallace** of Toledo, killed in July 1984 east of Twelve-Mile Camp when a bulldozer he was riding on overturned and crushed him.

—**Walter Northrup** of Woodland, killed in May 1985 when a log rolled off his truck while he was removing his binders and struck him in the chest.

—**David Clark** of Woodland, killed in September 1985 near the Muddy River when struck by a falling tree.

—**Russ McCall** of Castle Rock, killed when crushed by a rolling log while setting chokers near Clatskanie, Oregon, in August 1988.

—**Owen Woodard** of Castle Rock, killed when hit by a snag while falling timber near Nineteen-Mile Camp in October 1990.

—**Ronald Sixkiller** of Woodland, killed near Longview in March 1996 when a tree he had cut rolled over him.

—**Jim Traub** of Longview, killed in June 1997 near the Kalama River while on his way to work when his pickup went over a 300-foot embankment.

—**Tony Cherrington** of Castle Rock, killed near Adna in April 1998 when a tree his partner was falling struck another, sending a top down on him.

—**Daniel Williams** of Longview, killed near Olympia in July 1999 when, after loosening his binder chains, two logs rolled off his truck and struck him in the head.

And **Robert L. Hansch,** killed October 19, 1966, while cutting timber near Neah Bay.

In July 1998, the national media told the story of security guards John Gibson and Jacob Chesnut, killed by a gunman who went on a shooting spree in the Capitol Building in Washington, D.C. Like Gibson and Chesnut, loggers know the risks that accompany their job. They take these risks for identical reasons: to feed their families, to make their house payments, to put their children through college, to save enough for a much needed vacation. But out this way there are no special ceremonies to honor the dead, no television coverage, no appearances by the President at graveside services, no promises from congressmen to provide support for widows and their children, no mournful sound of taps wafting across a burial field.

The men whose names I listed have no granite wall. A few dozen words in a single issue of the local paper tell their stories. They were the best we had to give, but the flag at city hall has never once flown at half-staff for them.

Will the Last One Out
Please Turn Off the Lights?

I N HIS 1955 BOOK *The Last Wilderness*, Murray Morgan lauded changes in a logging industry previously characterized by instability and impermanence. "At the turn of the century most logging camps were said to have three crews—one coming in, one on the job, and one going out. Now," Morgan boasted, "it's not unusual for a man to work a lifetime with one company."

When you have lived your life in a single place, history can be a powerful force. People wear blinders, latching onto any evidence that good things will last. More than a few northwesterners, buoyed by the words of Murray Morgan and others, firmly believed that logging would never suffer a permanent slowdown. Yes, the old growth would eventually be logged out, but somehow, setting after setting would be born, section after section of good straight timber. This was the promise of reforestation. It was also an anthem of denial, a head-in-the-sand response to accusations of overcutting and the onset of change. Years after the writing on the wall became clear, wishful thinking dominated the Northwest. We have finally entered a new era, one that tolerates no wishing and little hoping. Enduring, adjusting, and coping are today's most highly-prized commodities.

County governments in Washington, Oregon, Idaho, and northern California have long depended on federal timber dollars. Laws prohibit these counties from collecting property taxes on publicly owned forestland within their boundaries, but a ninety-two-year-old government program has always granted them 25 percent of the revenue that logging on those lands generated.

During the past two decades, state and federal agencies have reduced their timber sales drastically. As a result, rural counties have not only lost thousands of jobs but also millions of dollars in logging revenue that previously funded schools and highway projects. In 1987 and 1988, Oregon's Lake County received $5.3 million a year in federal timber revenue; the county collected only $300,000 in 1998.

In April 2000, the U.S. Congress finally took action. A bill sponsored by Oregon Democrat Ron Wyden and Idaho Republican Larry Craig provides $576 million per annum to rural Western communities through 2006. Although the collection ratio will drop from 25 to 15 or 20 percent of timber revenues, payments will be based on revenues from the 1980s, when logging activity reached its peak. Legislators intend for the plan to sustain timber communities through a weaning period during which they will be expected to encourage environment-friendly development.

The Craig-Wyden bill also aims to placate Northwest residents who have pressured Congress to increase harvest rates in federal forests. Already the hostility of the 1980s and 1990s has edged toward acceptance. Rural communities no longer hold town meetings opposing regulations that limit timber sales and eliminate jobs. Logging now accounts for only 3 percent of employment in the Pacific Northwest; the ranks are thinning. The Craig-Wyden legislation will reduce the pain for taxpayers not involved in logging, making it even more difficult for standard bearers to muster troops. As the years slip by, impotence replaces anger; loggers and their families can only wait to see how things play out.

Amid the weighty economic issues, one ecological fact stands out: the gift of old-growth forest has been wiped away. Yet from an environmental perspective, the situation remains dynamic. Local gyppo Whoopy Gould says that Weyerhaeuser foresters are hinting at a move to a thirty-five year rotation schedule, down from the current forty-five to fifty years. "These days, when a tree reaches thirty-five years, it can meet all the demands of the current market," Gould explains. It is not cost-effective for timber companies to allow replants to grow for more than fifty years, let alone five hundred. Every season they can lop off the cutting rotation increases profit. Although he avoided confirming the thirty-five-year figure, Weyerhaeuser's John Keatley would not deny that the company plans to reduce the harvest rotation. "It's definitely going to get shorter. Mill technology is able to do more with small timber. Add to that the fact that trees are growing faster than ever. A five- or ten-year adjustment is certainly within the realm of possibility for rotation reduction."

Recent changes in market demands and prices have encouraged timber companies to reduce their harvest schedules. When old growth was no longer readily available during the 1980s, a number of sawmills invested in equipment designed to handle diminutive logs; those that didn't likely went out of business. Today's mills can produce high-quality lumber from logs as small as six inches in diameter. They "stew" the logs in hot water and run them through lathes that peel off wood in thin layers called veneer. Then they glue the layers together to fabricate beams and plywood with fewer defects than products milled from larger trees. Production of laminated veneer has doubled since 1995, and many experts believe that "engineered" lumber will keep increasing its share of the market. The tight, clear grain of old-growth lumber still sets the standard for quality. Second- and third-growth trees often have knots and other defects, and mills are unwilling to pay substantially more for large number-two-grade logs when they can more easily handle smaller number threes and generate similarly high-quality finished products.

Home Depot, the nation's largest lumber retailer, announced that as early as 2001 it will stop selling products made from old-growth trees. While this looks like a positive step, it only encourages timber owners to shorten harvest rotations. They have no economic incentives to grow older forests. "We have to be able to compete with the rest of the world," says George Fenn, a tree farmer who lives near Elkton, Oregon. "Chile, Argentina, New Zealand, they're all going to the short rotations."

Many people outside the timber industry hold a dim view of the trend and its potential effects. The U.S. Forest Service and various universities have studied harvest rotations and have concluded that longer rotation schedules protect watersheds, fish, and wildlife. Conservationists fear that shorter rotations will heavily damage the landscape. Logging operations will disturb the soil more often; more frequent harvests will allow plant life fewer years to regenerate, resulting in increased run-off, flooding, sedimentation, and stream damage. Moreover, wildlife that thrives in mature forests will have even more difficulty surviving.

The largest log Weyerhaeuser Company harvested was cut northwest of Mount St. Helens in 1944. It measured 124 inches in diameter at the stump and scaled out at 71,684 board feet. Industry experts predict that harvested logs will soon average ten to twelve inches in diameter on the butt end. —Courtesy Longview Public Library

Moving in the opposite direction from timber companies, the Washington Department of Natural Resources has announced that it plans to lengthen its harvest schedule from sixty years to more than one hundred, a direct result of what DNR forester Richard Grabianowski calls "obvious environmental concerns." In the 1970s, when Bert Cole ran the DNR, environmental concerns never reached the front burner. Cole decided to clear-cut the pristine ancient forest of the Olympic Peninsula as rapidly as possible. Though it comprised only 15 percent of the DNR's holdings, the peninsula supplied 40 percent of the agency's annual harvest. Cole seemed unfazed by the knowledge that his rampage would cause timber production and employment for loggers who relied on state contracts to drop 50 percent before the year 2000. By the time Cole's tenure ended in 1980, the DNR had earned a reputation as the "Department of Nothing Remaining."

In 1998, current state lands commissioner Jennifer Belcher described the department's mission as having little to do with maximizing timber production; instead, the DNR will focus on maintaining and safeguarding water conditions, air quality, and fish and wildlife. In 1996, the average annual harvest rate on state land west of the Cascades fell to only 1.03 percent. The DNR does not expect it to rise significantly. "I believe we have to either secure our national heritage for future generations or risk losing it forever," Belcher says. Terry Ruff, Forest Practice Coordinator for the DNR, says Belcher's philosophy permeates every facet of agency policy, and the transition from timber producer to habitat protector has not been an easy one. "It's difficult to balance things," Ruff says. "On one hand, we're supposed to produce income for counties and school districts, while at the same time being responsible for environmental goals."

The U.S. Forest Service is also edging away from viewing timber production as its central charge. Claire Lovendal, supervisor of the Gifford Pinchot National Forest, condemns the agency's massive overcutting during the 1980s. "We blew it. We knew at the time that was not the way to manage an ecosystem. But . . . it was the thing to do politically." Environmentalists, scientists, citizen advocacy groups, and the media have chastised the Forest Service for its cozy relationship with the timber industry and forced the agency, after years of denial, to confess that its timber sales program actually *loses* millions of dollars annually. In 1999, the agency drafted new guidelines making the restoration and sustainability of watersheds and forests its primary goal. U.S. Forest Service chief Mike Dombeck espoused the new position, saying, "The health of our land must be our first priority. Failing that, nothing else really matters."

In spite of such pronouncements from agency heads, the political warfare has not subsided. In particular, debate still rages over the perceived success or failure of the Clinton administration's 1994 Northwest Forest Plan. Agriculture Secretary Dan Glickman, who oversees the U.S. Forest Service, is one of a handful of optimists who believe the N.F.P. is working well. "You may remember eight or nine years ago, people were at proverbial loggerheads. There was almost a revolution between timber interests and environmental interests. That is no longer the case." Glickman believes Forest Service scientists have made good progress toward protecting threatened and endangered plants and animals, one of the N.F.P.'s goals. Fred Dorn, contracting officer for the Gifford Pinchot National Forest, also praises the plan. "It got to the point [where] we were trying to micromanage every area for every species. The N.F.P. made us change the way we looked at forest management. It forced us to examine things in a more holistic way."

But logging companies feel they were sold out. They complain that the Clinton administration failed to live up to its pledge to make 1.1 billion board feet of timber available for bid each year. In 1995, the year after the plan took effect, the Forest Service released only 600 million board feet nationwide. In 1998, the total dropped to 287 million board feet. During the late 1980s, before the implementation of restrictions to protect spotted owl habitat, federal timber accounted for nearly 60 percent of the logs cut in Oregon; loggers harvested approximately 5 billion board feet a year on national forest and Bureau of Land Management tracts in that state alone. A decade later, only about 13 percent of Oregon's harvest came from federal land. In 1988, the Seneca Sawmill Company of Eugene, Oregon, bought 100 percent of its timber from public lands; the company now gets less than 10 percent of its supply from state and federal sources. Between 1989 and 1999, 330 Oregon sawmills closed, fully 45 percent of the total. In a September 1999 *Seattle Post-Intelligencer* article, Northwest Forestry Association president Jim Geisinger said, "The Clinton administration has placed so many restrictions on the Forest Service that it's impossible for them to deliver even the small amount of timber that is called for in the Northwest Forest Plan."

Norman Johnson, a forestry professor at Oregon State University who helped draft the 1994 plan, says the industry mistook the N.F.P.'s intent. "Timber harvesting is a secondary objective of the plan," Johnson explains. He says the plan never guaranteed the 1.1 billion board feet figure. Rules governing species and landscape protection make the harvest goal virtually unattainable. "If the analysis shows that you can't provide the protection that you thought [you could], you don't get rid of the protection. You lower the harvest level."

Environmentalists point out that timber companies have no right to complain about broken promises. After industry executives saw the potential impact of the Northwest Forest Plan, they lobbied legislators sympathetic to their concerns to slip a salvage logging rider through Congress in mid-1995 by attaching it to a spending bill. The legislation allowed the removal of fire-scarred or insect-damaged trees. Proponents touted it as a necessary step in preventing catastrophic forest fires. The rider also supplied product to small mills whose access to public logs the N.F.P. had curtailed. But the provision went far beyond salvage. It released earlier timber sales—even those including old growth in sensitive habitat—that the government had cancelled due to environmental concerns. In an unprecedented step, the measure also overrode all existing environmental laws that would have impeded those harvests. The *Seattle Post-Intelligencer* denounced the rider and those who supported it. "Besides ridding the woods of environmentally sensitive old growth, all that has been accomplished by the industry and its congressional handmaidens with this bald-faced act of bad faith is to reopen the bitter battles for the Northwest woods."

The salvage logging rider expired at the end of 1996, but environmentalists' concerns persisted. They, too, felt the government was not keeping to the word of the N.F.P. In 1998, thirteen conservation groups filed a lawsuit against the federal government charging that 20 percent of the timber harvested on federal land actually comes from Late Successional Reserves, which the N.F.P. set aside to guarantee habitat and species protection. Doug Heiken of the Oregon Natural Resources Council believes the suit was necessary. "If the government would stop breaking their promises and just follow the requirements of the Northwest Forest Plan," Heiken says, "fewer of our ancient forests would be clear-cut, more forest creatures would be safe, more wild salmon would survive and spawn, and our drinking water would be cleaner."

An August 1999 ruling by U.S. District Court Judge William Dwyer upheld the new paradigm. Dwyer found that the U.S. Forest Service and the Bureau of Land Management had violated the Northwest Forest Plan by failing to adequately survey logging's potential impact on seventy-eight species of plants and animals; he ordered the temporary shutdown of logging on thirty-four timber sales in western Washington. The decision eventually postponed more than one hundred sales in Washington, Oregon, and California, and delayed the harvest of 300 million board feet of timber. Environmentalists, timber industry representatives, and government officials have since worked out a deal that will provide some species protection while allowing the sales that Judge Dwyer deferred to go forward. Environmentalists agreed to drop survey demands for nine species; federal officials agreed to extend earlier survey efforts in more than one hundred areas slated for logging.

Dwyer's ruling appalled timber industry supporters. Idaho Senator Larry Craig called it ludicrous. "These sales [are] on hold while the Forest Service tries to figure out how to search for slugs, slime, and salamanders." The Northwest Forestry Associ-ation's Jim Geisinger blames Dwyer's decision for the probable closure of several mills in Oregon that have no lumber supply for 2000. The district court ruling adds to the mounting pressure on the Forest Service to manage existing habitat more cautiously and more judiciously. For independent logging contractors, this means having even fewer state and federal timber sales to bid on. The gyppos' increasing reliance on contracts with private landowners such as Hampton, Longview Fibre, ITT-Rayonier, Simpson, and Weyerhaeuser has taken a good measure of the independence out of being independent operators.

The timber industry as a whole has transformed in a big way during the last two decades, prompted not only by environmental restrictions and the eradication of the old growth, but also by technology and international economic trends. Today's industry focuses on increased productivity and decreased operating expenses. Mack Hogans, senior vice-president at Weyerhaeuser's corporate office in Federal Way, Washington, says the company has eliminated 10,000 jobs in the last decade, 1,400 of them in Washington. In the Longview area, the company has reduced its work force by 50 percent since 1980 through layoffs at the mills and in the woods. An article in the August 3, 1998, edition of the *Longview Daily News* announced that Weyco's new technology "will continue to trim timber jobs." Virtually every other major player in the industry is charging down the same path.

When the Washington State Employment Security division released its predictions of the top fifteen rapidly declining jobs for 2000 through 2010, fallers and buckers came in at number eight, shovel and yarder operators at number fourteen. Chris Johnson, labor economist for Employment Security, says that while he still sees the wood products industry as a driving force in the region, he does not see growth in its future; instead, he predicts "a gradual decline." Weyerhaeuser officials anticipate an upturn in harvests during the coming decade as a result of high-yield forestry practices that Charles Bingham spearheaded in the 1960s and 1970s. However, with technology advancing at a dazzling pace, increased harvests will not likely call for increased employment.

While Weyerhaeuser Company has significantly contributed to national and global economics, no single area has felt its influence more strongly than southwest Washington and its timber towns. Nearly every local logger has either worked directly or indirectly for Weyerhauser—as a member of Weyco's union force or as a hire of a contractor doing business with the company. For that reason, the company's fortunes here cannot be separated from the fortunes of the residents. Since 1929, Weyerhaeuser has invested $2.5 billion in Cowlitz County; it has paid $1 billion in taxes and contributed $2.6 million through its charitable foundations. Clearly, however, Weyerhaeuser has shifted its focus dramatically since it came to the Northwest in 1903 to log salvage at Yacolt. Through the end of World War II, the southwest Washington operation remained its hub, responsible for the bulk of the company's production and profit. But in the early 1950s, the company bought large tracts of timber in the southern United States. It currently owns 5.4 million acres of forestland, including 3.4 million acres in southern states and 2 million acres in Washington and Oregon. During the last fifty years, the importance of the company's local operation has continued to decrease.

When the Columbus Day Storm salvage operation coincided with the expansion of foreign markets in 1962, Weyerhaeuser unfurled its sails and rode the wind. By 1997, Asian markets accounted for almost 15 percent of the company's sales. Weyco officials predict that global demand for forest products will outdistance supply for at least another decade. Corporate hopes center on Latin America and Asia, where increasing literacy rates may soon increase the demand for pulp products. The average American uses more than seven hundred pounds of paper per year, while the average Chinese uses only fifty pounds; fore-casters expect modernization in China and elsewhere to foster demand for many products, including paper and lumber. Consequently, the company has announced plans to "continue to acquire forestlands in strategic locations." In 1997, besides maintaining long-term leasing rights on 22.9 million acres of forest-land in the Canadian provinces of Alberta, Saskatchewan, and British Columbia, Weyerhaeuser bought nearly 200,000 acres of timber in New Zealand. "We've positioned ourselves to be the forest products purveyor for the Pacific Rim," says George Weyer-haeuser Jr., great-grandson of company founder Frederic Weyerhaeuser and the company's senior vice-president of technology. Foreign competitors are stepping up their timber acquisitions, and Weyerhaeuser must take bold steps to maintain its hold on the market. European countries, exporters of virtually no wood products as recently as 1995, made significant gains by offering dried spruce wood at a much lower price than the Northwest's Douglas fir, which has traditionally been Japan's construction material of choice. Led by Austria, Sweden, Norway, and Finland, Europe now claims 15 percent of the Japanese market.

Weyerhauser has discovered the benefits of owning timber-land abroad, especially in places such as New Zealand, Chile, Uruguay, Argentina, and others close to the expanding Asian and Latin American economies. "There are environments where trees grow much better than they do in the Northwest," John Keatley says. Buying into hospitable climates with fewer environmental restrictions and easy access to new markets puts the company in a win-win financial situation. Clearly, a smaller portion of Weyerhaeuser's success will hinge on Northwest timber-lands, giving the company more flexibility in meeting its needs and increased leverage in responding to wage and benefit demands from loggers in southwest Washington.

The timber companies' power in negotiations with loggers, both organized and independent, has grown immeasurably since World War II. The 1986 Northwest contract is now the milestone against which every labor agreement in the area, before and after, is judged. That contract, in addition to laying off thousands of timber workers and reducing wages and benefits by 20 percent overall, dealt the union's strength a crippling blow. "We got complacent," one timber faller told me. "We started thinking it was always going to be the way it had been in the seventies.

[That] made it a lot harder for people to come back to earth and cope with the changes."

Union membership in the United States has dropped 21.1 percent during the past ten years, plunging this country's level of unionization to one of the lowest among industrial nations. Currently, only 13.9 percent of American workers carry a union card. The International Woodworkers of America, the Northwest timber workers' former union, merged in 1994 with the International Association of Machinists and Aerospace Workers. Del Whinery, president of the Shelton-Longview branch of the IAMAW, says the reason for the change was simple: "During the Reagan years, we lost 60,000 members. The merger gave us a little more bargaining power." The fact remains, though, that union timber workers are becoming a nonentity in both name and numbers.

Except in technical fields with a high demand for workers, a decline in earning power has accompanied the overall decline of union membership. And with more companies contracting work out and using temps, fewer and fewer workers receive employer-paid benefits. Michael Moore, author of *Downsize This!* and creator of the documentary *Roger and Me*, which assailed General Motors Corporation's treatment of its employees, views the rosy economic news coming out of Washington, D.C., these days with cynicism. The government neglects to mention that stock market surges and lofty employment numbers have cost working people dearly. "No one, these days, can remember what job security used to feel like," Moore writes, "because everyone lives in total fear that he or she could be next. No one is safe. . . . Health benefits? Paid vacations? You've already kissed those good-bye."

The facts support Moore's opinion. The number of workers with a pension plan slid from 50 percent in 1979 to 42.9 percent in 1989. During that same ten-year span, the percentage of employees covered by a company-sponsored health insurance package dropped from 68.5 to 61.1 percent. The erosion of employer-paid benefits continued throughout the 1990s. Even as high-tech firms lure computer programmers and website managers with the promise of stock options and benefit packages, blue-collar workers in American industries find themselves with inadequate health insurance and pension plans. In 1999, a number of major corporations, citing double-digit increases in the cost of health care plans, announced that they would be unable to continue providing the same level of medical coverage to their workers. Some opted for less expensive benefit packages that provide less inclusive coverage; others passed the price increases on to their employees.

"I see a future for logging here," contractor Whoopy Gould says, "though there won't be nearly as many people in the work force. And in another three to five years, I don't think you'll see any company logging." Tom Cooley and other Weyco and Simpson employees cringe at the possibility that the logging companies will do to loggers what Ronald Reagan did to air traffic controllers: liquidate their crews and rely exclusively on independent contractors as a cost-cutting device, leaving loggers with no job security and fewer benefits.

Union president Del Whinery predicts a continued mix of union and contract logging, but he sees storm clouds on the horizon. Simpson Timber Company, which has operated on the Olympic Peninsula for more than a century, is another of the last timber companies to employ union loggers. Simpson has already taken a step that Whinery believes Weyerhaeuser will duplicate: it has eliminated its cutting and hauling operations and relies exclusively on contractors to handle those tasks. Union loggers do only the yarding. Whinery predicts other changes will occur as well. "I think Weyerhaeuser and Simpson will keep doing shovel logging with their own crews because it's very profitable, but I wouldn't be surprised to see all of the high-lead stuff go to contractors." The end result would be the elimination of the companies' riggingmen, chasers, and yarder operators.

When the union president is more inclined to resignation than resistance, there is little reason for optimism.

Although he is a critic of Wobbly proportions, former company logger Jim Carter refuses to believe that Weyerhaeuser will completely phase out its union work force. "All the way through 1998 they were buying new yarders and shovels. They wouldn't be buying it unless they were planning to use it," Carter says. "Besides that, if they went all gyppo then the gyppos could get together and say, 'We're not logging one more stick until we get more money.' There's no way the company would put themselves in that position."

Whoopy Gould agrees that a unified, empowered gyppo organization could make things difficult for companies like Weyerhaeuser and Simpson, but he doubts gyppos will ever unite. It would require a compromise on the part of men who are very independent. Weyerhaeuser, for its part, seems content to play both sides against the middle. "It's like a game," one company employee said. "They pit the contractors against the union loggers and just keep working the pay rates down as far as possible."

Gould says Weyerhaeuser's contracting out of an increasing share of its operation has not made life easier or more profitable for gyppos. If state and federal timber sales remain slow—which they surely will in the face of court battles over logging on public lands and regulations aimed at protecting watersheds— private landowners such as Weyerhaeuser, Longview Fibre, and Simpson will be the only players at the table. The competition for contracts with these companies is already vicious. Weyerhaeuser extends gyppos a slightly different version of the take-it-or-leave-it contract it forced on its own loggers in 1986: either log it at the rate we offer, or someone else will. The negotiations are like a hardball version of musical chairs, and fewer and fewer independent contractors can find a seat. "We're all competing against each other," Gould says, "and because of that we're logging for what we did twenty years ago. You wouldn't believe how efficient you have to be just to survive." Gould says he can no longer afford to log Weyerhaeuser timber; he can't make a decent profit on the rate the company pays.

One gyppo I talked to guessed at the timber companies' strategy. "I don't think the companies will bring the pay rates up until some of us start going broke. And they'll only do it then so that enough of us survive to keep the operation going."

In the meantime, loggers walk on egg shells. They go through the motions each day, convinced that things can only get worse, yet clinging to the narrow possibility that they will somehow beat the odds and survive. Loggers certainly aren't the first to have experienced this type of crisis. Buffalo hunters, steel workers, and many others have been down the same road. Circumstances change; "progress" happens; it's as simple as that. When you look at their situation from a distance, you can easily say "Well, that's the way it goes. They'll just have to make the best of it." Visit Castle Rock, Washington, and you will find out what your casual dismissal ignores: the pain that accompanies the understanding that for many people, what lies down the road is a dead-end.

Eyes Forward

I N Alden Jones's book *From Jamestown to Coffin Rock*, long-time Weyerhaeuser employee Howard Ketchum explains the mindset that drew him and so many others to careers in the logging industry:

> When you lived around a logging town, that's all the young fellows ever seemed to think about was getting in the woods. I didn't want to go to school. . . . If I had it to do over again, I'd see things different.

Three-quarters of a century later, the wisdom of Ketchum's hindsight is dawning on young men in the Northwest, including those in my family. Eight of my cousins went to work in the woods during the 1960s and 1970s. Those same eight have eleven male children; only one—Sonny LeMonds—works in the timber industry.

Bob and Jim LeMonds, Don Strain, Tom Cooley, and Bob Hansch all made half-hearted attempts to get an advanced education, hoping to break logging's hold on them and their families. Their plans crumbled in the face of ready work, good wages, and an industry that appeared to offer a promising future. For their sons, the bait is far less tempting, and fewer young men are willing to bite. A gyppo operator for twenty-eight years, Whoopy Gould has seen interest in the field decrease and the quality of his employees decline. "I used to get twenty-five or thirty calls if I had a job opening," he says. "Now I'm lucky if I get one. And a lot of the guys today don't produce like guys did fifteen or twenty years ago."

In the past, a father's passionate railings couldn't convince his son to stay out of logging. Today, the sons don't need to be told. Perhaps those times when the old man *didn't* speak carried the weight. Perhaps watching him come home scared into silence by the fear of layoffs, embittered by the belief that employers, politicians, and government bureaucrats were selling him out, and drained and defeated by an inner voice that said he might not be able to take care of his family, finally turned the tide. If a recent high school graduate boasts to a veteran logger of his interest in a long-term career in the woods, he will be showered with ridicule. That fewer young men are setting their sights on a career in the woods is a promising sign: maybe the region is ready to let go of its past.

Although it might seem callous, I'm not especially concerned about the fate of loggers in their twenties and thirties; they are young and resilient enough to adapt to a new paradigm. The men I will continue to worry about long after I finish this manuscript are those in their forties and fifties who have worked as loggers their entire adult lives and may not be able to envision themselves making the transition to anything else. For them, the idea of returning to school—to a world of big words, fast computers, and incomprehensible mathematics—is both intimidating and, in many cases, unrealistic. These men are both intelligent and wise, but they are also unprepared and extremely apprehensive.

In 1998, the federal government offered $3.8 million in educational assistance to 875 unemployed wood products workers in five Washington counties. More than 400 of those people lived just north of us in Lewis County, where Pacific Lumber and Shipping had laid off hundreds of loggers and millworkers in the timber-dependent communities of Morton, Randle, and Packwood. The grants, made possible by the Timber Recovery Act of 1991, paid college tuition and up to half the employees' wages while they received a combination of classroom instruction and on-the-job training. The government offered a similar deal in Cowlitz County after Weyerhaeuser cut 1,100 jobs here during the mid-1980s, and again when the spotted owl listing and the state export ban led to an economic downturn in the early 1990s. In its eight years of existence, the Timber Recovery Act created programs that enrolled 13,831 people in advanced training courses. Of those, 5,200—including Ron Downing—

graduated with a degree from the institution they attended. Individual states administered the grants and established a list of fields for which unemployed timber workers could be trained. In Washington, these included tourism and hospitality, computer programming and support, health care, civil engineering, and aerospace work. In February 2000, the Washington legislature passed a worker retraining bill to fill the gap created when the Timber Recovery Act expired in 1999. The new bill offers laid-off timber workers an additional thirty to seventy-four weeks of unemployment benefits, provided they are retraining in a high-demand field.

Although these programs represent a positive step, even a best-case scenario is less than promising. What if timber workers succeed in making the transition? What if they complete the training and get high-demand jobs as certified nurse's aides, long-haul freight truck drivers, counterworkers and landscapers at hospitality and tourist businesses? Will the wages and benefits they earn support their families? Or will they become members of America's fastest growing class, the working poor, treading water in part-time positions that pay little more than minimum wage, with neither means nor hope at their disposal?

Abandoning a way of life is difficult, but the Northwest has no choice. We can only look forward and move ahead. My mother's family left Russia when a century-old welcome mat for Germans was yanked from beneath their feet. My father's parents fled the Midwest after drought and the stock market crash of 1929 destroyed a farming culture that had existed for generations. It is painfully obvious that southwest Washington will never again see a forest like the one that stretched up the Toutle and Kalama River drainages toward Mount St. Helens, never again see the same level of employment in the timber industry, never again feel the rosy glow of an economy that offered a middle-class lifestyle without the prerequisites of an advanced education.

Maybe a decade or two from now things will stabilize. Those men in their forties and fifties I worry so much about will be drawing social security and telling stories from their recliners. I hope their sons and grandsons will not only have found less dangerous, more certain work, but will also be better equipped to adjust and move on in the event the world comes crashing down once more.

I have learned this from my conversations with loggers: if you are looking for the past, you should refer to books and photographs. Only a fool would expect it to come back around again.

Glossary

backcut. A cut back through a tree. After the faller cuts the face, he moves to the opposite side of the tree and finishes the job by sawing back through toward the face. When a faller saws a backcut in a tree, he "backs it up."

barberchair. When a tree breaks off before the faller finishes his cut. In addition to damaging the wood, the premature fall may cause the trunk to kick back, injuring the faller. Also known as an alligator.

bell. A sliding, bell-shaped piece of metal that fastens around the choker knob. Once the chokermen loop the choker cables around a log and fit the choker knob into the bell, the logs are ready for yarding.

bight. The zone inside the triangular path of the mainline and haulback cables on a logging site; the area is considered off-limits because of dangers posed when temporarily slack or tangled cables begin to move.

blocks. Pulleylike devices that cables run through.

brush. The woods in general, or a site being logged.

buck. To saw downed timber into marketable logs.

buckle guys. A set of guylines hung one-third of the way down from the top of a spar tree; their purpose was to prevent the spar from buckling under the pressure exerted by the yarder.

bull-buck. The supervisor of a cutting crew.

bunks. The supports on a log truck and trailer that the logs rest against. Connected to the truck's frame above each axle, the bunks include the stakes that hold the logs in at the sides.

busheling. A method of calculating a timber faller or bucker's pay according to the amount of board feet he has produced.

butt rigging. The heavy metal knobs and rings that connect the chokers to the mainline cable.

calks. High-topped, spike-soled boots.

camp push. The superintendent of a logging camp.

cat. A bulldozer.

catskinner. A bulldozer operator.

chaps. Leg protectors worn by cutters to prevent injury.

chaser. A logger who works on the landing; the chaser unhooks the chokers from logs as they come in from the brush, then cuts off any limbs the fallers might have missed.

chokerjaggers. Strands or "threads" of steel that have unraveled from a choker or cable; they can penetrate gloves, clothing, and skin.

chokers. Cables that drag logs from the brush to the landing. Attached to the mainline by the butt rigging, the chokers are run out to the brush, where the chokermen secure them around the logs, then pulled back to the landing, where the chaser unhooks them.

cigar raft. The huge, ocean-going, cigar-shaped bundles of logs pioneered by Simon Benson to move product from the Northwest to mills in California. The rafts, pulled by tugs, could measure 1,000 feet in length and 55 feet in width; piled high and partially submerged, a single raft could contain as much as six million board feet of timber.

cold deck. A pile of logs, either on or off the landing.

crummy. A bus used to transport loggers from town to the woods.

cunit. One hundred cubic feet of wood. The cunit has replaced the board foot as the standard unit of measurement for timber.

cutter. A timber faller.

cutting the corner off. When a faller's backcut in a tree reaches the face sooner on one side than on the other; the holding wood causes the tree to twist on the stump and fall in an unplanned direction, damaging wood and endangering loggers.

deadfall. A fallen snag or a mass of tangled brush, branches, and fallen trees. Also, a trap that uses a falling weight to crush prey.

donkey. Another name for the yarder.

donkey sled. The log foundation on which the donkey sat.

dump. A place where trucks off-load logs for sorting and/or further transportation. Formerly, train cars often dumped logs in a pond or river to await water transport.

eye. A loop spliced into a cable so it can be hooked or shackled.

face. The open-mouth cut made by the faller to set the direction for the tree's descent; also called the undercut.

face up. To cut the face or undercut in a tree.

faller. A timber faller; also known as a cutter.

feller-buncher. A machine on treads with an arm that clips trees at the base (working like a pair of scissors) and lays them down, eliminating the damage to the wood that falling causes. Like roto-saws, feller-bunchers are designed to cut quantities of small timber (up to approximately thirty inches in diameter) on flat ground.

forwarder. A machine with bunks and self-loading capabilities that carries bucked logs from the brush to the landing or road. On flat ground, the forwarder can do the job of the yarder.

gap. The Weyerhaeuser term for the difference between what the company pays to have its union crew do a job and what it would have cost to contract the job out.

grapple. Pincerlike metal tongs that pick up logs.

green timber. Live, standing timber.

ground logging. A logging method prevalent in the Northwest from around 1910 to 1923; a steam yarder on skids pulled logs to the landing, with the mainline and haulback cables running through the brush at ground level.

G.T. The guyless tower, invented in the 1980s to yard small trees on flat ground; it requires no supporting guylines. Smaller than a standard tower, the G.T. can be run by two men instead of a crew of six. The operator sends a grapple on a mainline out into the brush; a hooktender guides him in picking up logs to yard to the landing. Shovel-logging has largely replaced the guyless tower.

guylines. Cables that secure a spar or tower during yarding; the guylines connect the top of the spar to a circle of surrounding stumps.

gyppo. An independent logging contractor; also, his employees, independent truckers, and other nonunion logging workers. The word may be a derivative of gypsy; others believe it originated with the Wobblies, who thought nonunion contractors were out to "gyp" or cheat the union loggers.

harvester. A rubber-tired machine that combines the capabilities of a roto-saw and a processor; a harvester can fall, buck, and bark trees.

haulback. A thick cable that carries the rigging from the landing back to the brush, where the chokermen will snare the next turn.

haywire. Lightweight cable used to pull heavier cable (such as the mainline or haulback cable), particularly when a crew is moving lines around a spar to create a new skid road.

head faller. The veteran man on a two-person cutting crew.

high-ball. To hurry, often without regard for safety, as in high-ball logging.

high-lead logging. A logging method that uses a spar tree or steel tower and elevated blocks and cables to yard logs. Elevating the operation means the front end of a log is carried above the brush, thereby avoiding some of the hangups common in ground logging.

high-lead tower. A mobile, steel spar.

hooking. Planning skid road changes and moving the cables and other equipment around the spar to create a new skid road and log another part of the setting; also referred to as "tending hook."

hooktender. The head man on the rigging crew, responsible for planning and supervising skid road changes; more commonly known as the hooker. On smaller operations, one man may fill both the hooktender and riggingslinger positions.

horse logging. A logging method common in the early twentieth century before the advent of steam machinery; it relied on horses to yard logs.

jillpoked. A jillpoked log has one end buried in the ground and the other sticking up in the air.

kerf. The slit made by a saw in a log.

landing. A cleared site to which logs are yarded from the brush. The logs wait at the landing for trucks (or, formerly, rail cars) to transport them to a dump or yard.

line horse. During the days of single-drum yarders, the horse that dragged the yarding cable from the landing back out to the rigging crew.

loading machine. A machine that lifts logs onto trucks or rail cars. Also known as a shovel.

mainline. A thick cable that runs from a drum on the yarder out to the brush; the rigging on the mainline pulls logs to the landing.

pass line. Light cable used to raise blocks and heavier lines when the crew is rigging a spar tree.

peavey. A pry-bar-like lever with a hook attached. Peaveys are used for rolling logs.

processor. A machine that limbs and bucks tree-length logs, either on the landing or in the brush.

pull haywire. To realign the mainline and haulback cables to a new skid road using lightweight cable called haywire (the haulback and mainline cables are too heavy to pull manually).

pull rigging. To supervise the rigging crew, choosing which logs to choke for each turn and making sure the work goes smoothly; what a riggingslinger does.

ramrod. To direct or take charge of.

red fir. Smaller-dimension Douglas fir.

riggingslinger. The second-in-command to the hooktender on a rigging crew; he tells the crew which logs to choke for each turn.

rig-up crew. A crew consisting of a climber, hooktender, yarder operator, and others who rigged spar trees.

road. The path the logs travel as they are yarded to the landing; also called the skid road.

roto-saw. A machine on treads that falls timber up to approximately thirty inches in diameter using a round saw blade.

running saw. Cutting timber; also referred to as "working on the saw."

scale out. To total or add up to.

second faller. The bucker and apprentice member of a two-man cutting team; also called second cutter.

section. An area of land measuring one square mile.

setting. The area that a single crew is logging. Also called a side.

shackle. A C-shaped metal fastener closed with a steel pin; the shackle is used for hanging blocks and connecting cables.

shingle bolts. Logs bucked to short lengths so they can be split or cut into shingles.

shovel. A machine equipped with a boom that loads logs onto trucks; also called a loading machine.

side. A logging operation manned by a single crew. A company might operate several sides. Also called a setting.

siderod. The foreman on a bigger operation; he is responsible for supervising one or more sides.

single-jacking. The practice of having each faller work alone as part of a larger crew. Single-jacking marks a departure from the old-growth days, when two cutters worked together on each tree.

skid road. The rough path over which the yarder drags turns of logs to the landing.

skidder. A machine that drags or skids logs to the landing. Initially, skidder and yarder were synonymous; now, a skidder is a tractorlike vehicle that yards logs.

skids. The log supports that the old yarding machines rested on.

snag. A standing, dead tree.

sniper. During the ground logging days, the riggingman who beveled the ends of logs with an axe so that the logs would ride more easily over stumps and debris on their way to the landing.

snoose. Chewing tobacco.

sort. The grade or category of a log, as determined by species, dimension, and condition.

spar tree. A large standing tree on the landing that anchored the lines on high-lead settings before the advent of the steel tower. The rig-up crew limbed, topped, and secured the spar to a circle of stumps with guy lines; the crew then hung blocks on the spar tree and ran the lines through them that would drag logs to the landing.

speeder. A cartlike device that transports equipment or passengers by rail.

springboard. A two-by-six board with an iron hook (or, occasionally, half-driven nails) on one end. A timber faller inserted the board into a hole hewn in the side of a tree, then stood on the springboard—using it as a level work platform—while he made his cuts in the tree.

squirrel chunk. A short log hung from a strap on the spar tree; the squirrel chunk counterbalanced the boom on the loading machine.

strap. A short length of cable with eyes spliced onto each end used to hang blocks.

strip. A patch of timber worked through by a faller on any given day.

sucker. A limb that grows upward from the trunk of a tree, forming half of a U.

swing the blocks. To adjust the mainline and haulback blocks on the spar so loggers could yard a different section of the 360 degrees around the tree. The climber typically swung the blocks either once or twice per setting.

tag out. To link two or more choker cables together in order to reach logs off the skid road.

tower. The mobile, steel equivalent of the spar tree used in high-lead logging.

turn. A group of logs yarded simultaneously using several chokers.

undercut. The face that a logger cuts in a tree to direct its fall.

whistle punk. The rigging crew member who communicated with the yarder operator by pulling on a light wire connected to a steam whistle on the donkey. The whistle punk signalled the yarder operator to stop, start, or slacken the rigging. Loggers now use handheld transmitters to accomplish this task.

white finger. A numbness of the fingers and hands caused by the long-term use of chain saws.

widowmaker. A loose limb or top hanging in a tree that wind or the force of another tree falling can dislodge. The impact of a limb that is only an inch or two in diameter can cause serious injury or death.

Wobblies. Members of the Industrial Workers of the World, an organization that worked to unionize loggers and miners before the Great Depression.

woods. Logging territory; "working in the woods" means being involved in the logging industry.

yard. To pull logs from the brush to a landing.

yarder. Also known as a donkey, the yarder sits on the landing and pulls in logs from the brush.

yellow fir. The most massive of the Douglas fir trees.

Selected References

Books

Allen, Alice Benson. *Simon Benson: Northwest Lumber King.* Portland, Ore.: Binford & Mort, 1971.

Andrews, Ralph. *Glory Days of Logging.* Atglen, Penn.: Schiffer Publishing, 1994.

Andrews, Ralph. *This Was Logging.* Atglen, Penn.: Schiffer Publishing, 1982.

Booth, Brian ed. *Wildmen, Wobblies, & Whistle Punks: Stewart Holbrook's Lowbrow Northwest.* Corvallis, Ore.: Oregon State University Press, 1992.

Dietrich, William. *The Final Forest: The Battle for the Last Great Trees of the Pacific Northwest.* New York: Simon and Schuster, 1992.

Goodwin, Ted. *Stories of Western Loggers.* Chehalis, Wash.: Loggers World, 1977.

Heilman, Robert Leo. *Overstory Zero: Real Life in Timber Country.* Seattle: Sasquatch Books, 1995.

Jones, Alden. *From Jamestown to Coffin Rock: A History of Weyerhaeuser Operations in Southwest Washington.* Tacoma, Wash.: Weyerhaeuser Company, 1974.

Moore, Michael. *Downsize This!* New York: HarperPerennial, 1997.

Morgan, Murray. *The Last Wilderness.* Seattle: University of Washington Press, 1955.

Prouty, A. M. *More Deadly Than War! Pacific Coast Logging: 1827–1981.* New York: Garland Publishing, 1985.

Pyle, Robert Michael. *Wintergreen: Rambles in a Ravaged Land.* New York: Charles Scribner's Sons, 1986.

Roberge, Earl. *Timber Country.* Caldwell, Idaho: Caxton Printers, 1977.

Roberge, Earl. *Timber Country Revisted.* Olympia, Wash.: Washington Contract Loggers Association, 1991.

Urrutia, Virginia. *They Came to Six Rivers.* Kelso, Wash.: Cowlitz Historical Society, 1998.

Van Syckle, Edwin. *They Tried to Cut It All.* Seattle: Pacific Search Press, 1980.

Webber, Bert and Margie. *This Is Logging and Sawmilling*. Medford: Ore.: Webb Research Group, 1996.

Newspaper and Journal Articles

"Aid offered to help unemployed timber workers find jobs." *Longview (Wash.) Daily News*, July 2, 1998.

Bernton, Hal. "New demand for small logs changes practices, prices." *Oregonian*, October 24, 1999.

Bernton, Hal. "Settlement will restrict federal timber harvests." *Oregonian*, December 21, 1999.

Brettman, Allan. "Forest supervisor talks about 'love.'" *Longview (Wash.) Daily News*, January 31, 2000.

Brettman, Allan. "Water quality tops trees as priority, Forest Service chief says." *Longview (Wash.) Daily News*, September 16, 1999.

Brown, Leslie. "Skeptics eye forest-industry initiative." *Tacoma News Tribune*, October 12, 1995.

Brown, Leslie. "So now, back to the woods." *Tacoma News Tribune*, January 29, 1996.

Chapman, Jeffrey. "Forest Under Siege." *USA Today*, March 1991.

"Clinton's Northwest Forest Plan under fire." *Environmental News Network*, July 10, 1998.

Conlin, Joseph. "Old Boy, Did You Get Enough Pie? A Social History of Food in Logging Camps." *Journal of Forest History*, October 1979.

Crouse, Mike. " 'Can do' is needed." *Log Trucker*, October 1999, p. 5, 54.

"Forest plan calls for surveys of species, including elusive slugs." *Longview (Wash.) Daily News*, December 13, 1999.

"Forest products industry anxiously greets new millennium." *Longview (Wash.) Daily News*, January 2, 2000.

"Gene-altered trees raise thickets of promise, concern." *Washington Post*, August 7, 2000

Hines, Mark. "Modern machinery making logging safer." *Daily Astorian (Ore.)*, September 26, 1999.

Hogan, Dave. "Oregon's forested counties could gain millions." *Oregonian*, November, 2, 1999.

Hughes, John. "Fight over forest surveys continues." *Longview (Wash.) Daily News*, November 29, 1999.

Iritani, Evelyn. "Wood products industry a symptom of global glut." *Los Angeles Times*, October 26, 1998.

Keene, Roy. "Forest Plan instructive first step." *Seattle Post-Intelligencer*, September 22, 1999.

"Logging lost $88 million." *Longview (Wash.) Daily News*, June 11, 1998.

Lowe, Clyde. "Labor Unions' Trials, Triumphs of Last 100 Years Are Traced." *Longview (Wash.) Daily News*, August 19, 1953.

McClelland, John. "Life of an early logger fraught with risks." *Longview (Wash.) Daily News*, May 4, 1998.

McClelland, John. "Longview's labor movement launched during Depression." *Longview (Wash.) Daily News*, September 8, 1998.

McClelland, John. "Ryderwood was a lifeline for Long-Bell." *Longview (Wash.) Daily News*, April 27, 1998.

McClure, Robert. "Glicman defends Northwest Forest Plan." *Seattle Post-Intelligencer*, September 2, 1999.

"Poll: Washington voters rank environmental issues highly." *Longview (Wash.) Daily News*, November 12, 1999.

"Progress slow but measureable in Northwest Forest Plan." *Vancouver (Wash.) Columbian*, December 19, 1996.

"Report: State's natural heritage in danger." *Longview (Wash.) Daily News*, October 6, 1998.

Rice, Randi. "Backbone of Longview." *Longview (Wash.) Daily News*, January 18, 2000.

Robb, Karen. "Area companies hope future holds increase in demand for lumber." *Longview (Wash.) Daily News*, July 23, 2000.

Spencer, Hal. "Retraining program ends for laid-off timber and fish workers." *Longview (Wash.) Daily News*, June 29, 1999.

Swisher, Larry. "Bill would give needed boost to timber communities." *Longview (Wash.) Daily News*, April 15, 2000.

"Taking stock of the Clinton forest plan." *Longview (Wash.) Daily News*, November 28, 1999.

"Top 15 rapidly declining jobs." *Longview (Wash.) Daily News*, July 8, 1997.

Wallis, Robert E. "Green Commonwealth." *Pacific Northwest Quarterly*, Summer 1996.

"Weyco: New technology will continue to trim timber jobs." *Longview (Wash.) Daily News*, August 3, 1998.

"Wood exporters try to lure back Japan." *Longview (Wash.) Daily News*, July 4, 2000.

Pamphlets and Brochures

Department of Labor and Industries. *Safety Standards for Logging Operations*. Washington, D.C., 1997.

Munson, Mike, ed. *Forest Facts & Figures*. Olympia, Wash.: Washington Forest Protection Association, 1999.

Washington State Department of Natural Resources. *Forest Practices Illustrated*. Olympia, Wash., 1997.

Weyerhaeuser: An industry leader for nearly a century. Tacoma, Wash: Weyerhaeuser Company.

Where the Future Grows: A History of Weyerhaeuser Company. Tacoma, Wash.: Weyerhaeuser Company, 1989.

Online Sources

Bolin, Mike. "Pro Logger Training Program Cuts Down on Injuries."
http://www.ag.uiuc.edu/news/issues/863457472.html

"Census of Fatal Occupational Injuries Summary."
http://www.stats.bls.gov/news.release/cfoi.nr0.htm

Frazier, Todd M., and Robert J. Mullan. "Occupational Injuries and Deaths Among Loggers, United States."
http://www.cdc.gov/epo/mmwr/preview/mmwrhtml/00001717.htm

"OSHA Technical Links-Logging."
http://www.osha-slc.gov/SLTC/logging/index.html

Ward, Ken Jr. "Logging is state's most dangerous job." *The Charleston West Virginia Gazette.*
http://www.wgazette.com/static/series/timber/LOGDANGER.htm

Index

Ambrose, Stephen, xvii–xviii
American Forestry and Paper
    Association, 130–31

Barley Logging Company, 20
Barr, Bob, 26–27
Benson, Simon, 11, 27
Berndt, Amelia, 8, 21
Berndt, Henry, 7–8, 19–23, 39
*Best Companies to Work for in
    America, The*, 109–10
Bingham, Charles, 67–68, 173
B.L.R.S., 117
block, haulback, 46
block, high-lead, 46
bucking, *21, 22;* risks accompany-
    ing, 119, 160–61; skills, 20
buckle guys, 46
Bunyan, Paul, mythology, xviii
Bureau of Labor Statistics, 158
busheling, 61–62
buy-out, Weyerhaeuser: com-
    pany comments regarding,
    123; compensation, 98, 113,
    123, 138; loggers' response to,
    123, 138; wage cuts, 123, 138

Carpenter, Dwight, 50, 93–94
Carter, Jim, 3–4, 141–42, 176
Castle Rock Stihl, 64–65, 81, 108,
    113–14
Caswell, Mert, 36–37, 77, 87
chasing, 134, 147

chokersetting: conditions, 91,
    134; risks accompanying, xv–
    xvii, 155–56, 160–63; skills,
    xv; wages, 42, 91, 134
Citizen Soldiers (Ambrose), xvii–
    xviii
clearcutting, 168, 130–31; defense
    of, 69–70, 128; Measure 64, 128;
    opposition to, 128; public opin-
    ion regarding, 10, 128–29
Clemons Tree Farm, 39, 67–69
climbing, *45;* equipment used in,
    44; problems faced during,
    95–96; rigging a spar tree, 44–
    47; risks accompanying, 47–
    48, 160–63; skills, 43–48;
    wages, 43, 92
Clinton, President Bill. *See*
    Northwest Forest Plan
Cole, Bert, 168–69
Columbus Day Storm, 1962. *See*
    Hurricane Frieda
Competitive Logging Program:
    criticism of, 110, 142–44;
    purpose, 98, 142–43; success
    of, 142–43; wages, effect on,
    98, 123, 142–143; workplace
    atmosphere, effect on, 98–99,
    101, 142–44
Cooley, Sam (author's uncle), 22,
    134
Cooley, Tom (author's cousin),
    39, 133–49, *135, 137,* 176, 179

contractors, independent: costs
  incurred by, 53, 65–66;
  environmental regulations,
  effect of, 54–55, 124–25, 172;
  export bans, effect of, 124–25;
  hiring difficulties for, 179;
  layoffs, 66, 124–25; quality
  control problems with, 63, 66;
  wages and benefits paid by,
  67, 83–84, 113–14; Weyerhaeuser's use of, 27, 62–63,
  122–23, 141–44, 176–77
Craig, Larry, 166, 172
Craig-Wyden Bill, 166
cut-and-run logging, 9, 22–23, 38
cutting. *See* timber falling

deaths and injuries from logging,
  34–35, 70, 125–28; high-ball
  logging, effects of, 155–56;
  loggers' response to, 158–59;
  rationalization of, 156; reduction of, 156–58; statistics, 155–
  58; white finger (hand and
  arm vibration syndrome), 70,
  109, 127
Department of Labor and
  Industries, U.S.: costs of
  insurance coverage, 65–66;
  criticism of, 72; death and
  injury statistics, 156–58; role
  of, 72–73
Department of Natural Resources,
  Washington: changing philosophy of, 169; Cole, Bert,
  168; harvest rotation, 168–69;
  Olympic Peninsula, logging
  of, 168–69
Diamond Timber, 83, 87
Dietrich, William, 69
Dobbins, Harold, *21*
Downing, Fred (author's uncle),
  21, 41–42, 89–90, 102

Downing, Larry (author's cousin),
  39, 42, 49–50, *51*, 89–102, *97*,
  145, *154*
Downing, Ron (author's cousin),
  39, 41–57, *51*, 60, 91–92, 102,
  124, *154*, 180
drag saw, 27, *28*
Dwyer, Judge William, 171–72

Ells, George, xiv–xv
employment, logging: in Cowlitz
  County, 3, 25–27, 30, 39;
  decline of, 2–4 54, 172–73;
  export market, influence of, 2;
  in Lewis County, 180; mill
  closures, 170, 180; predictions
  regarding, 149, 173, 176–77;
  retraining programs, 55, 180–
  81; technology, influence of,
  2–3, 148, 172–73; in Washington State, 2–3, 172–73
environmental damage caused
  by logging, 55, 69
environmental regulations
  governing logging: criticism
  of, 70; effect on independent
  contractors of, 55, 124–25;
  export bans, 54–55; Forest and
  Fish Agreement, 1999, 70,
  129–30; Forest Practices Act,
  1974, 69; industry concerns
  regarding, 130–31; northern
  spotted owl, 3, 54–55, 180;
  public opinion regarding,
  128–30
equipment, logging. *See* rigging;
  machinery
export bans, effects of, 54–55, 180
export market, 2–3, 77–78, 141,
  173–74

feller-buncher, 146
Final Forest, The (Dietrich), 69

Forest and Fish Agreement, 1999:
criticism of, 70; described,
129; support for, 129; Weyerhaeuser comments regarding,
129–30
Forest Service, U.S.: change in
philosophy of, 169; formation
of, 10; legal action involving,
171–72; prediction of timber
shortfalls by, 38; relationship
with timber industry, 169;
responsibilities of, 10–11;
timber program, financial
losses, 169; overcutting by, 78.
See also Northwest Forest Plan
forwarder, 147
4-L (Loyal Legion of Loggers and
Lumbermen), 112
Fotheringill, Dick, 43, 91–92
From Jamestown to Coffin Rock
(Jones), 26, 46, 67, 179

Global Positioning System
(G.P.S.), 147
Gould, Allen, 36, 41
Gould Jr., Allen "Whoopy," 65–
67, 145, 166, 176–77, 179
Grays Harbor, 16, 156
Grays Harbor Commercial
Company, 157
ground logging, *12, 13;* described,
11–13; equipment, 11–14
guyless tower (G.T.), 118
guylines, 45–46
gyppos. *See* contractors, independent

Hall, Keith, 62, 70–71
Hampton Tree Farms, 83, 172
Hansch, Bob (author's cousin),
152–55, *154*, 163, 179
Hansch, Otto (author's uncle),
21 *152*, 152–55
Hare, Earl, 105–7

harvester, 147–48
high-climbing. *See* climbing
high-lead logging, *26;* advantages
of, 26; described, 43; introduction of, 26–27; rig-up process
for, 43–47; steel towers,
transition to, 51, 92
high-yield forestry: criticism of,
69, purpose of, 67, results of,
68, 173
Hinkley, Mike, 96, *97*
hooktending, xvi, 51–52, 118
horse logging, 11, 41–42
Horsley, Greg, 114–15, 124–25, 127
Hurley, Jack, 52–53, 96
Hurricane Frieda, 42, 78–79, 173

Industrial Workers of the World
(Wobblies): activities of, 11,
goals of, 10, influence of, 21,
111–12, response to, 11, 112;
strikes led by, 111–12; Wesley,
Everest, lynching of, 112
International Paper (I.P.), 53–54
International Association of
Machinists and Aerospace
Workers (IAMAW): contract of
1986, 110, 122–24, 138, 174,
criticism of, 12, loss of mem-
bers by, 175
Paul Bunyan mythology,
response to, xviii
International Woodworkers of
America. *See* International
Association of Machinists and
Aerospace Workers
ITT-Rayonier, 54, 172

Jones, Alden, 26, 46, 67, 179

Keatley, John, 128, 143–44, 148,
166–67, 174
Ketchikan Pulp, 90
Kinzua Logging Company, 30–32

labor relations. *See* unionization and labor relations

Last Wilderness, The (Morgan), 165

Late Successional Reserves, 3, 171. *See also* Northwest Forest Plan

LeMonds, Bill (author's cousin), 39, 117–32, *120*, 114, 138

LeMonds, Bill (author's grandfather), 25–29, 33–34

LeMonds, Bob Jr. (author's cousin), 39, 75–88, 179

LeMonds, Bob Sr. (Big Bob, author's uncle), 25, 27–30, 33, 35–37, *36*, 75–81, 85

LeMonds, Cliff (author's cousin), 25, 33, 104

LeMonds, Jim II (author's cousin), 39, 103–16, *106*, 179

LeMonds, Jim Sr. (author's father), xiii–xv, xvii, 21, 25–40, *32*, *36*, 39, 75–77, 79–81

LeMonds, Julia, 75, 78–79, 82–83

LeMonds, Shari, 117, 126, 132

LeMonds, Sonny (author's nephew), 79–87, 179

Lewis County, layoffs in, 180

Liberty Logging, 83, 87

loading machine, 135–36, 140, 146; hiring of operators for, 144–45; risks accompanying operation of, 140–41, 161; skills needed to operate, 136–38

logging camps, 15; closing of, 38; conditions in, 14–18, 21, 90; food served in, 17–18 ; purpose of, 14; Ryderwood, 27, 151

logging equipment. *See* rigging; block, haulback; block, highlead; buckle guys; guylines; mainline; pass block; pass line; pass rope; shackle; tree plates

logging, legislation restricting, 54, 129

logging, types of jobs in. *See* bucking; chasing; climbing; hooktending; loading machine operation; truck driving; sniping; timber falling

logging machinery. *See* machinery, logging; drag saw; fellerbuncher; guyless tower; harvester; loading machine; processor; roto-saw; steel tower

logging sports, 49–51, 92–93; changes in, 94; event locations, 93; noteworthy performances in, 50, 93; purses paid, 50, 93

Long, George, 10

Long-Bell Company, *26*, 27, 151

Longview Fibre, 90, 115, 124, 172, 177

Lower Columbia Trucking, 115

Loyal Legion of Loggers and Lumbermen (4-L), 112

machinery, logging: fellerbuncher, 146; forwarder, 147; guyless tower (G.T.), 118; harvester, 147–48; loading machine (shovel), 135–36, 140, 146; mainline, 26–27, 46; roto-saw, 146; yarder, 11–14, 139

McCormick Logging Company, 19, 23

McLean *&* Shaffer, 27, 33, 104

Measure 64, 128

Mezger, Walt, 2, 62–63, 68, 77–78, 125

mills, lack of timber, effect of, 170, 172; retooling of, 167

More Deadly Than War! (Prouty), 155–56

Mount St. Helens. *See* St. Helens, Mount

Nesbit, Dick, 105, 117

northern spotted owl, effects of rulings to protect, 3, 54–55, 180

Northern Pacific Railroad, 9

Northwest Forest Plan: court ruling regarding, 171–72; criticism of, 170–72; intent of, 3; effects of, 3; support for, 169–70

Occupational Safety and Health Administration. *See* Department of Labor and Industries, U.S.

old growth, 28, 52, 67, 71–72, 107, 124, 136, 140, 171; decimation of, 168; largest tree logged by Weyerhaeuser, *168*; policies regarding, 167

Pacific Lumber and Shipping, 180

Pacific Northwest Logging Congress, 155

Pacific Northwest Regional Planning Committee, 38

pass block, 44–45

pass line, 45

pass rope, 44–45

Phillips, Betty, 123, 131, 142–44

Pope and Talbot, 9, 27, 33

processor, 146–47

Prouty, A. M., 155–56

railroads: influence on westward expansion, 8; land grants to, 8; land sales by, 8–9; logging by, 14, 19–20, *19, 20*, 38

retraining programs, 55, 180–81

rigging for logging: buckle guys, 46; chokers, 139; guylines, 45–

46; haulback block, 46; high-lead block, 46; 45–46; main-line, 26–27, 46; pass block, 44–45; pass line, 45; pass rope, 44–45; shackle, 45–46; tree plates, 45–46

Roberge, Earl, 69, 158–59

Roller, Ed and Ernie, 19, 42, 60, 90, 92

Rosboro Lumber, 87

roto-saw, 146

Rush, Don, 122–24

safety. *See* deaths and injuries

Safety Board of Washington State, 156

salvage logging rider, 171

Schaeffer, Louie, 27–28, 30, 33, 85

Schafer Brothers, 156

shackle, 45–46

shovel logging, 146, 176

Simpson Timber Company, 39, 172, 176–77

sniping, 13

Snyder, Bill, 30–32

spar trees: danger of collapse, 46; phasing out of, 51, 92; raising of, 46–47; rigging of, 44–47; size of, 43

spotted owl. *See* northern spotted owl

springboard, 29, *29*

St. Helens, Mount, eruption of: effect on employment, 59, 79–80, 109–10, 121; effect on equipment, 108, 121, 138; loggers' attitudes regarding, 53, 97–98, 107, 138, logging deaths resulting from, 162, salvage operation following, 121; Weyerhaeuser, policy change resulting from, 64, 110; Weyerhaeuser, losses suffered by, 121

steel tower, 51, 92
Strain, Don (author's cousin), 39,
 59–73, *65,* 90, 179
Sustainable Forestry Initiative,
 130–31

technological advancements, 38;
 electronic chokers, 147;
 employment,effect on, 2–3,
 148, 172–73; feller-buncher,
 146; forwarder, 147; Global
 Positioning System (G.P.S.),
 147; harvester, 147–48; log
 trucks, 85–86; in mills, 167;
 processor, 146–47; roto-saw,
 146; safety, effect on, 158;
 shovel, 136, 146
They Tried to Cut It All (Van
 Syckle), 44
timber companies: American
 Forestry and Paper Association and, 130–31; environmental regulations, response
 to, 130–32; export ban, effect
 of, 125; insurance costs for
 employees of, 65–66; labor
 relations, 122–24, 174, 177;
 Measure 64, opposition to,
 128; Northwest Forest Plan,
 criticism of, 170; overcutting
 by, 23, 54; salvage logging
 rider and, 171; Sustainable
 Forestry Initiative and, 130–
 31; U.S. Forest Service,
 relationship with, 169
Timber Country Revisited
 (Roberge), 69, 158–59
timber falling, *106, 120;* apprenticeship for, 61–62, 72, 96,
 105–6; busheling, elimination
 of, 61–62; contract cutters, 63,
 11; death and injury rates,
 158; difficulty of, 52, 96, 106;
 insurance costs for, 65–66;

mechanized cutting, 146–48;
 production rates, 61, 72; risks
 accompanying, 52–53, 70–72,
 99–100, 108–9, 125–28, 153–
 54, 160–63; single-jacking
 (team cutting), 108–9, 119–20,
 153–54; skills, 62, 105–6, *106,*
 120
timber harvests: criticism of, 69;
 rationale for, 69, 166–67;
 shortening of, 67, 69 166–67;
 smaller dimension, effects of,
 72, 107, 136, 139–40
timber prices, 66, 111
timber production: Clemons
 Tree Farm, 67–69; Forestry
 Inventory System, 68; high-
 yield forestry, 67–69, 173
Timber Recovery Act, 180–81
tree plates, 45–46
truck driving: conditions, 35–38,
 78–79; distances traveled, 36,
 75, 83–86, 87; expenses, 81–
 82; financial hardships of, 36–
 37, 78–79, 86; layoffs, 141;
 risks accompanying, 86, 161,
 163; technological advancements in, 85–86, wages, 78,
 80, 83–84, 114

U.S. Department of Labor and
 Industries. *See* Department of
 Labor and Industries, U.S.
U.S. Forest Service. *See* Forest
 Service, U.S.
unionization and labor relations:
 buy-out by Weyerhaeuser, 98,
 113, 123, 138; "closing the
 gap," 141–44; contract of 1986,
 98–99, 122–24, 138, 174;
 decline of power of unions,
 63–64, 101–2, 143–44, 173–76;
 Depression Era, 112; effects
 of, 21, 42; rise of, 111–13; wage

and benefit losses, 98–99, 123, 174–76; World War I, 112

Van Syckle, Edwin, 44
Vernon, George, 2, 62

Weyerhaeuser Company: acquisitions, 9, 173–74; buy-out, 98, 113, 123, 138; change in focus, 173–74; Clemons Tree Farm, 39, 67–69; competition faced by, 174; Competitive Logging Program, 98–99, 101, 110, 123, 141–44; costs incurred by, 65–66; equipment, transition to smaller, 63, 118; export bans, effect of, 125; Forest and Fish Agreement, 1999, response to, 129–30; hiring practices, 144–45; high-yield forestry, implementation of, 67–69; improved efficiency of, 38–39, 63, 143, 172; influence in Cowlitz County, 173; independent contractors, use of, 27, 63–64, 101–2, 141–44, 172; labor relations, 61–62, 98–99, 113, 123, 138, 141–44, 173,

177; legislative influence of, 10; mechanized cutting, transition to, 148; origins, 9; Pacific Rim exports, 77–78, 125, 141, 173–74; silviculture, 38–39, 67–68; timber renewal, 10, 38–39, 67–68, 173; wages and benefits paid by, 42, 61–64, 83–84, 91–92, 98, 123, 138, 141–44, 149; work force reduction by, 63–64, 109–11, 122–24, 172–76; Yacolt salvage operation, 9
Weyerhaeuser, Frederic, 9, 174
Weyerhaeuser, George, 122–23
Weyerhaeuser, George Jr., 174
Weyerhaeuser, Phil, 39
white finger, 70, 109, 127
Wobblies. *See* Industrial Workers of the World
workers' compensation: costs, 65–66; origin, 157
Wyden, Ron, 166

Yacolt Burn, 9, 71
yarder: line speed of, 139; steam, 11–14, *12, 13, 26*

About the Author

James LeMonds has lived most of his life in Castle Rock, Washington, a logging town in the shadow of Mount St. Helens. The son of a log truck driver, LeMonds first faced the danger and grueling conditions of work in the woods during two summers spent as a chokersetter—which quickly cured him of any desire to leave college for the life of a logger. Author of *South of Seattle* (ISBN 0-87842-363-X), he has written for the *Tacoma News-Tribune,* the *Oregonian, Seattle Weekly,* and other regional publications. He holds a master's degree in education from Lewis and Clark College and teaches English at R. A. Long High School in Longview, Washington.